CLASS, STATE AND AGRICULTURAL PRODUCTIVITY IN EGYPT:

A Study of the Inverse Relationship between Farm Size
and Land Productivity

CLASS, STATE AND AGRICULTURAL PRODUCTIVITY IN EGYPT:

A Study of the Inverse Relationship
between Farm Size and Land Productivity

GRAHAM DYER

Foreword by Terence J. Byres

FRANK CASS

LONDON • PORTLAND, OR

First published in 1997 in Great Britain by
FRANK CASS & CO. LTD.
Newbury House, 900 Eastern Avenue,
London IG2 7HH England

and in the United States of America by
FRANK CASS
c/o ISBS, 5804 N.E. Hassalo Street, Portland, Oregon 97213-3644

Transferred to Digital Printing 2004

British Library Cataloguing in Publication Data

A catalogue record for this book is available from the British Library

ISBN 0–7146–4707 1 (cloth)
0–7146–4245 2 (paper)

Library of Congress Cataloging in Publication Dataze

Class, state, and agricultural productivity in Egypt: a study of the
   inverse relationship between farm size and land producitivty /
   by Graham Dyer : foreword by Terence J. Byres.
         p. cm. – – (Library of peasant studies ; no. 15)
   Includes bibliographical references and index.
   ISBN 0 7146 4707 1. – – ISBN 0 7146 4245 2 (pbk.)
      1. Farms, Size of–Egypt. 2. Agricultural productivity– –Egypt.
   3. Peasantry– –Egypt. 4. Agricultural and state– –Egypt.   I. Dyer,
   Graham, 1958–   .   II. Series
   HD1470.5.E3C58   1996
   338.1'6– –dc21   96–39385
                                                                           CIP

Contents

List of Tables

Acknowledgements

My foremost debt of thanks is to my friend, colleague and supervisor, Professor Terry Byres at SOAS, who has been a constant source of advice and inspiration. It was Terry who planted the seeds of this thesis and who has over many years developed the central ideas at the core of my understanding of the inverse relationship, and the analytical framework within which such a study has to be located.

This work also has its origins in my M.Phil. thesis at Cambridge University and my thanks are due to Professor John Sender who was my supervisor there, and for his continuing help and advice as a colleague at SOAS. I am greatly indebted to Samir Radwan, Chief of the Rural Employment Policies Branch, Employment and Development Department, International Labour Office, in Geneva, for providing me with the original data on which his joint study with Eddy Lee on the anatomy of rural poverty in Egypt was based. Samir also greatly facilitated my fieldwork in Egypt during the summer of 1990. Many thanks are also due to his colleagues Albert Wagner and Patrick Cornu for preparing the tape files and instructions. I appreciate immensely the enabling help of Ajit Ghose, formerly at the ILO in Geneva, and Ruchira Chatterji, formerly at Cambridge University.

I would like to thank Dr Yunis Batriq, Cultural Attache, and Dr Elsaid Elbaz, Agriculture Councillor, at the Egyptian Embassy in London for their advice and letters of introduction to Dr Yusuf Wali, the Egyptian Minister of Agriculture; Dr Hassan Khadr, the Under-Secretary of Agriculture, Agricultural Economics Department; and Dr Mohammed Salim at the Central Agency for Public Mobilisation and Statistics, who authorised and facilitated my fieldwork with letters of introduction to the Agricultural Administrations in Giza and Qena governorates.

I received immensely useful advice from Professor Alan Richards, formerly at the American University in Cairo, Dr Richard Adams at the International Food Policy Research Institute in Washington, and Dr Nicholas Hopkins at AUC who have all had long experience of working in rural Egypt. I would also like to thank Professor Heba Handoussa, head of the Department of Economics and Politics at AUC, and Dr Souraya Turki, head of the Department of Sociology at AUC for providing academic hospitality.

I am indebted to the help, advice, hard work and friendship of the members of my fieldwork team: Dr Amin Girgis of the Statistics and Computing Section of the Giza Agricultural Administration; Sabri al-Shoni, Agricultural Engineer in the Giza Agricultural Administration; and Mohammed Sayyid, agricultural extension worker (for agricultural machinery) in the Qus District Agricultural Unit. Thanks also go to Atef Abu al-Azam, Director of the Statistics Department, Giza Agricultural Administration; Abdel Azim, Director of the Saff District Agricultural Unit; and especially Hassan Abdel-Fattah Hassan, Director of the Shubak al-Sharqi Cooperative, and Antar Mahdi, Supervisor in the Shubak al-Sharqi Cooperative for their time and help. In Qena, my thanks go to Faruq Aref, Director of the Qena Agricultural Administration; M. Makram, Director of the Statistics Section in Qena Agricultural Administration; Murtada Abd al-Naim, head of Public Relations in Qena Agricultural Administration; and Abdel Aziz Arabi, Director of the Qus District Agricultural Unit. I owe especial thanks to Abd Ali Majr, head of the Agriculture Unit and Director of the Higaza Cooperative; Rabia Nur, Agricultural Supervisor in Higaza Cooperative; and Abu al-Fadl of the Village Bank in Higaza. Above all, I thank the farmers of Shubak al-Sharqi and Higaza who welcomed me into their homes and gave me their time and information.

I would also like to thank Mohammed Zeidan at the Agricultural Museum in Cairo, and Ahmed Rammah at the Agricultural Research Centre, for their advice and help; and the library staff at AUC and the USAID depository in Cairo for their kind and efficient help.

Finally, this book is dedicated to my family: Nada, Souraya and Jihane without whose love, support and patience this work would not have been possible.

Foreword

The existence of an inverse relationship between farm size and land productivity has been observed in the agricultures of a large number of countries, both in the past (at least as far back as the nineteenth century, and possibly before that) and more recently. It has been claimed that this is a universal phenomenon: true of any settled agriculture where there are clear differences in the size of operational holding, and at all times. That is to say, it is represented as being neither regionally nor historically specific. There is here a most interesting problem, that might be investigated by historians. It has already received analytical attention from contemporary social scientists (especially by economists), essentially with respect to contemporary developing countries.

Some considerable effort, and no little statistical ingenuity, have gone into demonstrating the aforementioned double universality, in the poor country context. From the apparent pervasiveness and persistence of an inverse relationship, in such countries, many conclusions have been drawn: about the nature of 'peasant' agriculture, and about desirable policy implications. Most notably, it is held to demonstrate the superior 'efficiency' of small-scale, 'peasant' agriculture, and to support powerfully the case for redistributive land reform; while it has been an important strand in the case made against collective agriculture in socialist countries.

The very existence of an inverse relationship has been disputed, in different ways. But, that it can be found, quite conclusively and remarkably widely, seems to be clear (although there may be tricky definitional questions as to what constitutes 'size of holding').

The conclusions derived from it have, also, been questioned. This is, in part, because of doubt over its postulated historical universality. There is, indeed, a body of evidence showing that, while such an inverse relationship can be demonstrated in a wide variety of countries, across several continents, over long stretches of time, circumstances have arisen in which the inverse relationship appears to break down and disappear. All of the aforementioned conclusions are clearly, then, thrown into considerable uncertainty. The deriving of conclusions from a relationship that no longer exists is, to say the least, problematic. We do need to view the inverse relationship – as with a whole range of crucial questions in agrarian political economy – from a dynamic rather than a static perspective.

Such doubt further derives from fundamental disagreement over the reasons for the inverse relationship, where it does continue to exist. Thus, if the most plausible explanation is one that need not inhere in small-scale, or 'peasant', agriculture – if such agriculture can, in principle, exist independently of the relevant causal influences – then conclusions drawn about the nature of such agriculture are likely to be false. Moreover, the redistributivist case and the relevant strand in the anti-collectives case become unconvincing (such advocacy must, then, lose this particular support). Or if the explanation is one that is unlikely to persist in a post-land reform situation, then that policy implication becomes open to dispute. Such questioning cannot be easily dismissed.

While the inverse relationship has been observed and discussed with reference to a large number of countries, it is in India that the most comprehensive, penetrating and authoritative scrutiny has taken place. Nowhere else has there been a debate on this issue that can remotely match – in intellectual depth, range and technical quality – that pursued in India : carried out, as so often, in the pages of the *Economic and Political Weekly* (formerly the *Economic Weekly*, in whose pages the debate was started in 1962, in a contribution by Amartya Sen).

Graham Dyer here draws upon that debate and considers the relevant issues in relation to the Egyptian countryside. In so doing, he contributes to our understanding of the dynamics of the inverse relationship and to the literature of agrarian political economy. His book derives from the Ph.D. thesis which he completed successfully in 1995.

The data upon which part of the study is based have been drawn from an ILO study of 18 villages conducted in 1977, in Egypt's two major agro-ecological zones, Upper and Lower Egypt; and on fieldwork done by the author, in two villages, in 1990, one in Qena governate and the other in Giza governate (the former in Upper Egypt, and the latter in Lower Egypt). Of the two villages chosen by the author for fieldwork, one was expected to show a positive relationship between size and productivity and the other an inverse relationship. That proved to be the case and permitted a dynamic, rather than a static, examination of the inverse relationship.

This study is important in several respects. We may single out four of these which identify it as a welcome addition to the existing body of literature.

The first is that it extends analysis of the inverse relationship seriously to Egypt. Hitherto, consideration of this phenomenon for Egypt has been meagre and there has been no more than a 'shadow debate' (to use Graham Dyer's phrase). It is unlikely that a debate on Egypt of Indian proportions will emerge. But we do now have a serious study of the inverse relationship in Egypt; and, indeed, for the first time, in North Africa/the Middle East. That is a gain for the literature on agrarian change in developing countries.

Secondly, the author clarifies a number of conceptual, statistical and methodological issues raised in treatment of the inverse relationship. He does so, in part, by focusing on the Indian debate; and, in part, through his handling of the Egyptian data. The problems are many and treacherous, and require the most careful handling. He proceeds with economy and insight. Anyone now working on this will gain from reading the relevant parts of the book.

His third contribution is to provide a trenchant critique of those explanations of the inverse relationship which seek to explain it in terms of qualitative and quantitative factor differences between farm-size categories. He argues, convincingly, that such explanations are theoretically flawed and characterised by conceptual confusion. The approach is clinical and lucid. Again, a most valuable service is provided for those who wish to pursue analysis of the inverse relationship.

Fourthly, his major, methodological contribution lies in the manner of his deploying a political economy, analytical framework, set in the context of agrarian transition. The approach is class-based: that is to say, it seeks to locate farm size within a matrix of social class. In so proceeding, he transcends approaches which simply reify size and abstract from property relationships. The inverse relationship is shown to be historically specific: to be the product of an emerging capitalist agriculture, in which, however, non-capitalist forms of surplus appropriation continue to prevail; and in which all farms have access to more or less similar technology. Where the inverse relationship breaks down, more thoroughly capitalist forms of appropriation have emerged; and differential access to a new, and more powerful technology, exists.

It is one of the essential aims of the *Journal of Peasant Studies* and the *Library of Peasant Studies* to advance the political economy of agrarian change, in the analysis of contemporary conditions and processes in the Third World. Graham Dyer operates squarely within that tradition. The editors are delighted to see his book published in the *Library of Peasant Studies*.

TERENCE J. BYRES

INTRODUCTION

The Present Study: Nature and Rationale

The inverse relationship between farm size and farm productivity is widely accepted as a 'stylised fact' of agriculture in developing countries, a generalised phenomenon observed in many countries characterised by widely differing agro-climatic conditions, agrarian structures and cropping patterns. This study uses primary fieldwork data to examine both the factors which give rise to such a relationship, and the impact of economic and technological change on the inverse relationship in the context of Egyptian agriculture.

The significance of the inverse relationship as a crucial developmental issue cannot be overemphasised. It is important not only in terms of the debate surrounding economies/diseconomies of scale, but because land ownership in backward agriculture is practically synonymous with control of labour, wealth, and social and political power. The inverse relationship constitutes a major component of the economic rationale for redistributive land reform, and has obvious importance for policy issues such as co-operative and other forms of land reorganisation, involving discussion of factors such as market imperfections and the institutional framework of traditional agriculture.

This book is in two parts. Part one, comprising the first three chapters, critically discusses the inverse relationship debate, with particular emphasis on India. The Indian literature on the inverse relationship is by far the most extensive, and it is within this debate that most of the analytical approaches to the inverse relationship have originated, even if only embryonically. These chapters are an essential preliminary analysis to the examination of the Egyptian situation.

The second, core part of the book uses fieldwork data from rural Egypt (both an extensive 18-village survey conducted by the ILO in 1976 and the author's own intensive two-village survey conducted in 1990) to support a new political economy approach to understanding the factors behind the inverse relationship and to examine how the inverse relationship breaks down in the dynamic context.

Chapter I discusses the nature and extent of the evidence for an inverse relationship in the agrarian sector of developing countries, and the suggested policy implications of such a relationship. We demonstrate that the suggested policy implications are heavily dependent on a number of unconvincing assumptions. They are also dependent on a particular theoretical perspective on the inverse relationship. Further, after examining the causal explanations for the inverse relationship and placing it in the context of agrarian transition in later chapters, we shall see that the inverse relationship rationale for redistributive land reform disappears.

This chapter also clarifies the issues involved with an examination of the major conceptual, statistical and methodological problems associated with the inverse relationship debate. Neither the existence of the inverse relationship, nor its implications, have gone unchallenged. Indeed, Amartya Sen, who is regarded as the prime mover of the debate, was one of the first to admit that the inverse relationship was by no means a well established fact and had not been proven beyond the legitimate doubts of exacting statisticians.

The necessity for care in interpreting the inverse relationship findings is imposed by a number of important conceptual, statistical and methodological problems associated with the data. Classification by farm-size implies that the characteristics of a farm depend predominantly on its belonging to a certain size-group. Size of farm however is a very general variable and to treat it as the only significant parameter would be a mistake. Other significant problems include the level of aggregation of the data, and the use of OLS regression techniques on grouped data.

Despite these problems, the inverse relationship has been confirmed in Indian agriculture at the time during which the studies cited in this chapter were conducted, and its statistical validity has been adequately established by an analysis of the disaggregated data. It is not necessarily, however, a phenomenon that will persist indefinitely. Clearly the inverse relationship is a phenomenon that needs to be explained, and not explained away by 'exacting statisticians'.

A number of conjoint relationships are revealed by the various studies mentioned, involving other factors of production besides land. These relationships tend to be clustered, suggesting some a priori explanations for the inverse relationship along factor-intensity lines. This sets the context for a critical examination of the major theoretical explanations of the inverse relationship in the following chapter.

Chapter II turns to the theoretical debate with a critique of those explanations of the inverse relationship which attempt to explain the inverse relationship in terms of qualitative and quantitative factor differences between farm-size categories. It is postulated that small farm-size categories, however they may be defined, utilise qualitatively superior factors of production, either in terms of physical resources such as soil quality and irrigation, or in terms of management, labour, and production technique. The main thrust of such an approach has been to explain why such factors are concentrated on small farms.

I demonstrate in this chapter that the explanations of the inverse relationship based on qualitative factor differences are severely flawed. The various approaches are both theoretically inadequate and their assumptions remain unsupported by the empirical evidence. The essentially untestable hypotheses relating to superior management on small farms rest on an uncritical acceptance of the inverse relationship data, relying on a residual hypothesis tested by weak and unreliable proxy variables without consideration of other factors which a more critical analysis of the data suggests are important.

The alternative hypothesis concerning differentials in land or soil quality between farm sizes rests on conceptual confusion over the meaning of fertility and on the distinction that must be made between the macro and micro levels of aggregation. At best, indirect and imprecise data have been used to support a priori reasoning which neglects factors which would tend to undermine the hypothesis.

We continue the theoretical critique with an examination of those explanations based on differential factor input intensities between farm size categories, comprising a range of variant cheap labour theories. This approach postulates that small farms apply production inputs, especially land and labour, more intensively in cultivation. The debate has centred around Amartya Sen's model which postulates different behavioural strategies as between farm-size categories. A more explicitly neo-classical variant of this approach will also be discussed.

Clearly, the empirical evidence does on the whole provide support for an explanation of the inverse relationship based on factor intensities, and in particular, a labour-based explanation. The clustering of empirical relationships around cropping intensities and labour input intensities (the latter subsuming capital and irrigation factors) in association with the inverse relationship finding certainly justifies the focus on patterns of labour use.

However, the models presented in this chapter which attempt to explain how the inverse relationship is generated via labour utilisation are theoretically flawed while crucial elements in their underlying assumptions are also subject to empirical refutation. The critical problems arise from the production function methodology employed. Conceptually, these approaches depend on a spurious calculus involving the marginal product of labour and the wage rate. As we will see, the former is an operationally useless concept in agricultural production, while the latter is only one and probably not the most important variable taken into account in determining labour use. The question must encompass a more complex set of market and non-market relations than the suggested behavioural assumptions incorporated in the models allow.

These essentially static choice-theoretic frameworks have proven to be seriously defective. This would suggest that the framework of analysis is inappropriate. There is clearly a need to go beyond farm size as the relevant stratifying variable to examine the underlying relations and forces of production.

Chapter III turns to an examination of the inverse relationship in the context of agrarian transition, and attempts to transcend the limitations of the debate. We present a new approach to explaining the existence of an inverse relationship within a political economy perspective, and show how in the dynamic context, the inverse relationship breaks down.

We propose an alternative class-based approach to understanding the inverse relationship. This class-based approach proceeds from the proposition that the peasant farm is embedded in the socio-economic context of an emerging capitalist agriculture in which however, non-capitalist forms of surplus appropriation are still prevalent. Where capitalist farming is emerging out of a semi-feudal agriculture, the coexistence of both the modes shapes the labour market, while the characteristics of the labour market itself influence the form and process of transition.

The class-based approach attempts to locate farm size within a class matrix. The fundamental determinants of factor-use intensities are the nexus of property rights and tenurial conditions that shape market characteristics, resource endowments, and the nature and extent of market participation by different peasant strata. Within the process of peasant differentiation, poor peasants end up with smaller and smaller below-subsistence plots of land, and are forced to intensify cropping intensity and labour input in order to achieve subsistence levels of income. This stratum of poor peasants may also be characterised by compulsive market involvement or 'forced commerce'. Exploitative relations of production and exchange, with landlords, merchants and moneylenders extracting surplus via high rents, usury and price wedges, either singly or conjointly, compel poor peasants to achieve higher than average yields, market a high proportion of high-value cash crops, and sell labour off-farm in order to pay off cash and debt obligations as well as reach subsistence income.

In those areas where we find an inverse relationship, it is the case that all farm sizes have access to a more or less similar technology. Large and small farms use the same set of production inputs, and the small farms achieve higher output per acre via higher cropping intensity and higher application of labour effort per acre. With the introduction of a new technology which favours large farms due to its associated economies of scale, the so-called advantage which the small farms have with respect to labour input intensity, may be matched or more than matched by the new advantages which large farms have with respect to technology. In this situation, we might expect the inverse relationship to break down and eventually disappear, and with it part of the case for redistributive land reform.

Chapter IV turns to the core part of the thesis with a critical survey of the inverse relationship debate in the Egyptian context. We examine the nature and range of evidence for an inverse relationship between farm size and productivity in the Egyptian countryside. In contrast with the extensive Indian literature on the inverse relationship is the rather meagre resonance that the debate has had in Egypt. This relative paucity, however, has not prevented calls by several writers for redistributive land reform in the Egyptian countryside. The Egyptian evidence ranges from simple assertion, by invoking the authority of Berry and Cline, to full-scale field studies.

The studies examined in this chapter present apparently strong, but contradictory evidence on the relationship between farm size and productivity, with some contributors supporting the existence of an inverse relationship while others vehemently deny its existence. However, all the participants in the Egyptian debate reveal crucial conceptual and methodological flaws in their analyses, echoing many of the errors and misconceptions we have examined in the previous three chapters. It is important to consider these in some detail since they are flaws which recur wherever the inverse relationship has been examined and discussed. We draw heavily on the critical analysis of the debate surrounding the inverse relationship which we have discussed thoroughly in the previous three chapters.

Nevertheless, these inconclusive and partial results do suggest that the inverse relationship may be an important phenomenon in rural Egypt, although not in the way conceived of by the authors looked at in this chapter.

Chapter V identifies the central features of the political economy of the Egyptian countryside, as a necessary prelude to discussion of the fieldwork data. We consider some of the central features of the political economy of the Egyptian countryside, which have been identified by other researchers and which are central to our own analysis. In other words, we here survey the evidence with respect to the mechanisms and institutions which have been central to rich peasant dominance in contemporary Egypt. This is an important prelude to the treatment of the ILO data and the author's study villages in the following chapters. As we shall see, the influences identified in this chapter were crucial in the study villages, both with respect to the causal factors behind the inverse relationship and to its disappearance.

We shall see that despite significant land reform measures, important elements of semi-feudal agriculture remain strong: sharecropping tenancy, personalised oral contracts, and an indebted poor peasantry. Access to land and resources lies through the patronage of the rich peasants and those landlords who managed to evade land reform legislation. This is the environment, the matrix of exploitative relationships, in which the inverse relationship flourishes.

Our hypothesis is that in the early stages of transition, institutional biases act strongly in favour of the larger farmers. Several studies show that the main beneficiaries of the land reform legislation, and subsequently, the co-operative and rural credit system in Egypt were the rich farmers. The control of the latter by the rich peasantry, those owning over ten feddans of land, ensured their dominance with respect to the diffusion of the new technology. While at an earlier stage, intrinsic advantages of scale are not unimportant, these become increasingly significant over time, enabling the large farmers to maintain relatively high investment and growth rates. In this two-stage process, the first impact of agrarian transition is the weakening and disappearance of the inverse relationship. Later, when scale advantages operate for a substantial length of time the relation turns significantly positive.

Chapter VI employs an extensive ILO data set covering 18 villages in six regions of Egypt to show a more complex and heterogeneous pattern of the relationship between farm size and productivity. We subject the data used by Radwan and Lee in their 1986 study to much closer examination, in order to discover the nature and extent of the inverse relationship in the Egyptian countryside, and its relationship to technological change. This will provide a stronger empirical support for our hypotheses. Then, in the following chapters, we can explore, at the more disaggregated level of individual villages, just why such an inverse relationship exists, where it exists, and how it is changing.

Analysis of the data at a more disaggregated level produces results at variance with widely held views on the size–productivity relation. We find in the Egyptian rural sector striking parallels with the process of agrarian transition in India, with regard to the technological factors. The heterogeneous pattern of technological change in Egyptian agriculture is mirrored by the pattern of occurrence of an inverse relationship between farm size and productivity. Where technical change in agriculture is at a relatively undeveloped stage, we appear to have evidence of a significant inverse relationship. In those regions where technical change is relatively more advanced, the inverse relationship is absent. We can advance the hypothesis, on the basis of the evidence in previous chapters, that technical change in these latter regions has led to the breakdown of a previously existent inverse relationship.

Finally, in Chapters VII and VIII, intensive village fieldwork data from 1990, collected by the author, is used to provide support for the political economy approach to explaining the inverse relationship and its breakdown in the Egyptian context. In order to test the various hypotheses associated with the inverse relationship, two village surveys were carried out in the summer of 1990. On the basis of the results from the ILO data, a village (Higaza al-Qibli) was chosen from Qena governorate which was expected to show a positive relationship between farm size and productivity. A second village (Shubak al-Sharqi) was chosen from Giza governorate which was expected to shed light on the inverse relationship.

Land reform in Shubak has created a situation in which relatively little social differentiation and elite land accumulation has occurred. Thus, land reform has actually had the effect of slowing down capital accumulation, inhibiting saving and investment. Shubak is characterised by small scattered land possessions prohibiting the application of modern technology and leading to the fragile formation of capitalism. Land fragmentation has weakened the ability of large farmers to adopt new agricultural methods, slowing down the intensification of capital utilisation. Significant elements of semi-feudal agriculture remain to provide the compulsions driving poor farmers to intensify land and labour use, thus generating an inverse relationship.

The village is dominated by middle and rich peasant farms which have not developed into capitalist farmers. These farms are not fully commercialised and operate with essentially the same techniques of production as the poor farmers with less than three feddans of land. Clearly, the evidence from Shubak shows us that the larger farmers are not qualitatively different from smaller farmers, but only quantitatively differentiated.

In contradistinction, Higaza clearly falls into a capitalist path category. This village has a relatively greater concentration of land, a larger area and population, and higher levels of new technology use, particularly mechanization. The co-operative system was dominated by the rich peasants allowing the large farms to accumulate land and other means of production such as machinery. Thus, Higaza has exhibited a different outcome with increased social differentiation and the potential disappearance of the small farmer rather than his survival.

Higaza has also benefited from development efforts in the form of loans for machinery and other modern inputs because of its integration into an industrialised agriculture dominated by sugar capital. The mode of production has changed because capital has penetrated the village and changed the system of production instead of being merely externally imposed via market relations. The middle and rich peasant family farms have given way to capitalist enterprises organised by the family, but based on wage labour and capitalist accumulation, manifested in the intensive use of machine inputs.

The 'traverse' from Giza to Qena, representing a development of the forces of production, both determines and is determined by the development of the relations of production. In particular, rich peasants, either as proto- or fully-developed capitalist farmers monopolise productive resources and dominate access to the new technology through their control of the co-operative and rural credit systems. The utilisation of this new technology accelerates rich peasant accumulation and deepens the process of social differentiation. The productivity advantages thus gained lead to a reversal in the size–productivity relationship characteristic of a relatively backward agriculture.

In conclusion, we show through both theoretical critique and empirical analysis, that in the static context, the inverse relationship is not the product of superior efficiency on the part of small farms nor is it due to better quality land on the small farms, but arises from the desperate struggle of poor peasants for survival on below-subsistence plots of land in a relatively backward agriculture, and the matrix of exploitative relations within which they operate. Redistribution of land on the basis of the inverse relation argument therefore, far from alleviating poverty and creating employment opportunities, will only deepen and perpetuate extreme levels of exploitation and poverty. Furthermore, in the dynamic context of the development of the forces of production, in the shape of Green Revolution technology, the inverse relationship is likely to disappear. The inverse relationship argument for redistributive land reform no longer has any rationale in the context of changing production conditions.

I

The Nature of the Inverse Relationship and Its Apparent Policy Implications

INTRODUCTION

The empirical evidence for the existence of an inverse relationship between farm size and farm productivity[1] is both historically and geographically widespread, ranging from pre-revolutionary Russia and China to contemporary poor countries in Asia, Africa and Latin America. Indeed, the inverse relationship is widely regarded as a 'stylised fact' of traditional agriculture [*Bardhan*, 1973: 1370], a generalised phenomenon observed in many developing countries characterised by widely different agro-climatic conditions, agrarian structures and cropping patterns [*Cornia*, 1985: 514–15; *Ghose*, 1979: 27].[2]

One commentator notes:

> A striking feature of the agricultural systems of virtually all poor countries is that yields per acre rise as average farm size declines. That is, the smaller the farm, the greater the average productivity of land. Conversely, the larger the farm, the greater the average productivity of labour. Since land is usually the factor in most acute shortage, the farms with the highest yields per acre are normally the most efficient. Even in countries where the average farm is very small, such as in India, it has been demonstrated that those farms which are smaller than average are economically the most efficient' [*Griffin*, 1974: 228].[3]

The modern debate comprises a large theoretical and empirical literature which came into being in the Indian context.[4] Central to the modern Indian debate on farm size and productivity is the 17-volume Farm Management Studies (FMS) data collected by the Directorate of Economics and Statistics and the Research Programmes Committee over three years: 1954–55, 1955–56 and 1956–57.

The Indian debate proper begins with Sen's seminal 1962 article in the Economic Weekly [*Sen*, 1962].[5] There he notes the following observation: 'By and large, productivity per acre decreases with the size of holding.' Sen further notes that this trend holds in most areas for value-added too. I cite the statistical basis for Sen's argument in Table 1, Appendix A.

Khusro [1964] and Bharadwaj [1974a] carry out more detailed studies using OLS regression techniques on the grouped FMS data. Table 2 in Appendix A [*Bharadwaj*, 1974a: 92] lists the OLS regression coefficients for yields per acre on farm size for the entire data set.[6] While all regression coefficients are negative, not all are statistically significant. Khusro [1964: 59] finds no exception to an inverse relation in all seven states,[7] concluding: 'It is this consistently recurring phenomenon of declining slopes in all seven States without exception that lends itself to the generalisation that in Indian farming of the 1950s gross output per acre declines with an increase in farm size' [1964: 54]. The constant generation and analysis of data since then continues to confirm the finding of an inverse relationship.[8]

I.1 SOME APPARENT POLICY IMPLICATIONS

The significance of the inverse relationship as a crucial developmental issue cannot be overemphasised. It is important not only in terms of the debate surrounding economies/diseconomies of scale, but because land ownership in backward agriculture is practically synonymous with control of labour, wealth, and social and political power [*Bachman and Christensen*, 1967: 263]. Such a relationship has obvious importance for policy issues such as land ceilings and redistribution, as well as co-operative and other forms of land reorganisation, involving discussion of factors such as market imperfections and the institutional framework of traditional agriculture [*Bardhan*, 1973: 1371]. The apparent implications of such a relationship constitute a major component of the economic rationale for redistributive land reform and a small farm bias in agricultural development strategy.

Cornia [1985: 532] writes:

> Because of the demonstrated superiority of small *vis-à-vis* large farming, land redistribution would have, if thoroughly implemented, immediate beneficial effects in terms of output growth, enhanced income distribution and, as a result, of alleviation of rural poverty. It would also bring about a resource use more in line with the factor endowment of developing countries by increasing labour absorption ... while forestalling premature labour-displacing mechanisation.

Lipton [1974: 304] regards small farms as 'superior' because they select both higher labour intensity and produce higher output per acre and output per unit of capital, thereby economising on what poor countries are short of (land and capital), absorbing idle resources (labour), and producing more of what is needed (food).

Berry and Cline [1979], regarded by many as the definitive statement on the inverse relationship, argue that the finding of systematically higher land productivity and comparable levels of total factor productivity on small farms as opposed to large farms suggests 'that the expansion of the small-farm subsector of agriculture may be a more effective way of increasing both employment and output than pro-large-farm strategies and thus warrants serious consideration in almost all developing countries' [1979: 4]. According to these authors, in LDCs, small farms are likely to have higher total factor productivity, and so are the optimal size for output maximisation, as well as for labour absorption and income distribution [1979: 16].

Given that small farms generate higher land productivity and total social factor productivity (the authors do admit an extremely important caveat to this statement: 'except in the very smallest farms in some countries' [1979: 128]), the authors propose the redistribution of land to the small farmers who apply labour more intensively, and the improvement of small farm access to credit and new technology. Both strategies will improve equity and increase output levels [1979: 128].

With such land redistribution, the authors claim that:

> The optimal postreform farm size, in the absence of technical returns to scale, will be merely the total agricultural area divided by the total number of families in the agricultural labour force (after adjusting for land quality). That is, since total factor productivity falls as farm size rises in the relevant range, the most productive agrarian structure will be that composed of the smallest farms possible, consistent with full allocation of the available land and labour force, i.e., total area divided by the total number of farm families [1979: 18].

They add in a footnote: 'An equal distribution of available land among the entire rural labour force on a family farm basis will generally result in parcels significantly larger than the smallest prereform farms' [1979: 226, fn. 23]. Berry and Cline then reason: 'If the equal distribution of all available land among all families implies a labour/land ratio equal to that of the same sized farms in the existing agrarian structure, the land productivity of these latter farms can provide a rough prediction of average land productivity after redistribution ... ' [1979: 18].

Estimates of output gains after land redistribution follow a two-step procedure: first, the average farm size is computed by dividing the available land by the number of families in the rural labour force;[9] secondly, a statistical estimate of output per acre for that farm size is applied to the former result. Berry and Cline present [1979: 132–3, Table 5–1] estimates of the potential gains from such equalizing land redistribution, ranging from 10 per cent for Pakistan to 79.5 per cent for north-eastern Brazil, including

19 per cent for India, 23 per cent for the Philippines, 25 per cent for Brazil as a whole, and 28 per cent for Colombia and the Muda river area of Malaysia.

The only caveats to the above procedure for calculating output gains given any prominence in Berry and Cline are those arising from price changes following shifts in output mix, and changes in labour input intensities [1979: 18–19]. However, the set of assumptions required for this astonishingly simplistic calculation to hold are both numerous and highly unlikely to occur in reality.

The first and most obvious problem with this procedure is that the estimates are not constrained by product mix or land quality. In other words, the total land available which is defined as all land currently being used for agricultural purposes including pasture and woodland, can be converted to arable cultivation. Indeed, even marginal and waste land or land unsuitable for arable purposes can be so converted. Clearly, such a computation is inadmissible; the latter category of land would have to be excluded from the calculation, and the remainder would have to be disaggregated by type or use, between arable and pasture for example. Very different figures are likely to result. Indeed, where such product disaggregation has been carried out, as in Cline [1970] for Brazil, the potential output gains from land redistribution have been disappointing.[10]

Furthermore, none of the foregoing calculations take into account the possibility of there being a minimum efficient scale or of there being a floor determined by subsistence income. In terms of the inverse relationship evidence, the optimal size of farm would be around one acre [Sen, 1962]. But when other criteria are considered, relating to viability, we find that the level of the floor rises considerably. One criterion might be that of minimum income. That is, the farm should be able to provide an adequate level of income for a peasant family – a subsistence income. This may turn out to be significantly larger than the optimal size based on the inverse relationship phenomenon (output maximisation). Other criteria might involve employment absorption: that is, the farm should be able to gainfully employ the working members of the average rural family; or technology absorption: that is, the minimum farm size should be such as to make efficient use of draught animals or machines. Consideration of these criteria may significantly raise the minimum feasible size of holding.[11]

Note here, we have a clear conflict between the various criteria, in particular that based on the inverse relationship, on the one hand, and those based on subsistence requirements or resource use on the other. Thus, the concept of viability sets a limit to redistributive land reform.[12]

To draw on the inverse relationship to justify redistributive land reform, the general equilibrium effects also need to be considered: landless labourers have normally been excluded from access to redistributed land, and if land reform is implemented at the expense of large farms, then the landless may be worse off due to a fall in employment opportunities.

Even if the inverse relationship is empirically valid because small farms use more inputs per acre,[13] land redistribution without ensuring the availability of extra inputs may not produce the expected results [*Bardhan*, 1973: 1371]. Estimates of output gains after redistribution of land assume that the required inputs exist and that no losses occur due to the process of redistribution. Such estimates do not take into account the extra investment costs of providing irrigation to unirrigated land, or of providing extra inputs (seeds, fertilisers, pesticides and so on). Smallholder farming is not a cheap option. It requires investment in both production and infrastructure [*Lipton and Lipton*, 1993: 1525]. The process of land redistribution itself may involve extra costs in terms of cadastral survey, boundary marking and the provision of access to plots, as well as the potential for the disruptive effects of land reform to reduce output.

The estimates further assume that the current input–output characteristics on existing farms of the 'optimal' size would also characterise farms of that size after land reform. This question relates not only to the availability and distribution of production inputs, but also to the whole area of motivation governing labour effort. If incomes were to rise on the small farms, this may relax the subsistence income or debt obligations constraint and allow small farmers either to relax labour effort with a lower application of labour per acre, and, hence, lower output per acre, or to reduce the proportion of output marketed.[14] In such circumstances, while on-farm family consumption might increase, the supply of marketed surplus may well fall with serious consequences for economic activity outside agriculture.

One area dismissed rather cursorily by Berry and Cline is the question of the possible dynamic losses of redistributive land reform affecting negatively the rate of saving and capital accumulation, and the adoption of new technology. Yet the supposed static productivity advantages of small farms may seem inconsequential if a small-farm system cannot generate sufficient investments and the necessary increases in agricultural output. The authors however doubt the existence of any possible dynamic losses arising from land distribution because (1) there appears to be no evidence for higher agricultural growth rates in countries with higher than average farm size, and (2) there is evidence in Green Revolution areas that small farmers adopt the new technology rapidly [1979: 134–5].

The first point is quite irrelevant. Average farm size provides no indication of the distribution of farm size or the weight of large farms in that distribution. What needs to be compared is the relative output growth rates of a group of large capitalist farms with a group of small peasant farms in one country. Berry and Cline cite evidence of simulation experiments with rural savings data for Brazil and India by Cline and Bhalla[15] which indicate that income redistribution would have only a limited impact on rural savings rates and total savings [1979: 28]. However, as Sen [1964] and Bharadwaj [1974a] have shown, the vast bulk of small farms in India are highly indebted deficit farms. It is therefore most likely that any post-reform average or marginal rate of rural saving would be very low. Indeed, Bhalla disposes of this annoying problem of deficit farms by excluding them from his analysis (this reduces his NCAER sample by over 50 per cent).

The second assertion is also highly dubious. The authors assert that small farmers adopt the Green Revolution technology very soon after the large farmers, thus re-establishing an inverse relationship in the form of an S-curve [1979: 28]. They claim that the association of mechanisation with the adoption of new technology is erroneous, simply just another manifestation of factor market imperfections, and that the existence of the latter imply the need to channel new inputs towards the small farms [1979: 27–8].

However, the empirical evidence would appear not to substantiate this assertion. Patnaik [1987: 120–25] has demonstrated that although some farms in all size groups have adopted the new technology, those small farms are in fact, in terms of scale and hired labour use, rich farms.[16] It is the rich farms who both adopt the new technology thus reaping the initial benefits and who maintain that advantage. The evidence in chapter III shows clearly that the inverse relation has broken down in those Green Revolution areas as large farmers adopt both the new technology and mechanise. Indeed, Berry and Cline do admit that large farms are able to capture economies of scale with the introduction of mechanised technology [1979: 138].

Finally, there are important political constraints to redistributive land reform. A rural power structure dominated by landlords or rich peasants may simply undermine land reform legislation through evasion and avoidance. However, Lipton's view that 'avoidance can sometimes help reform [as] threats of ceilings can induce substantial sales to poorer farmers' [1993: 645] or that such a process can be implemented 'if the rich farmers see their interests in such a process and/or are too weak to stop it' [1993: 653] would, faced with the evidence, appear to be wishful thinking of Daedalus-like proportions.[17]

I.2 CONCEPTUAL, STATISTICAL, AND METHODOLOGICAL
    PROBLEMS

Neither the existence of the inverse relationship, nor its implications, have gone unchallenged. Indeed, Sen was one of the first to admit that the inverse relationship was by no means a well established fact and had not been proven 'beyond the legitimate doubts of exacting statisticians due to the fact that average data can be misleading' [1964a: 323].

Barraclough [1973: 266], after noting that the CIDA studies in Latin America corroborate the finding of an inverse relationship, warn: 'great care must be taken in interpreting these data. When comparisons are made for relatively homogeneous areas limited to the same types of farming and tenure conditions these inter-farm differences often diminish and in some cases even disappear.'[18]

A notable conceptual problem with respect to the inverse relationship has been introduced into the debate by Utsa Patnaik [1972: 1613–24].[19] She argues forcefully that, if instead of taking acreage as the measure of farm size (size grouping) we take either annual value of gross output per farm or the value of tangible capital stock (scale grouping), we then get (may get), in certain circumstances, 'diametrically opposite results'.[20] Note the conditionality flagged in this statement by the inclusion of the phrase 'in certain circumstances' and the use of 'may' in parentheses.

On the second measure of size (the scale grouping) output per acre rises (may rise) sharply with increasing scale of production. It may be the case, she says that 'an intensive application of capital on the smaller holding results in its being larger [than a holding of higher acreage] on every economic index except acreage' [1972: 1614].

The reason for this is, she argues, that holdings of 'varying levels of intensity, i.e. with varying production techniques and even varying organisation' [1972: 1617] are lumped together within the same size category. So it is, then, she argues, that the size grouping approach blurs (may blur) certain distinctions: between intensively and extensively cultivated holdings; and between different categories within the peasantry, so obscuring the extent of differentiation [1972: 1615]. It is possible to identify, say, a rich peasant with 80 acres and a rich peasant with just eight acres [1972: 1614].

If all of this is so, then the outcome is as follows, with the inverse relationship emerging on the size grouping, and certain crucial aspects concealed, which are clear on the scale grouping:

> When grouped by size, a small number of high-productivity holdings of small size, lumped with similar sized but low productivity extensively run holdings (which constitute the majority), raises the average yield for the small size group as a whole; while the large extensive farms, lumped with similar sized but much more intensive high-productivity capitalist farms, lower the average yield for the large-size group as a whole ... Not only with respect to yield, but also as regards all inputs, capital intensity and labour productivity, we find

the same striking differences in the results of grouping by size and by scale respectively' [1972: 1620].

Patnaik is making a very important point. It is, indeed, the case that 'when we are studying a process of agricultural change ... it becomes especially important to analyse the available data according to scale of production' [1972: 1621]. Two holdings of the same size may well differ in their class status. A holding may be smaller in size but larger as an economic unit [1972: 1614]. But note how she formulates the argument:

> What we are saying is that in the past, the set of rich peasants and the set of farms above 20 acres in UP probably had a very large number of common elements: while at present owing to the changes taking place in use of techniques and intensification of production the intersection of the two sets is getting smaller. Therefore the identification of the properties of one set with those of the other is now less justifiable and may be downright misleading [1972: 1624].

Observe the difference stressed between the past (a static situation) and the present (a dynamic one): in the Indian case, between the pre-'new technology' situation and the period when that 'new technology' had begun to spread and have an impact. That differentiation has a certain plausibility. The validity of her argument surely relates to circumstances of change. One might argue, even on her logic, that in the relatively static situation of the 1950s, when the inverse relationship was first established in the FMS studies size was a useful measure, encompassing 'sets with a very large number of common elements'; while in the 1970s (when she was writing and when the 'new technology' was beginning to spread) her logic began to take on significance. She stresses:

> If techniques were absolutely uniform for all holdings then of course no problem of distinguishing between size and scale would arise. However techniques are far from uniform ... The possibility of adopting new, usually much more capital intensive techniques exists [by the 1970s] for the farms with an investible surplus [1972: 1615].

This is the crucial point. We would wish to argue that techniques were tending to uniformity in the 1950s (certainly, they tended to uniformity to a far greater extent then than in the 1970s); and so size is then a useful stratifying variable: an acceptable index of economic status (class position). And where techniques of production have been only partially transformed, farm size may still be the relevant stratifying variable. Great care must be taken by the researcher to avoid grouping farms with different systems of production together. Methods used later in the analysis of the fieldwork data, in the Egyptian context (Chapter VII), include computation of rank correlation coefficients between the set of farm sizes and the set of farm scales of production, and the computation of diagnostic statistics to identify outliers in the data set. The exclusion or separate treatment of these cases of course require theoretical and empirical support.

One further issue of crucial significance that needs to be flagged at this point, as it relates closely to the question of agrarian change, is the actual breakdown and disappearance of the inverse relationship in the context of the 'new technology'. This widely documented phenomenon [*Chadha,* 1978; *Roy,* 1979; *Khan,* 1979; *Dyer,* 1991] will be discussed in Chapter III. Suffice it to state here that abundant evidence from India and Pakistan shows that following the introduction of the Green Revolution technology, the inverse relationship has disappeared, markedly so in those areas where the new technology has penetrated most deeply.

This, of course, is a very different phenomenon from that described by Patnaik. The latter approach generates a statistical breakdown of the inverse relationship by switching from an area definition of farm size to a scale measure (warranted by the possibility that a sub-group of holdings of small size have secured important productivity advantages through intensive application of capital, thus increasing their economic scale). The former approach, however, posits that it is the larger farms, due to their greater surpluses and access to and control over capital, which capture the productivity gains from the new technology, thereby structurally reversing the direction of the size–productivity relationship, despite the continued intensive application of family labour on the small farms.

The statement by Barraclough above, raises the crucial distinction that needs to be made between aggregated and disaggregated levels of analysis. At highly aggregated levels of analysis, whether at the cross-country [*Cornia,* 1985], national or regional level, a relatively high degree of land heterogeneity is to be expected. Those areas with better than average soil quality, in particular, water availability, and hence higher than average natural land productivity, are historically likely to have attracted greater population settlement. Higher population density will, given limited land resources, lead to small average farm size over long time periods. Contrariwise for areas of relatively poor agricultural land where population settlement is likely to be less dense and average farm size larger. Hence, at this 'macro' level, an inverse correlation between land productivity (as measured by output per acre) and farm size is to be expected.

Note that this type of natural inverse relationship at the 'macro' level is fundamentally different from the inverse relation at the centre of this study. At the aggregate level, the direction of causality runs from land productivity (itself caused by better soil quality) to small average farm size. However, at the micro level (village level for example) the causality is postulated to run in the opposite direction: specific factors associated with smaller than average farm size are producing higher than average farm productivity.[21] Roy [1979: 5, Tables 1.1–2] notes data for Indian states which show the 'macro' relation. Moving from the macro to micro scale, the direction of causation is reversed: 'while exogenous factors are assumed to cause the inverse relation at the macro level, endogenous factors are assumed to cause the same inverse relation at the micro level'. So the inverse relationship at the 'macro' level is caused by diversity in natural conditions.

There are two further dimensions to the problem of aggregation. There is the related problem of aggregation over villages leading to a spurious inverse relationship. Even if no inverse relationship existed within villages, but there were different soil fertilities between villages, and high fertility villages had smaller average farm size, then an inverse relation would be shown by data aggregated over the villages. Alternatively, if fertility (average land productivity) was the same over villages, and the inverse relationship holds in each village, but villages have different size-ranges, then such a relationship could be eliminated [*Chattopadhyay and Rudra, 1976*: A110]. Rudra [1968b] implies that the inverse relationship does not exist within any particular village, but arises as a spurious relationship when data for different villages are aggregated.[22]

There is also the problem of grouped averages. Most of the analysis of the FMS data was carried out using size class averages for the principal variables, farm size and output per acre. Grouped data may generate an aggregation bias when the in-group variance is in fact greater than the between-group variance. Thus, farm level data which show no overall relationship between farm size and output per acre, may when grouped into size classes show a spurious inverse relation. Barbier [1984] shows that the overall relation is very sensitive to size-class boundaries.

Rudra [1968a: 1041] suspects the process of aggregation is responsible for what he calls the 'spurious correlation' of the FMS data. He writes: 'the farm management data do not permit of the generalised conclusions that have been drawn, the inferences having been made without adequate examination of the tables themselves' [1968b: A-33]. Nevertheless Chattopadhyay and Rudra still use grouped data to reject the *prima facie* arguments of the FMS data and Sen [1976: A-110].

In the same study, Rudra criticises the use of simple linear regressions and log-linear regressions in the FMS studies which imply certain assumptions about the nature of the relationship being tested [1968a: 1041].[23] Chattopadhyay and Rudra regard rank correlation tests as superior as the latter assume no specific functional relation between output per acre and farm size [1976: A-107].[24]

In a later study, Rudra presents data on rank correlation coefficients between farm size and yield per hectare *for individual crops* [1968b: A-35, Table 1]: producing only four statistically significant negative coefficients. Note, however, that there is a clear distinction to be drawn between physical yields of individual crops and total crop production in value terms (this reflects the importance of cropping intensity and crop pattern). Unlike the inverse relationship in value terms, little evidence has been produced for an inverse relationship in terms of the physical yields of individual crops.

1.3 THE INVERSE RELATIONSHIP VINDICATED AND SOME CONJOINT RELATIONSHIPS: CLUSTERED FACTORS

While Rudra is correct to assert the need to disaggregate the data, the divergence between his results and those of the FMS would persist even with disaggregation. Rudra's concept of yield per acre is biased toward eliminating the inverse relationship. Yields have been calculated as gross value of output per gross cultivated area [*Rudra*, 1968a: 1041]. Gross cultivated area or gross cropped area includes farm size plus those parts of the operated area multi-cropped.[25]

However, factors such as double (or multiple) cropping and the percentage of land cultivated reflect the economics of farming. They are not exogenous factors affecting the economics of farming. A farmer who cultivates land more intensively via double cropping and raising the percentage of land cultivated may be argued to be using land more efficiently [*Rao*, 1968c: 1413]. Rudra's procedure corrects for the efficiency of land use by using gross cropped area.[26] Moreover, it is important to establish why land is cultivated more intensively. Rudra's procedure however, obscures cropping intensity differentials between farm size groups which may be of critical significance.

Hanumantha Rao notes that if an inverse relationship exists between cropping intensity (the ratio of gross cropped area to net cropped area or farm size) and farm size, then Rudra's results are not surprising. If however such a relation does not exist for Rudra's villages then possibly no inverse relation exists. 'The relevant question in this case is ... whether these five [*sic*] villages are to be regarded as more typical of Indian farming than those studied by the FMS in different parts of the country' [*Rao*, 1968c: 1413–14].[27]

Nevertheless, much of Rudra's criticism of the earlier FMS studies has a great deal of validity. While Chattopadhyay and Rudra challenge the universal validity of the inverse relationship, they do not reject that validity in all circumstances: in some places, at certain times, and for certain size ranges the inverse relationship holds [1976: A-104]. Their findings, too, important as they are, are no basis for generalising over the whole country.

Other writers have sought to answer some of the criticisms by using disaggregated data for individual farm households at the village level.

Saini [1971] and Bhattacharya and Saini [1972: A63] analyse disaggregated FMS data for 25 data sets in nine States, concluding: 'Thus, by and large, the inverse relationship between farm size and productivity is a confirmed phenomenon in Indian agriculture and its statistical validity is adequately established by an analysis of the disaggregated data' [1971: A81-2].[28]

The general conclusion after the spilling of much ink is that the inverse relationship between farm size and productivity has been confirmed as a valid empirical phenomenon in India, but not in the way conceived of in the earlier studies. Rudra and Sen in a joint paper [1980: 393] conclude: 'While ... the inverse relation is more frequently confirmed than rejected, it would be a mistake to take it to be an empirical generalisation for Indian agriculture as a whole.' The inverse relationship findings in the Indian FMS, then, are not entirely conclusive. Moreover, some exceptions and complications are introduced by considering other factors besides land [Sen, 1964b: 441]. But those findings do suggest a persistent phenomenon that needs to be explained.

A wide range of relationships between farm size and other important factors are revealed by the various studies mentioned above that may throw some light on the theoretical understanding of this phenomenon. The major findings of the FMS studies and the wider debate which followed can be summarised as follows:[29]

(1) An inverse relationship between output per net cropped acre for the total value of crop production and farm size exists for *most* regions of India, and for a wide range of other countries

(2) That inverse relationship appears to be weakened when gross cropped area is used as the land measure in the productivity calculation.

(3) No inverse relationship is evident between the physical yield per acre of individual crops and farm size. Indeed, in most cases, physical yields of individual crops appear to be constant or even increasing across farm size.

(4) There is a strong inverse relationship between cropping intensity and farm size, where the cropping intensity index represents the ratio of gross cropped area to net cropped area.

(5) A further inverse relationship is evident between units of labour input per acre and farm size. As farm size increases, less human labour input is applied per acre.

(6) A related phenomenon is the declining ratio of family labour to total labour as farm size increases. The ratio of hired labour input to total labour increases with farm size.

(7) Along with increasing labour input intensity on the smaller farms, is a higher intensity of application of capital inputs (including animal labour power, seeds, fertilisers, and farm buildings).

(8) This latter association does not apply to purchased intermediate inputs which tend to increase proportionately or more than proportionately with farm size.

(9) An inverse relationship has also been noticed between the percentage of cultivated area irrigated and farm size.

It is already fairly obvious that these findings are closely interdependent. All the studies mentioned in this chapter find these relationships clustered, suggesting a priori explanations for the inverse relationship based on factor input intensity, which will be discussed in the following chapter.

SUMMARY AND CONCLUSIONS

This chapter has critically surveyed the range and nature of the evidence for an inverse relationship between farm size and land productivity. We have seen that the evidence for an inverse relationship between farm size and land productivity is both geographically widespread and historically pervasive. Empirical support for the finding has been heavily documented for the contemporary developing regions of Africa, Asia and Latin America, as well as for earlier periods in Europe, Japan, and North America.

The contemporary significance of the inverse relationship as a crucial developmental issue cannot be overemphasised. Such a relationship has obvious importance for policy issues. The apparent implications of such a relationship constitute a major component of the economic rationale for redistributive land reform and a small farm bias in agricultural development strategy. This it is claimed will have a positive impact on output, income, employment absorption, and poverty alleviation.

The suggested policy implications are however heavily dependent on a number of unconvincing assumptions. They are also dependent on a particular theoretical perspective on the inverse relationship which will be examined in Chapter II. Nevertheless, these implications of the inverse relationship, accepted at face value without critical examination of its nature or causal factors, are subject to severe qualifications. Any positive impact may be severely constrained by efficiency considerations relating to minimum feasible farm size, input availability, dynamic general equilibrium effects on saving, investment and employment, and the nature of technical and social change in agriculture. Further, the next two chapters attempt to show that, after examining the causal explanations for the inverse relationship and placing it in the context of agrarian transition, the inverse relationship rationale for redistributive land reform disappears.

Neither the statistical evidence for the inverse relationship, nor its apparent policy implications, have gone unchallenged. This chapter has examined the principal conceptual and methodological problems associated with the data. Classification by farm-size implies that the characteristics of a farm depend predominantly on its belonging to a certain size-group. Size of farm however is a very general variable and to treat it as the only significant parameter would be a mistake.

Despite these problems, the inverse relationship has been confirmed in Indian agriculture at the time during which these studies were conducted, and its statistical validity is adequately established by an analysis of the disaggregated data. It is not necessarily, however, a phenomenon that will persist indefinitely. Clearly the inverse relationship is a phenomenon that needs to be explained, and not explained away by 'exacting statisticians'. These latter however did perform the useful function of questioning the FMS data critically. It would be a mistake to regard the inverse relationship as an empirical generalisation for Indian agriculture as a whole, however.

A wide range of relationships between farm size and other important factors are revealed that may throw some light on the theoretical understanding of this phenomenon. This range of clustered relationships suggests a possible labour-based explanation for the inverse relationship which will be discussed in the following chapter.

Further limitations of the FMS data include an over-emphasis on technical relations, input-output data, and only cursory information on tenancy and variation of tenurial terms and conditions across farms. The concentration on size of holding and technical relations on individual farms neglects information on property relations and underplays other aspects such as tenurial status, farm investment size, scale of output, rent burden, and non-price factors. An important point raised is whether productivity differentials will persist over time making small farms historically viable or whether they are based on a specific conjuncture of factors and are subject to change. The FMS years of reference are prior to the Green Revolution. Thus possibly production conditions have changed, both in technological and property aspects in certain regions.

This would suggest that the framework of analysis is inappropriate – an examination of the inverse relationship in the context of agrarian transition would perhaps be more profitable. We must go deeper than the size of holding categories to the underlying social relations of production. The next chapter examines the main theoretical approaches to the inverse relationship and in Chapter III, I attempt to transcend the limitations of the debate.

NOTES

1. This relationship is hereinafter referred to throughout this study simply as the inverse relation or inverse relationship. Other inverse relationships between key economic variables associated with the current debate are specified in full. While the inverse relation has been introduced as one between farm size and farm productivity, the latter component usually refers to land productivity. Given the overwhelming importance of land as the major factor input in the agriculture of poor countries however, this may be justified.

2. Cornia's study of 15 developing countries found that output per acre systematically declines with increasing farm size in all countries except Bangladesh and Peru [1985: 517–23]. We cite Cornia's evidence in full in Table 1 in Appendix A in order to show the precise basis for the statement. Evidence exists also for the following countries: Poland, Iran, Indonesia, Pakistan, Argentina, Chile, Guatemala, Korea, Sri Lanka, Thailand, Mexico, Brazil, Kenya, Philippines, Colombia, Malaysia, Egypt, and others [Dyer, 1995: 21].

3. Citing Lau and Yotopoulos [1971] and Paglin [1965].

4. The Indian debate on the inverse relation has been by far the most extensive. It began in the pages of the *Economic Weekly* (later *Economic and Political Weekly*) with Sen's 1962 article. It continued over the years with Mazumdar [1963], Sen [1964], Agarwala [1964a; 1964b], Khusro [1964], Mazumdar [1965], Paglin [1965], A.P. Rao [1967], C.H.H. Rao [1966; 1968a; 1968b; 1968c], Rudra [1968a; 1968b], C.H.H. Rao [1972], Bhattacharya and Saini [1972], Patnaik [1972], Rudra [1973], Bharadwaj [1974a], Chandra [1974], Chattopadhyay and Rudra [1976; 1977], Chadha [1978], Rudra and Sen [1980], Barbier [1984]. Other major contributions are Sen [1966], C.H.H. Rao [1966], Bhagwati and Chakravarty [1969], Saini [1971], Bharadwaj [1974b], Bhalla in Berry and Cline [1979], Saini [1979], Roy [1981], Carter [1984], Patnaik [1987], Bhalla [1988], Bhalla and Roy [1988]. See Ellis [1988] for a useful, but flawed, survey.

5. In the Indian context, precursors to Sen include Charan Singh, Raj Krishna and E.J. Long. Long concludes that the data 'clearly calls into question the supposition in much land reform discussion that large farms are more "efficient" than small farms' [1961: 118]. Bachman and Christensen take this further, citing Mann who finds generally higher output per acre on small family farms than on the large co-operative farms in Punjab [1967: 245].

6. I cite the Bharadwaj data in full in Appendix A as they usefully summarise the findings from the entire Indian FMS data set in the form of OLS regression equations. Bharadwaj fits a log-linear regression for each district for all three years: $\log Y = \log a + b \log X$ where Y = yield per net acre (yield is gross value of output) and X = *average* size of operational holding for the relevant size group. The use of grouped and averaged data is further discussed below.

7. While the regression coefficients are all negative, only three regressions (out of 21) are statistically significant: Bombay, Madras, and Punjab. See Table 1B in [Khusro, 1964: 55–7] for the full regression results.

8. See note 4 above which includes the major contributions to this extensive empirical support for an inverse relationship in the Indian context.

9. In determining the number of family parcels it is assumed that each family has 2.5 workers [Berry and Cline, 1979: 130]. Land available is defined as total farm area in the 1960 FAO World Census of Agriculture.

10. In seven out of twelve regional crop sectors, production changes were either negative or insignificant [1970: 146–8].

11. In a famous exercise, Khusro [1973] estimates the average size of the minimum feasible holding in India, in terms of minimum income unit, or the 'size of farm below which its output is too small to maintain the family at whatever is considered to be a reasonable standard of living' [1973: 38], at about 15 acres [1973: 67]. Likewise, the minimum work

unit, or the size of farm below which family manpower cannot be fully employed, is estimated at 7.5 acres, the dividing line between adequate and inadequate family labour absorption [1973: 60]. Finally, the minimum plough unit, or size of farm below which the farm becomes too small to absorb effectively the services of a pair of bullocks, is estimated conservatively at an average for all-India of 7.5 acres [1973: 52].

12. In Javanese conditions, for example, equal redistribution of land would leave no livelihood holdings at all, and the output effects of bringing ¼ acre farms up to ½ acre were found to be disappointing [*Lipton, 1974: 283*]. And in the Egyptian case, three acres is considered as being the minimum feasible size of farm on the income criterion, according to informal interviews with farmers during fieldwork in 1990.

13. A crucial distinction needs to be made here between purchased and on-farm-supplied inputs. See below and the discussion in Chapter II for the importance of this distinction.

14. See Dharm Narain, *Distribution of the Marketed Surplus of Agricultural Produce by Size-Level of Holding in India, 1950–51*, Asia Publishing House, Bombay, 1961.

15. W.R. Cline, 'Interrelationships between Agricultural Strategy and Rural Income Distribution, Food Research Institute Studie', Vol.12, No.2, 1973, and S. Bhalla, 'An Analysis of Savings in Rural India', mimeo, Washington, DC, 1975, using NCAER data.

16. I return to this question of farm size versus farm scale in Chapter III where we move on to a political economy approach to the inverse relationship in the dynamic context.

17. See T.J. Byres, 'Of Neo-Populist Pipe Dreams: Daedulus in the Third World and the Myth of Urban Bias', Journal of Peasant Studies, Vol.6, No.2, Jan. 1979.

18. Citing H. Morales Jara, 'Productividad presente y potencial en 96 predios de la provincia de O'Higgins y su relacion con el tamano de las propriedades', (tesis de Ing. Agron., Universidad de Chile, 1964; J.O. Bray, *La intensidad del uso de la tierra en relacion con el tamano de los predios en el Valle central de Chile* (Santiago: Universidad Catolica de Chile, 1960); A. Corvalan Morales and R. Parra Herrera, 'Introduccion a la determinacion de areas agricolas homogeneas en Chile: Aconcagua-Chile' (tesis de Ing. Agron., Universidad de Chile 1963).

19. The argument in this section has been developed by T.J. Byres in an unpublished manuscript.

20. In adopting such an approach, Patnaik is following Lenin's treatment in *New Data on the Laws Governing the Development of Capitalism in Agriculture*, which relates to the USA and the apparent inverse relationship found there in the US Census data on agriculture of 1910–11. See Volume 22 of *Collected Works* (Moscow, 1964), pp.58–71. One needs to take a position on whether or not Lenin was correct with respect to US agriculture at that time. He probably was. He, of course, himself used size, quite happily, as a stratifying variable in *Development of Capitalism in Russia*. But while Lenin may well have been correct with respect to the US in 1910–11, the same may not have been true of India in the mid-1950s; although it may have begun to have validity in parts of India by the 1970s.

It is interesting that Patnaik's reasons for so questioning the inverse relationship – that is, in relation to arguments about co-operative agriculture and so on – seem to be similar to Rudra's (whom she quotes with apparent favour [1972: 1615]. But her approach is, of course, very different to his. She also wishes to oppose the populist arguments about small farms being more efficient and so on [1972: 1613].

21. Note however that Roy [1979] does attempt to show that the direction of causality at the 'macro' level is indeed operative at the micro level. We will discuss this land-based approach to understanding the inverse relationship in chapter II.

22. Bhattacharya and Saini [1972: A-72] note that intercept terms vary significantly between villages due to soil fertility and other factors. Indeed, the variation in intercepts explains a higher proportion of variation in productivity than net or gross cropped area.

23. None of the studies on the inverse relationship gives any justification for assuming a linear relation, whether log-transformed or not. This criticism also has some significance for the reliability of t tests [*Roy, 1979: 27*]. The validity of t tests are dependent on the validity of the underlying regression relations. Rudra writes [1968a: 1043]: 'There may be many reasons to expect some sort of association (between yield per acre and farm size), but none whatsoever for any linear relation.' Scatter plots reveal the absence of any systematic relationship between the two variables.

24. The hypothesis to be tested is not that f(x) has any particular functional form with a negative coefficient, but that given (x1, y1) and (x2, y2), both x1 > x2 and y1 < y2 hold. Thus the suitability of rank correlation tests [*Rudra*, 1968b: A-37].

25. 'The reason we have not taken farm size as the divisor is that we would like to treat the extent of double cropping, proportion of uncultivated land to cultivated land, etc, as distinct factors affecting the economics of farming and not subsume all of them in the factor "size of farm"' [*Rudra*, 1968a: 1041]. This procedure however, obscures cropping intensity differentials between farm size groups which may be of critical significance.

In fact, inspection of the FMS tables themselves (in *Farm Management in India. A Study Based on Recent Investigations, Appendix III*), reveals that where the gross cropped measure is used, the inverse relationship disappears.

26. This can be seen from the table below in which two farms of the same size have the same output per gross cropped area, even though farm A has higher output per net cropped area [*Rao*, 1968: 1413]:

		A	B
(1)	size of holding (acres)	10	10
(2)	output per farm (Rs)	750	500
(3)	output per acre (2/1)	75	50
(4)	% of holding cultivated	100	80
(5)	% cultivated land double cropped	50	25
(6)	gross cropped area (acres)	15	10
(7)	output per gross cropped area	50	50

27. Rudra [1968b: A-38] answers Rao, but not convincingly. While the FMS studies use both net cropped area and gross cropped area, they are used in different contexts (see note on physical yields of individual crops and total value yields below). Rudra also points out that while higher cropping intensity on small farms is one of the factors leading to higher yields (hence the importance of using net cropped area in yield measurements), there are other reasons for the inverse relation mentioned by the FMS studies: such as higher labour input intensity and higher fertility. Therefore using gross cropped area should not 'correct' entirely for efficiency of land use. However, labour input and cropping intensity are highly correlated (see section I.4 below), and the differential fertility hypothesis is insignificant at the 'micro' level.

28. Saini in an earlier study uses disaggregated FMS data for Uttar Pradesh (Meerut and Muzaffarnagar districts) and Punjab (Amritsar and Ferozepur districts) for the years 1955–56 and 1956–57 (this paper is a shorter version of Saini [1969a]). All land coefficients were significantly below unity indicating a strong inverse relationship [*Saini*, 1969b: A-120].

29. See tables in Bharadwaj [1974a: 91–125, Appendices B-H]. Given their conciseness, the tables relating to the principal findings listed in the text are reproduced in Tables 3 and 4 in Appendix A.

II

Theoretical Approaches to the Inverse Relationship

INTRODUCTION

In the previous chapter, we saw that the empirical data points to a number of clustered relationships involving factors of production. That evidence has spawned a vast theoretical literature which has attempted to explain how the inverse relationship arises. It is both convenient and logical to examine the principal theoretical approaches to the inverse relationship under three broad conceptual headings: (1) the first approach attempts to explain the inverse relationship in terms of qualitative factor differences between farm-size categories; (2) the second, and more substantial approach, attempts to explain the inverse relationship in terms of differential factor use intensities between farm-size categories; (3) the third is a class-based political economy explanation of the inverse relationship. This is discussed in Chapter III.

Note here that the more usual categorisation of theoretical approaches in agrarian political economy, comprising neo-classical, Chayanovian, and Marxist paradigms, runs across the sets of explanations based on qualitative and quantitative factor differences. In this chapter, we intend to show that the first two approaches, both essentially static in nature, are either inadequate or fundamentally flawed as explanations for the inverse relationship. The third approach will be more fully examined in Chapter III when we move from the static context to the dynamic context of agrarian transition.

In section II.1, we discuss an influential set of explanations of the inverse relationship based on the proposition that small farms are characterised by better quality management, labour input, and technique than on the large farms. Section II.2 critically evaluates those explanations based on differential soil fertility between farm sizes. Related to that question are hypotheses concerning better irrigation on small farms.

The extensive list of complementary relationships revealed by the FMS data tends to suggest that the inverse relationship is associated with variations in cropping intensity and the quantum of labour and other production inputs per acre as the major explanatory factor. This has generated a group of explanations which we may call factor intensity explanations. One influential interpretation of the findings is that it is labour input intensity which explains higher cropping intensity, and much attention, therefore, has been directed toward the factors which explain labour input intensity.

Given the importance attached to labour use intensity, it is the rural labour market that has attracted most attention. It was to such questions that Amartya Sen directed himself by positing the existence of labour market dualism as the underlying explanation for the inverse relationship. In section II.3, we will outline the essential logic of the model developed by Sen, and confront the hypotheses associated with Sen's model with some empirical evidence on labour use in Indian agriculture. We also briefly discuss more explicitly neo-classical models – 'pricist' variants of the Sen model – which have been developed. Finally, in section II.4, we present a critique of the marginalist approach, within which both the Sen model and its neoclassical variants can be located.

II.1 MANAGEMENT AND LABOUR QUALITY HYPOTHESES

This section examines critically two separate, but as we shall see, inter-related explanations of the inverse relationship based on the proposition that small farms are characterised by better quality management and labour input than on the large farms.

Given the essentially untestable nature of the concepts of management and labour quality, the researcher is forced to utilise various proxies, and hence this approach tends to be residual in nature. Some form of 'diseconomies of large scale' peculiar to agricultural production are normally invoked as giving rise to an inverse relationship. Khusro [1964: 63, fn. 11] writes:

> with an expansion of farm-size and of all other inputs, might it not be that per acre returns decline owing to a fixity of entrepreneurship (the usual argument for diminishing returns to scale)? Entrepreneurship in underdeveloped farming being what it is, the point where it cannot cope with the expansion of other inputs ought to arrive at a smaller farm-size than in developed farming.

This view is supported by Hanumantha Rao [1966: 10–11]: 'If one agrees with Sen ... that the availability of capital cannot be a bottleneck for larger farms, then the productivity behaviour can be explained only in terms of the management factor and the income-leisure preferences among the larger farms.' Among the large farm groups, management may be insufficient to meet the increased needs of supervision and inefficient owing to dissociation of ownership from management and management from work [*Rao,* 1963: 2402].[1]

This argument appears to have two distinct components: the first is a proposition concerning the increase in complexity of organisation that comes with size, and which appears to have inefficiencies inherent in it, compared with the small farm situation; the second is a proposition relating to supervision problems and incentives which seem to become problematic as size increases.

Ellman states the first strand in the managerial diseconomies of scale argument as follows: 'the efficient large scale organisation of labour requires efficient planning, administration, and book-keeping work which is unnecessary under peasant farming where each peasant organises his own work for himself' [1989: 100]. This argument is frequently made with respect to agriculture, both large-scale capitalist farms as well as to collective farms. It is not an argument that one encounters with respect to industrial production. In principle, however, it applies just as much to a comparison between small-scale traditional artisanal units and large-scale modern units which spread management overheads. Yet it is not made in this context.

Clearly, complexity of organisation does increase with size, but why this should necessarily generate insuperable inefficiencies is not so clear. On the contrary, one might argue that the scope provided for division of labour and specialisation leads to the possibility of increased efficiency. If the logic of the argument applies to agriculture but not to industry, then identifiable differences must exist between the two, in relation to organisation and the internal problems of planning, administration and accounting. It is sometimes implied that such differences do exist in agriculture's spatial dispersion and the sequential nature of work over the course of the agricultural cycle. But why spatial dispersion is assumed to be a significant factor in agricultural production, and not in modern industrial production is unclear: after all, many modern plants cover vast areas and involve extremely complex management problems. Thus it is not at all self-evident that, simply in terms of organisation, large farms are inefficient. To that extent, the argument, in terms of organisation, is problematic.

Let us suppose however that the argument does have some validity. Its force then may hinge, to a certain extent, upon whether or not technical economies of scale exist. If there are indeed demonstrable potential economies of scale then these may compensate for possible managerial diseconomies. The greater the potential technical economies, the greater the compensation. That is, even if managerial diseconomies of scale could be shown to exist (in the sense that management becomes more difficult and more complex as size increases) that might not matter if technical economies of scale are possible. This implies a possible trade-off between technical economies of scale and managerial diseconomies of scale.

Thus, the argument simply in organisational terms is not wholly convincing, but the second part of the argument concerning incentives does seem, at first sight, to have considerable force. This part of the argument suggests that any economies of scale arising from indivisibilities will be offset by the agency costs of managing wage labour and enforcing effort on the part of the hired workforce. Supervision costs and incentive contracts, it is posited, will have profound implications for the optimal size of farm [*Mellor and Johnston*, 1984: 558; *Mellor*, 1966: 368; *Robinson* 1964: 1; *Nolan*, 1988: 41–2].

The obverse of the above approach is that small farms have a productivity advantage which relates to the quality of labour. This is a hypothesis in terms of qualitative factor difference which relates to incentive structures. It is a classic populist assumption suggested quite often in the literature, but is seldom stated with great clarity. More often, it is implied. Unfortunately, no evidence is presented in support of the proposition, or against which one might test the hypothesis.

Thus, for example, Khusro suggests that a unit of family labour is worth more, qualitatively, than a unit of wage labour. He says:

> Now, if it is true, as it probably is, that in agriculture a unit of family labour does more or better work than a unit of hired labour, the product will be larger for the former even if the quantities of labour applied were the same in both cases. In that case, a mere increase in the *proportion* of hired to family labour, as farm-size expands, gives a smaller per acre product [1964: 63].

Sen [1964a: 323] writes:

> Because of personal participation and supervision that a small business allows, a small holding may permit the use of some techniques – efficient ones – that cannot be used in larger holdings. Some techniques require not only inputs in the usual sense but also loving care, and Adam Smith had directed our attention to the 'affection' that small property inspires.

A more recent contributor argues: 'people will produce more as small family groups, working for themselves and receiving the whole product of their labour, than as employees in larger units ... This points to the frequent superiority of the smaller, self-managed family unit, as expressed in the 'inverse relationship': namely, the generally higher productivity of land, and to a lesser extent all factors taken together, farmed in smaller holdings' [*Lipton*, 1993: 1524].

Because family members are residual claimants to profits, they therefore have higher incentives to provide effort than hired labour. They share the burden of risk and have no search or recruitment costs in the labour market: thus, the claimed superiority of family over large wage labour-based operations [*Binswanger and Deininger,* 1993: 1452]. Due to the advantages of peer monitoring, agents such as family farmers benefit more from supervising each other in small groups than from external supervision by costly foremen. Small farms reduce unit labour-related transaction costs (search, screening, supervision, shirking) by providing nearby, informed, rapid and flexible family overview of labour, and by building on intra-family altruism and on the extended fungibility of family members between the household and the family farm [*Lipton and Lipton,* 1993b: 648].

It is further argued that individual peasant farmers have better knowledge of local natural conditions than managers of large farms, and that potential losses from imperfect information are minimised by the ability of the small farmer to adjust to micro variations in the natural environment [*Binswanger and Deininger,* 1993: 1452]. This is accentuated by weather variability which requires rapid and flexible response by the farmer.

Many of the foregoing arguments, if they have any validity at all, would appear to have more relevance for vast landed estates or extensive ranch-type farming involving thousands of acres. They will have much less relevance for the types of large farms we are considering, in the range from 10 to 50 or even 100 acres.

Supervision costs, under such conditions, would seem to be greatly exaggerated. The use of attached labour in a supervisory role, or even better, the use of family labour, in setting work tasks and ensuring execution is sufficient to ensure that the requisite labour effort has been expended on the part of the workforce. The threat of losing access to wage labour opportunities will provide the incentive for the worker to supply the quantity and quality of labour effort demanded. The often highly personalised relationship between employer and labourer, sometimes involving access to credit and land, help to provide 'nearby, informed, rapid and flexible' supervision of labour [*Bhaduri,* 1973].

On the small farm side of the equation, the idealised notion of 'family altruism' and 'fungibity of family members' ignores the unequal distribution of income within the farm household and intra-household exploitation. Further, the idea that small farmers have better information on the local environment is a dubious proposition, and is probably outweighed by the superior knowledge of large farmers concerning the use of modern technology.

The really critical problem, however, for these approaches is that if small farms were indeed characterised by superior management or labour quality, these should have been reflected in a productivity advantage with regard to individual crops. However, as Bharadwaj (Table 3a, Appendix A) has shown in her study of the FMS data no systematic or significant relation between farm-size and the physical yields of individual crops exists (in fact, irrigated wheat-gram and cotton in Punjab showed a positive relation). That they do not would seem to undermine further the hypothesis that the inverse relation arises from superior rural entrepreneurship of the small farmer.[2]

This approach is further undermined by the fact that the inverse relationship phenomenon is not limited to a simple comparison between small family labour farms and large hired labour farms. All the evidence shows that the inverse relationship runs across small family farms themselves. How the adherents of the above approaches might explain this has been left unwritten. Indeed, they seem not to have even recognised the problem.

Rao emphasises that the supposed managerial or supervisory disincentives are especially acute under labour-intensive techniques of production [1966: 11]. Indeed, much of the literature on diseconomies of scale comes from regions where agricultural mechanisation is incomplete and technical change has been slow [Binswanger and Deininger, 1993: 1452]. With traditional unmechanised technology, it is claimed that large landholders' supervisory capacity soon becomes binding [Binswanger and Deininger, 1993: 1468, fn. 2].

However, in the dynamic context of changing forces of production, with the introduction of more capital-intensive techniques, these constraints would be progressively attenuated. Indeed, the FMS evidence clearly shows that modern technology is concentrated on the large farms [Bharadwaj, 1974b: A-14]. This a topic which will be further explored in Chapter V.

II.2 LAND FERTILITY HYPOTHESIS

A second qualitative approach centres on the proposition that small farms are located on land of superior productive potential. Consideration of this factor leads us to the fertility-based explanation of the inverse relation.

There is some evidence in the FMS Bombay Report for intrinsic soil differences between farm sizes: small farms appear to have a higher proportion of medium and deep soils, and the uncultivated area is higher on the larger farms, but this should be interpreted cautiously as uncultivated land includes current fallow[3] as well as uncultivable bunds and irrigation canals. Indeed, it is difficult to distinguish between qualitative land differences and those arising from the application of fertility-augmenting inputs. Furthermore, superior soil quality may not be picked up by individual crop regressions because to some extent crop choice is dictated by soil type, and quality differences will be reflected predominantly in crop patterns [*Bharadwaj,* 1974b: A14-15].

Sen perceives some truth in the fertility based approach. Over time, a correlation between land fertility and size of holdings will be established via population expansion on more fertile land. Faster population growth on more fertile land (due to higher growth of income opportunities) leads to greater subdivision of the land. This is easy to see in interregional variation where population expands faster due to natural increase and immigration, but also within regions, claims Sen, where the ability of a farm household to withstand famine or crop disease is greater with more fertile land. Note that this approach ignores the crucial distinction that must be made between the inverse relation at the macro level, and that at the micro level (see Chapter II, section II.2).

Sen's argument regarding fertility differentials relies upon a rather dubious Malthusian link between income and family size and between level of income and fragmentation, and ignores alternative employment opportunities off-farm. An alternative hypothesis proposed by Bhagwati and Chakravarty [1969] suggests that large farms build up holdings by land purchase and foreclosure on loans leading to a high degree of fragmentation, and consequently low productivity.

Of course, neither version of the fertility hypothesis (Sen or Bhagwati and Chakravarty) holds the promise of economic betterment for the small farmer nor reflects any inherently progressive characteristics of the latter. However, while the fertility hypothesis based on partible inheritance or small farm distress sales may appear plausible, it is weakened by the fact that small farmers may sell land to other small farmers. Likewise, land reform laws may simply lead to the large farmers divesting their worst quality land. Bharadwaj also points out that according to the FMS database, whereas large holdings do tend to be composed of a greater number of fragments, the intensity of fragmentation (number of fragments per acre) is higher on the small farms (Table 4, Appendix A).

Khusro points out that the FMS survey deals with crude acreage figures with no correction for fertility.[4] He [*1964: 64*] claims to show, based on the behaviour of land revenue, that as farm size increases the proportion of bad or indifferent land increases and that this accounts for the decline in land productivity.[5] However, land revenue may be based on other considerations. Roy [*1979: 10, fn. 2*] cites the 1940 Land Revenue Commission: 'The absence of any systematic assessment in Bengal has led to a rate of rent, the incidence of which varies considerably from district to district and from holding to holding and has little relation to the productivity of land.'[6] Indeed, the land revenue figures may reflect neither natural soil fertility nor man-made improvements, but simply output per acre itself. In other words, land revenue figures may simply reflect that which we are trying to explain.

Having succinctly and clearly demonstrated the crucial difference between the macro level inverse relationship and the micro level relation, Roy [1979: 4] attempts to prove the thesis that at all levels of disaggregation, the inverse relationship arises along macro lines, that is, the main line of causation runs from soil fertility and therefore productivity to farm size. Thus, it needs to be shown that: (1) land is heterogeneous with respect to soil quality within the village; and (2) better quality land is parcelled into smaller operational units even at the village level.

Roy's conclusion is that it is not labour intensity that determines the inverse relation, but the fact that small farms are situated on better land (with higher water availability). Roy's chain of reasoning runs as follows: in the Indian context (as in tropical agriculture in general), the principal determinant of land productivity is soil moisture content rather than soil quality as a whole. Whereas soil quality variations tend to occur quite naturally at the macro level, soil quality and texture become more homogeneous at the more disaggregated level. This is not true of water availability however. The factor that causes most variation in soil water content at the micro level is topography.[7] Roy therefore needs to show that small farms are situated on land with higher soil water content, and hence on land of suitable topography. However, due to 'paucity of information', Roy is forced to use 'indirect forms of data' of an 'illustrative and ... indicative nature only' [1979: 68].[8]

Roy also admits that he will have to use similar indirect methods, using FMS data for West Bengal 1954–55, to demonstrate a connection between topography (as a proxy for soil moisture content) and cropping pattern [1979: 71, Table 2.5 and 73, Table 2.6], and between these and the inverse relationship (Table 5, Appendix A). Again this exercise represents a weak link in Roy's chain of reasoning. He writes: 'these correlations are of course necessarily vague due to imprecise data' [1979: 72].

He goes on to demonstrate that the distribution of this major asset is determined by (1) the pattern of tenancy and (2) the legal superstructure via partible inheritance. While plot size can indeed be a crucial control variable within tenancy agreements,[9] Roy's hypothesis is seriously impaired by the lack of robust data: evidence on tenancy is notoriously unreliable and tends to be at a highly aggregated level. Furthermore, data on soil quality are practically non-existent at the required level of detail.

However plausible the above hypotheses may seem, they nevertheless fail to establish an a priori foundation for explaining the distribution of land. They do not take into account the possibility that inheritance patterns may mean that heirs receive plots of all land qualities [Sen, 1981: 204]. Neither do they take into account the power relationships between the members of a particular family (between different parts of a family clan, or between genders for example). Neither is this form of partible inheritance necessarily operative in Muslim or Sikh areas or other areas where these types of laws do not exist or have been considerably modified. Furthermore, this type of explanation does not take note of the fact that often (as in the Egyptian case) the family farm continues to be operated as a single unit after inheritance (see Chapter VII).

Roy has persisted in his attempt to develop a land fertility-based explanation of the inverse relationship. In Bhalla and Roy [1988][10] data for 21,499 farms over all-India are used to test whether soil quality is a significant explanator of productivity differentials,[11] and to 'lend support to those who use fertility based arguments' to explain the inverse relationship [*Bhalla*, 1988: 60]. However, what these results in fact show is that despite the existence of the 'natural', macro-level inverse relationship, and despite the inclusion of soil quality indices in the model specification (which after all are there to control for soil quality differentials), there is still strong evidence for the existence of a significant inverse relationship in a high proportion of these relatively highly aggregated samples. And in almost one third of the district samples, we have a significant inverse relationship across farm size that needs to be explained.

Any discussion of the land fertility-based explanation of the inverse relation would be incomplete without commenting on the perhaps curious empirical finding that small farms appear to have a greater percentage of acreage under irrigation. Many studies have focused on this fact as an explanation for the inverse relationship [*Rao*, 1963: 2043; *Rao*, 1966: 7; *A.P. Rao*, 1967: 1990].

Bharadwaj [1974b: A-19] offers two possible explanations for the statistically significant inverse relation between irrigation ratio and size: (1) better irrigation leads to greater soil fertility which over time produces greater land fragmentation; and (2) abundant family labour is deployed to create and maintain irrigation facilities. However, the first explanation along the lines of the macro inverse relation, would not explain why within a given district, small farms have a higher percentage of irrigated area. Secondly, if such irrigation facilities require capital investment, then the purported advantage of the small farmer will be counterbalanced.

Bharadwaj also very interestingly directs attention to the possibilty that landlord strategies generate such a finding. Thus, she suggests:

> The landlord may prefer parcelling out the irrigated land among very small tenants for two reasons: while the bargaining position remains strong *vis-à-vis* the petty tenant, the latter may also have to resort to

very intensive cultivation in order to eke a subsistence out of the small plot leased to him. Thus the landlord may find it possible to maximise his returns (as a share of the total gross output on his entire land) if he leases out the land in smaller plots [1974a: 42].

This approach has a great deal of plausibility, and tends to fall within a class-based explanation, to be closely examined in Chapter III.

However, an inverse relationship between farm size and percentage area irrigated tells us nothing about the quality of irrigation facilities on various farm sizes, nor its effectiveness. The irrigation ratio is a rather poor index which does not indicate the effectiveness, source, quality, controllability or quantum of water supply. Indeed, Bandhudas Sen states: 'A large proportion of the area officially classified as irrigated is no better than unirrigated land, depending on rainfall as the source of water' [1974: 27]. Therefore quantitative comparisons of irrigation ratios are both imprecise and inaccurate.

II.3 LABOUR INTENSITY AND LABOUR MARKET DUALISM: THE SEN MODEL

Sen, in his seminal 1962 article, states that the FMS observations regarding the inverse relationship are to be expected given what he calls the 'mode of production' of Indian agriculture and its variation over farm size. He continues: 'we must focus attention on the systems of production underlying Indian agriculture' [1962: 245]. Sen later states [1966: 443] that it would be dangerous to analyse the peasant economy in terms of ideas borrowed from capitalist economies.

The Sen model[12] divides the rural economy into two parts: a modern, capitalist large farm sector based on hired labour, with the goal of profit maximisation; and a traditional peasant small farm sector based on family labour aiming to maximise gross output. While this approach, then, does hint at the question of determinacy alluded to above, Sen leaves the reasons for the primary motivation of output maximisation on the peasant farms unexplained, and concentrates on the causal factors behind higher labour input intensity.

On the large wage labour-based farms labour is hired in up to the point where the marginal product of labour is equal to the market wage, thus maximising profits. On the small family labour-based farms, 'provided labour has no outside opportunity of employment and provided there is no significant disutility of work in the relevant range of effort', labour will be applied beyond the profit-maximising point until its marginal product is zero [*Sen*, 1962: 245].

In a more sophisticated version of the model [*Sen*, 1966: 440], the small farms maximise utility in a trade-off between increased income from extra output and leisure. Thus on the family labour-based farm, the marginal product of labour is not equalised to the market wage, but is determined by the subjective evaluation of the marginal disutility of effort. Hence the market wage is no guide to the opportunity cost of family labour. The peasant household with under-employed family labour will accept lower returns in self-cultivation than in the rural labour market at the prevailing wage. Only in the case of output maximisation, will the marginal product of labour on family labour-based farms approach zero. The internal family worker wage will be the average product, greater than the marginal product, and setting a floor to the market wage.

This family labour allocation rule is similar to that advanced by Chayanov in his theory of the peasant economy.[13] Unlike Sen, however, Chayanov assumes the existence of family labour farms to the exclusion of wage labour-based farms. Nevertheless, they arrive at similar claims as to the relative superiority of the family labour farm. The subjective evaluation of labour is lower on the peasant farm than on the capitalist farm and this provides the former with greater resilience (via the ability of the peasant family to compress income).[14]

On this basis, the market wage does not reflect the 'true' opportunity cost of labour in the economy. Sen claims that capitalist labour allocation reflects this distortion, but peasant labour allocation is correct in calculating from the real cost of labour. Alternatively, of course, the wage gap may reflect the genuine social cost of hired labour and so there is no misallocation [1966: 443].

Thus, the inverse relation, according to Sen, is the natural result of an economy characterised by the existence of widespread surplus labour and family-based non-wage cultivation. The crucial factor is not size as such, but the system of farming (a large co-operative, for example, operating on the basis of family or non-wage labour may have higher yields than small capitalist farms [1962: 246]).

A number of writers have criticised the Sen approach as being analytically deficient given that even small farms do not rely on family labour exclusively, and a large number of small farms are engaged in off-farm income generating activities. It is pointed out by these authors that the Sen model requires the non-existence of off-farm employment opportunities and the absence of labour-hiring on the small farms [*Khusro*, 1964; *Bhagwati and Chakravarty*, 1969; *Rudra*, 1973; *Taslim*, 1989; *Mazumdar*, 1963: 1259].

Sensitive to the criticism that family labour farms and wage labour farms are not hermetically compartmentalised, and therefore that the wage rate may indeed be a decision variable for both sets of farms, Sen [1966: 443] does attempt to look for other explanations of the wage gap. He suggests that the wage gap may be to some extent explained by the efficiency wage hypothesis[15] or monopsonistic labour market behaviour and/or the presence of supervision problems [Sen, 1981: 210].[16]

The wage gap will be increased if family members on small farms discount market wages by the risk attached to job search. As long as the probability of finding a job is less than unity, it is to be expected that there will be lower output per acre on wage-based farms where the marginal product of labour and wage rate are equated. On the family farm, labour will be applied until the marginal product of labour is equated with the wage rate discounted by the probability of off-farm employment [Sen, 1964a: 323–5].[17]

The wage rate will not represent the marginal social opportunity cost of labour in the context of employment barriers [Sen, 1962: 246]. Indivisibilities in labour demand during the peak season, when agricultural operations are under a time constraint and there are risks and costs to the large labour-hiring farm in delay, may constitute an important labour market barrier. A partially unemployed farmer/labourer having to cope with coordination between off- and on-farm work and domestic chores will be at a disadvantage against the fully unemployed landless worker. The free time at the disposal of the farmer may be less than the minimum required by an employer [Bardhan, 1973: 1380].[18] The FMS data provides no information on free or unpaid labour services linked to rental or credit contracts. Such services may be extracted in the peak season, thus 'no simple "opportunity cost" concepts can be applied' [Bharadwaj, 1974b: A-17].[19]

Of course, the fact that small farms hire in labour does not imply that they should follow the MPL = w rule. Time constraints may necessitate the hire of labour for urgent tasks to avoid harvest failure, which is quite consistent with under-employment throughout the rest of the year. Further, certain operations require specialised skills requiring hired labour which cannot therefore be seen as a substitutive category. The hire of certain equipment, for example, may require hired labour.

Furthermore, there may be sociological factors behind labour market imperfections: barriers to employment of women and children on account of status, or reluctance to work outside the farm [Bardhan, 1973: 1380].[20] Family labour and off-farm labour are not always coterminous. Social convention and traditional behaviour may determine the allocation of tasks, dependent on class, caste and gender status.

Neither hypothesis then (that family and hired labour are exclusively separate categories so that family labour becomes a datum to the cultivating household, or that they are perfect substitutes so that the wage rate measures opportunity cost) is justified. The wage rate is only one determinant of labour use and possibly not the most important factor [*Bharadwaj,* 1974b: A-18].

A second major criticism directed at the Sen model is an extension of the above argument. Clearly, farms are neither exclusively family labour-based nor wage labour-based, but this can be taken further: examination of the FMS data shows that the proportion of exclusively family labour farms is negligible among the large farms (it is not even very high among the small farms) so that the labour allocation pattern posited by Sen on such farms cannot be used as a firm basis for an explanation of the inverse relation over the entire range of farm size [*Chattopadhyay and Rudra,* 1976: A-112].[21]

The Sen model may hold true for the range of farm size where the necessity of hiring labour in the slack season does not arise, but Khusro [1964: 63], in the Indian context, has shown that family labour is fully employed on the 7.5–10 acre size class, and hired labour is necessary beyond 10 acres. Once 15 acres is reached, the fixed quantity of family labour wears thin (per acre use of family labour is negligible both on 15 acre and 50 acre farms, with both depending on hired labour). So the use of family labour cannot be used as an explanation of higher productivity on 15 acre as against 50 acre farms.

Hossain [1977] restricts the opportunity cost explanation of the inverse relation to the range of small farms, but this does not explain the fact that the inverse relation is just as strong among the large farms relying on hired labour as between the small farms and large farms [*Taslim,* 1989: 56–7].[22] Nor does such an approach explain the lower labour use per acre on hired labour farms or the absence of any relation between labour use and the proportion of family labour as shown by Rudra and Bandopadhyaya [1973b: 989–91]. Labour input per farm, labour input per acre and output per acre show no systematic or meaningful pattern against the proportion of family labour to total labour. Statistical tests of labour input per acre against the proportion of family labour show that labour input per acre is not higher for family labour-based farms and there is no significant variation in labour input per acre across type of farm. Indeed, labour input per farm and output per acre are both less for the pure family based farm than pure hired labour farms. Thus there is no systematic dependence of labour input per acre or output per acre on labour composition, and therefore average output per labourer does not vary across labour composition [*Rudra and Bandopadhyaya* 1973: 992].

Taslim [1989: 58–62] in his study of Bangladesh[23] also finds empirical support for Rudra's results. A number of the propositions of the labour-based approach (specifically evidence for the links between labour intensity, yields and farm size) are supported, but the link between abundant supply of family labour and higher labour intensity at the heart of the family labour-based explanation is not supported. Evidence for the inverse relationship itself was inconclusive (statistically significant only at the aggregate level), but even if shown to exist, the evidence against the core hypothesis of the Sen approach shows that the opportunity cost of family labour explanation cannot be valid.

More explicitly neoclassical models exist which posit different sets of factor prices facing small and large farms as an explanation for the inverse relationship [Srinivasan, 1973; Bardhan, 1973; Griffin, 1974; Bhalla in Berry and Cline, 1979]. Here, the question is one of optimal use of factor inputs in the context of relative scarcity.

These authors present the following hypothesis as the main explanation for the inverse relationship: factor prices differ between the large farms and the small farms, such that the effective prices of land and capital are low for the large farms and the effective price of labour is low for the small farms. The presence of relatively abundant family labour on small farms and the relatively low implicit price of land for the large farmers dictate choices of technique with different factor intensities. Thus small farms have high labour/land ratios, whereas large farms use labour and land less intensively. Small farms with a lower opportunity cost of labour, can exploit more marginal land, cultivate a larger proportion of their land, and achieve higher yields.

In these factor market imperfection theories,[24] then, large farms go for production techniques with high land/labour and capital/labour ratios because factor market prices diverge from social opportunity cost, and this produces an inverse relation.

However, the principal thesis of differential factor prices between large and small farms, and its explanation in terms of the Sen framework, is highly problematic. If indeed factor price differentials were the main explanatory mechanism at work, then we would expect to find higher capital intensities on the large farms manifested in technological innovation, both biochemical and mechanical. However, as we will see in Chapter V below, in this context the inverse relationship breaks down. Indeed, this hypothesis would appear to be more appropriate as an explanation for the non-existence of an inverse relationship rather than its cause. Further, the supposed ability of the small farmer to exploit more marginal land (because of a lower opportunity cost of labour) is hardly conducive to higher crop yields.

Furthermore, the link between the ratio of hired labour to family labour and output per acre, and hence the link between supervision problems and productivity depends on the robustness of the proxy variable used in the correlation. Indeed, as Taslim himself recognises [1989: 68], the ratio of hired labour to family labour may not be an index of supervision problems, but instead reflect the ability of the farmer to hire wage labour. Employment of wage labour requires a fund of working capital. A low hired labour to family labour ratio may simply reflect the lack of access to such a fund. If such capital-constrained farms are characterised by lower productivity, then the above correlation is spurious. This, of course, points in the direction of a very different type of explanation for the inverse relationship which will be discussed below.

II.4 A CRITIQUE OF THE MARGINALIST APPROACH

One common element between the Sen model and these more explicitly pricist variants is that they share the same marginalist conceptions and categories. The critical problems arise from the production function methodology employed. Much of the FMS analysis is set out in terms of problems of resource utilisation in analogy with producers in competitive firms: production function analysis and optimality of labour use. They share a set of similar assumptions involved in the purported behavioural calculus at the centre of the models. The only difference between Sen's model and the factor market imperfection theories mentioned above is that the latter consider all relative factor prices whereas Sen considers only one price: the cost of labour, which varies according to the system of production. Note that the pricist variants do not recognise different farming systems in agriculture: 'We believe the agricultural systems in most parts of the third world are essentially capitalist' [Griffin, 1974: 83].

An important point of criticism of both the Sen model and the neoclassical variants concerns the simplifying assumption of a single crop and a single production cycle. This misses entirely the crucial significance of cropping intensity and cropping pattern. Roy [1979: 38–9] notes Sen's emphasis on 'for any one crop', and points out that Griffin [1974: 41] talks only of the relation between the output of a single crop per acre, in particular rice yields, and farm size, and deals with individual production cycles. Griffin claims that the subdivision of holdings would increase both employment and rice output. Thus, we see that both models were geared to explaining a non-existent relationship: while the inverse relationship can be observed in value terms, no such relationship exists with respect to the physical yields of individual crops. Of course, the models can be respecified to look at total value of crop output and labour input intensity, with a strong relationship between cropping intensity and labour application.

Production function studies, however, suffer from the problem that they are estimated with flow measures which obscures the role of indivisibilities in agricultural production [Sen, 1981: 204].The whole exercise of comparing the marginal product and wage rates is meaningless for agricultural production. Agricultural production is very different from industrial production. It is sequential in nature, subdivided both temporally and operationally. The production cycle in agriculture is prolonged and varies greatly between crops. No straightforward marginal productivity rules can be applied here as the productivity of family labour inputs prior to harvest time will depend on the timely application of the necessary amount of labour during the harvesting period. Labour demand at the harvesting stage is largely determined by elements of previous stages.[25] Labour at earlier stages thus has to be seen in the nature of fixed costs. Labour demand at harvest is a derived demand dependent on conditions earlier in the production cycle.[26] Under such conditions, the meaning of the marginal product of labour in agriculture becomes extremely hazy almost to the point of becoming operationally useless [Roy, 1979: 20–23].

A second common element is that both approaches assume the same production function for all farm sizes and systems of production. Both peasant and capitalist farms are assumed to be operating on the same production function, an assumption not identified by Sen in his 1962 or 1964 papers, but eventually admitted in his 1966 article. Sen focuses on two different systems of production: small peasant farms and large capitalist farms. It is not obvious therefore why these two systems are located on the same production function (the same marginal product of labour curve). Roy notes: 'the model is comparing farming methods which have fundamental differences in their organisation of production and qualitative differences in their division of labour' [1979: 19]. A theoretical justification for assuming the same marginal product curve for family labour-based and wage labour-based farms is not provided by Sen. If either class of farms use more capital or other inputs or enjoy some other advantage then that marginal product curve would be higher.

A similar problem undermines the more explicitly neo-classical variants of the production function approach. While labour homogeneity is assumed, this is not sufficient: the use of a single MPL curve requires concomitant assumptions regarding the organisation of production, homogeneity of all factors of production and equal factor intensities. Such models must also assume that different farms apply identical capital inputs per acre (both in quantity and type of capital) and that land is homogeneous regarding soil quality and irrigation. The isoquant diagram of Griffin includes land and labour holding capital constant, but if capital intensity varies across farm size then the isoquant will shift unequally.[27] Bagchi [1962] has shown that variation in the intensity of capital utilisation may make it difficult to analyse such relationships in neo-classical terms.[28]

Indeed, Sen himself was later to admit: 'it is illegitimate to eulogise peasant farming on the basis of an analysis in which every type of farm has access to the same production function and to the same factors of production' [1966: 444]. A peasant farmer may be constricted to a less efficient set of production conditions including lack of access to economies of scale, lack of technical knowledge or access to particular factors, or risk aversion to using new inputs.

The use of a single production function to compare two very different systems of farming, points to the identification problem at the heart of the Sen model and its disciples. This concerns the assumption that large farms are capitalist farms, and small farms are peasant family labour-based farms. This conceptual sleight of hand obscures the real relations at work which produce the inverse relation. This crucial point will be further discussed in Chapter V where we turn to a class-based approach to analysing the inverse relation. We must go deeper than the size of holding categories to the underlying social relations of production, in the dynamic context of agrarian transition.

A further set of problems arise from the proposed behavioural calculus of the farmer internal to the farm and to the methodology of comparison of the wage rate and marginal productivity. It is inappropriate to postulate effective leisure preference among poor peasants who are very close to subsistence; the effective limits are more likely to be biological [*Sen*, 1981: 207]. As we saw in section IV.2, family labour allocation is determined by objective factors like involuntary unemployment and intensity of poverty. Poverty and unemployment, rather than leisure preference, are the main reasons why small farmers intensify family labour use [*Sen*, 1981: 209].

SUMMARY AND CONCLUSIONS

We have seen in this chapter that the explanations of the inverse relationship based on qualitative factor differences are severely flawed. The various approaches are both theoretically inadequate and their assumptions are not supported by the empirical evidence.

Neither the qualitative differences in land nor in management and labour provide an adequate explanation for the inverse relationship. The differences in output per acre among farms cannot be ascribed mainly to inter-farm differences in soil quality or farm management. This essentially untestable hypothesis rests on an uncritical acceptance of the inverse relationship data, relying on a residual hypothesis tested by weak and unreliable proxy variables without consideration of other factors which a more critical analysis of the data suggests are important.

We have seen that any productivity advantage that might exist is certainly not supported by any evidence in terms of physical yields of individual crops or in terms of profitability. If indeed qualitative factor differences of this kind were involved, then one would expect to see discontinuities in the data at certain farm sizes and not a monotonically declining distribution of the observations. That we do not observe such discontinuities further undermines the technique-based approach.

The alternative hypothesis concerning differentials in land or soil quality between farm sizes rests on conceptual confusion over the meaning of fertility and on the distinction that must be made between the macro and micro levels of aggregation. The attempt to use land values or land revenue as proxies for soil quality have proven quite misleading. At best, indirect and imprecise data have been used to support a priori reasoning which neglects factors which would tend to undermine the hypothesis.

Clearly, the empirical evidence provides support for an explanation of the inverse relationship based on factor intensities and, in particular, a labour-based explanation. The clustering of empirical relationships around cropping intensities and labour input intensities (the latter subsuming capital and irrigation factors) in association with the inverse relation finding certainly justifies the focus on patterns of labour use.

However, the models presented above which attempt to explain how the inverse relationship is generated via labour utilisation are theoretically flawed, while crucial elements in their underlying assumptions are also subject to empirical refutation. The critical problems arise from the production function methodology employed.

The principal factor intensity-based explanation of the inverse relationship is the labour utilisation model developed by Sen. This essentially static framework has proven to be seriously defective. As Abhijit Sen [1981: 210] points out: there is 'an unexplained inconsistency between the a priori evidence that it is labour use which causes the inverse relation and the negative results from direct tests of labour-based hypotheses'. We have seen that Sen's opportunity cost model cannot be used to explain the existence of the inverse relationship among predominantly wage labour-based farms nor where most farms employ hired labour. Indeed, Rudra and Mukhopadhyay [1976: 34] show that labour-hiring is a generalised phenomenon on the small farms.

Conceptually, the cheap labour theories (both those of Sen and the more neoclassical variants) depend on a spurious calculus involving the marginal product of labour and the wage rate. As we have seen, the former is an operationally useless concept in agricultural production, while the latter is only one and probably not the most important variable taken into account in determining labour use. The situation encompasses a more complex set of market and non-market relations than the suggested behavioural assumptions incorporated in the models allow. This more complex enovironment will be explored in the next chapter where we turn to a class-based explanation of the inverse relationship in the dynamic context.

NOTES

1. In fact, the empirical evidence from both the FMS data and the Land Holdings Inquiry conducted by the NSS 16th round 1960–61, would suggest that such diseconomies are negligible. Indeed, Hanumantha Rao himself claims that Indian farming exhibits constant returns to scale rather than diminishing returns – scant support for any residual hypothesis pertaining to management diseconomies. See C.H.H. Rao, 'Size of Holdings and Productivity: Some Empirical Verifications', (unpublished and no date), cited in Khusro [1964: 63].
2. See also Roy [1979: 39].
3. If the percentage of area under current fallow increases with farm size then this would have some explanatory value for the FMS finding of declining output per acre with farm size. Note however, that this would be no indication of inefficient use of land on the part of the larger size groups, even where land was the limiting factor: under conditions of technologically backward agriculture, fallow periods are required for soil nutrient replenishment. Constant use of land would be quite unsustainable without increasing dosages of fertiliser. Given its importance, current fallow should perhaps be deducted from cultivable area for purposes of comparison. Nevertheless, there is little evidence to show that current fallow is a major cause of the inverse relationship.
4. A.M. Khusro, 'Some Basic Generalisations in Indian Agriculture', (unpublished, no date) cited in Sen [1964a: 325].
5. Bandhuhas Sen [1967: 77–8] notes that Khusro's results on fertility are biased by the fact that farms are still grouped by acreage rather than by land revenue and that the corrections for land quality (using land revenue data) have been made on grouped data rather than ungrouped for individual farms. When individual farms are regrouped by land revenue assessment, a significant inverse relationship is still in evidence. He further finds that while farms are not homogeneous with respect to soil quality and that the latter does affect output, when acreage and output are adjusted by a soil fertility index to take account of inter-farm differences in soil quality, there is still a significant inverse relationship between farm size and output per unit size.
6. Land Revenue Commission, 1940, cited in *FMS West Bengal Report*, 1955–56, p.9.
7. Roy mentions other factors as being important including evaporation demand, groundwater supply, irrigation, soil properties, crop characteristics, rainfall, and other inputs. It is not clear why Roy singles out topography as the prime factor. By topography, Roy means that land productivity, as a function of water availability, is inversely related to altitude. Roy admits that this may be an over-simplification [1979: 56].
8. Roy [1979: 59, fn.1] mentions that many studies have noticed heteroscedasticity and high variance within farm size groups which he offers as circumstantial evidence for his thesis concerning water availability. The presence of substantial heteroscedasticity and high intra-group variance when data relating only to irrigated land are used, however, would tend to suggest that other random factors are at work.
9. See Bharadwaj [1974b: A-15]. Very small plots compel the tenant to intensify input use to provide a subsistence income after paying rent obligations. This will be further explored in Chapter III.
10. Both writers seem to have shifted significantly their position on the causes of the inverse relationship. Roy [1981] had made some attempt to explore a political economy approach, particularly in relation to technological change in the Indian Punjab (see Chapter III). Bhalla in Berry and Cline [1979], on the other hand, was an erstwhile supporter of a neo-classical approach based on factor price differentials (see Chapter II).
11. The data were collected by the National Council for Applied Economic Research (NCAER) Fertiliser Demand Survey for the agricultural years 1975–76 and 1976–77. Significantly, no data were collected on the use of labour input which would have allowed direct testing of the labour intesity hypothesis.
12. A.K. Sen [1962] in a model remarkably similar to that developed by the Russian economist A.V. Chayanov [1966]: as pointed out by T.J. Byres in 'Output Per Acre and Size of Holding: the Logic of Peasant Agriculture under Semi-feudalism', unpublished manuscript, 1977, and in Patnaik [1979: 417, note 4].

13. Indeed, Roy [1979: 15–16, fn.1] traces these cheap labour theories to Chayanov, but notes that the constraints on family labour farms hiring labour past the point of intersection of income and drudgery curves is not explained.

14. Sen notes that Georgescu-Roegen has traced this line of thought to the historical 'Agrarian Doctrine' and related it to the logic of feudal agriculture [Sen, 1964b: 439].

15. See H. Leibenstein, The Theory of Underemployment in Backward Economie', Journal of Political Economy, Vol.LXV, April 1957, and also D. Mazumdar, The Marginal Productivity Theory of Wages and Disguised Unemployment, Review of Economic Studies, Vol.XXVI, June 1959.

16. Sen also mentions the possibilities of an institutionally determined minimum wage rate, or compensation for the loss of average product by out-migrating workers, as potential explanatory factors in some cases.

17. Roy [1979: 18], commenting on Sen's defence of the model, notes that the assumption of independence between p and w is questionable. It is just as likely that there is a functional relationship between the two variables.

18. The FMS data reveals the following employment patterns: the smallest farms rely heavily on off-farm work, with severe underemployment on the farm. On medium-size farms, total employment increases, both on and off farm, but the opportunities of off-farm work are inhibited by peak season work on-farm. The large farms are characterised by high employment on-farm [Bharadwaj, 1974b: A16–17]. Bharadwaj [1974b: A-17] notes however that on and off-farm employment are not independent categories. The availability of off-farm work affects the rhythm and intensity of on-farm work through choice of crop pattern, which commits family labour over crop cycles and this may limit off-farm employment opportunities. This is crucial when farms have a single earner (the FMS West Bengal Report, pp.54–7, shows that over a third of the farms have a single earner). Thus on and off farm work are not additive or simple alternatives [Bharadwaj, 1974b: A-17].

19. See also Chattopadhyay and Rudra [1976: 112–13].

20. See P. Visaria, 'The Farmers' Preference for Work on Family Farms, in Report of the Committee of Experts on Unemployment Estimates', Planning Commission, Government of India, New Delhi, 1970. The data cover nine villages in Ratnagiri district, Maharashtra state, and 14 villages in Kutch district, Gujarat, in 1966. Some 54 per cent and 80 per cent respectively, of male farmers, and 66 per cent and 84 per cent respectively, of female farmers expressed unwillingness to work off-farm. Cited in Bardhan [1973: 1380].

21. Rao [1966: 4–5] points out from his pro-small farmer viewpoint that since not only labour, but also capital and irrigation vary less than proportionately with size, the net MPL curve cannot be the same for different farm sizes. Higher capital input per acre (labour-absorbing investment) and the greater managerial efficiency of the small farm imply a net MPL curve higher for small farms than large farms. However, large farm access to capital could push their MPL curve outwards.

22. See below for Taslim's explanation of this empirical finding.

23. The survey data were collected by the Department of Economics, University of Dhaka, in 1982. The data cover two villages from each of Mymensingh, Comilla, and Rajashahi districts. Fifty households were selected from the village populations conditional on their involvement in the land-lease market (300 households in toto comprising pure landlords, cultivating landlords, owner tenants and pure tenants.

24. Even in the absence of market imperfections, Srinivasan has shown that labour intensification on the small farms is an efficient outcome. This explanation runs in terms of farmer behaviour in the face of production uncertainty: the choice of labour allocation between self-cultivation at an uncertain return and employment at a given wage. In order to maximise the expected utility of income, the farmer should devote a larger amount of labour per acre to self-cultivation as the size of farm decreases.

   This holds under Arrow-type risk-aversion postulates: absolute risk-aversion decreases and relative risk-aversion does not decrease as wealth increases. However, the plausibility of non-decreasing relative risk aversion is not self-evident, and the assumption of a given wage rate independent of the influence of production uncertainty is unsatisfactory.

25. See Roy [1979: 21]: at the final harvesting stage, the constraint on labour-hiring is not the

MPL = wage criterion, but whether these fixed costs can be covered. This means that not only will labour continue to be hired when the MPL is less than the wage rate, but also even when the wage rate is greater than the APL. The only limit to labour-hiring occurs when the gross revenue from a day's harvest is less than the cost of a day's harvesting.

26. See Roy [1979: 22]. The physical yield of a crop is already determined (plants per acre times yield per plant), and therefore the number of labour-hours required to harvest the crop is also predetermined (for any given technology). Whereas with Sen, higher labour input causes higher yield, there is in fact a reversal of causation: higher yields produce a greater demand for labour.

27. Indeed, the FMS data also shows higher capital intensity on small farms contrary to Griffin who claims that the shadow price of capital is lower for the large farms than the small farms.

28. Cited in Sen [1964b: 441–2].

III

A Class-Based Approach and the Breakdown of the Inverse Relationship in the Dynamic Context

INTRODUCTION

In this chapter, we propose an alternative class-based approach to understanding the inverse relationship.[1] We begin in section III.1 with some preliminary statements, rounding off the theoretical discussion raised in the previous chapters, and pointing the way beyond the marginalist approach. Section III.2 goes on to situate the inverse relationship within the context of the relations of production which characterise backward agriculture.

Finally, section III.3 focuses on Sen's (and others') extrapolation of an essentially static result to a dynamic context in which both the relations and forces of production are changing. The inverse relationship appears to arise in a situation where all cultivators are employing the same technology, but if large farmers have access to a superior technology then the Sen logic breaks down, and with it the inverse relationship itself.

III.1 BEYOND THE MARGINALIST APPROACH

We pointed out in the previous chapter, that three possible explanations in terms of factor intensity have been posited: (1) labour input; (2) cropping intensity; and (3) choice of crop mix. A crucial point in the debate over the causal factors behind the inverse relationship, but one that is more often ignored or obscured, is which of these explanations is determinant? These findings are clearly inter-related, but what is the direction of causality? No simple econometric analysis can tell us the answer.

There are two possible interpretations however. The first, labour-based approach, we have surveyed critically in the previous chapter. The second is that it is higher cropping intensity and a cropping pattern associated with either higher labour absorption or remuneration (and hence the higher income derived from production) which implies greater factor use intensity, in particular labour intensity. Bharadwaj [1974b: A-16], indeed, suggests that value productivity differentials between farms boil down to the differential cropping intensity components of crop patterns.[2] Here, the primary motivation is output maximisation, with cropping intensity appearing as the proximate cause of the inverse relation. Higher cropping intensities imply a higher intensity in the application of other factors of production, particularly labour.

Bharadwaj [1974b: A-16] notes from the FMS evidence that while there is a strong inverse relationship between labour input and size, this is not manifested in terms of individual crops. An explanation in terms of efficient factor substitution (with land fixed and the same production function with small farms operating with higher labour/land ratios and with higher productivity per acre but lower labour productivity) is undermined by the fact that there is no such relationship between labour productivity and size to be found in the FMS data. She concludes: 'Thus the higher use of labour on small farms cannot be explained in terms of land–labour substitution along a production-possibility frontier' [1974b: A-16].

Chattopadhyay and Rudra [1976: A-114], although taking a rather eclectic view of the inverse relationship,[3] make the following powerful and incisive statement which takes us beyond the confines of the marginalist approach:

> Among the forces that drive a small farmer to more intensive effort the most important one, of course, is his need for survival. There is a certain basic minimum of consumption that a poor peasant family has to have without which it will be simply wiped out. It is only understandable that such a poor peasant family, depending on a small piece of land, submerged in a vast population of surplus labour in the countryside, and thus not having any alternative sources of employment and income, would try to produce the maximum output on his piece of land. He would not only ignore any marginal productivity calculations insofar as family labour is concerned, he would employ hired labour whenever necessary to supplement family labour, and in doing that would pay no heed to marginal productivities. He would also try to apply non-labour and non-monetized inputs with maximum intensity, once again by using labour without any calculations. He would try to improve the quality of land by small-scale irrigation and other such means as can be procured with the help of labour. He will tend to leave fallow as little land as possible, and try to cultivate as many crops as possible and choose such crops which after meeting his minimum consumption needs would meet his minimum cash needs.

Further, under sharecropping, the 'tendency to intensify his effort would be all the more so because of the fact that he has now to meet his minimum needs with only a share of the results of his effort'. Aspects of this we will wish to pursue below.

Despite the criticisms of the methodology and assumptions employed in Sen's labour utilisation model and the neo-classical 'pricist' variants, the former does have the great merit of attempting to locate an explanation of the inverse relationship in terms of the different conditions of production facing farm households. These he explores within the logic of what he calls the 'mode of production of Indian agriculture' and its correlation with farm size [1962: 245]. However, Sen's notion of mode of production is conceptually nebulous and constrained by its choice theoretic framework based on relative resource endowments.[4] There is clearly a need to go beyond farm size as the relevant stratifying variable to examine the underlying relations and forces of production.

The class-based approach proceeds from the proposition that the peasant farm is embedded in the socio-economic context of an emerging capitalist agriculture in which, however, non-capitalist forms of surplus appropriation are still prevalent. Such a transitional state has been described by Bhaduri [1973] and Bharadwaj [1974b] as one of semi-feudalism, a situation in which the relations of production have more in common with feudalism than capitalism. Bharadwaj writes: 'where capitalist farming is emerging out of a semi-feudal agriculture, the coexistence of both the modes shapes the labour market ... while the characteristics of the labour market itself influences the form and process of transition' [1974b: A-11].

Agriculture remains backward inasmuch as 'the process of commercialisation has not culminated necessarily or rapidly in the pervasive dominance of capitalist relations' [Bharadwaj, 1985: 9]. The process of commercialisation has intensified peasant differentiation but has not generated a qualitatively changed peasantry: it has not resulted in a fully-formed capitalist agriculture in which rich peasants are transformed into capitalist farmers and poor peasants into wage labourers. Neither commercialisation nor the development of wage labour, however, are sufficient conditions for the development of capitalist agriculture.

This directly addresses Sen's and other writers' erroneous identification, on the basis of the labour-hiring criterion alone, of the large farms in their samples with capitalist farms. That identification needs an altogether more complex specification.

Thus, the transition from rich peasant to capitalist farmer cannot simply be assumed (as it is generally in many studies of the inverse relationship) – it requires demonstration. While the use of wage labour and market participation may be an important indication of the process of agrarian transition, the evidence contained in Bhaduri, Bharadwaj, Patnaik and others, as to the lack of capital intensification on the large farms, and to the continued existence of unfree relations between labour hirers and workers would suggest that Sen's (and others') elision of rich peasant/capitalist farmer is invalid.

III.2 THE INVERSE RELATIONSHIP IN THE CONTEXT OF BACKWARD AGRICULTURE

It is within the context of a backward agriculture that we must seek the factors that give rise to and sustain the inverse relationship. Within a semi-feudal agriculture, the normal competitive assumptions are fundamentally violated. It is therefore highly misleading to hypothesise that individual producers confront technical and market data in an impersonal environment and all are equally free to take decisions in all markets. Much of the discussion in this section leans heavily on the interlinked rural markets or mode of exploitation literature.[5]

In backward agriculture, dominant classes (landlords, moneylenders, traders, or combinations of these functions) ensure that subordinate classes (poor peasants and landless labourers) can only gain access to markets on a highly personalised basis. This asymmetric economic and social power of the dominant classes over the subordinate classes allows the former to insist that the latter accept manifestly unfavourable terms in one market as a condition of access to another – unfavourable in the sense that those terms are clearly inferior to freely negotiable terms in free markets. Here, the dominant class can take advantage of the economic compulsions to participate in markets (forced commerce) which the subordinate classes are subject to: in order to ensure survival, reproduction or the need to achieve a particular cash income target to repay debt or taxes.

The extent and type of market participation by different groups of peasant and the character of markets themselves will be significantly determined by local patterns of power while markets reinforce those patterns. The initial resource position defines bargaining position while relative bargaining power determines access to resources and thus current production activity and asset-income position. Market and social power are vested in the dominant rural classes. Poor peasant involvement in one market may restrict choice in production decisions in other markets.

Bharadwaj portrays a hierarchical structure of exchange relations reflected in market interlinkages. First, the rich peasants and landlords: 'In any market – we consider here output, land, labour and credit markets as the prominent ones – there are dominant parties mostly belonging to the substantial surplus households [those of landlords and rich peasants] who set the pattern as well as the terms and conditions of exchange' [1985: 12]. These operators are powerful enough to exploit markets from a vantage point and shape market relations via interlocking forces – exploitation in conjoint markets: land, credit, labour, input and product markets.

Next the middle peasants: ' ... the medium operators [middle peasants and some richer peasants] are basically price takers and "quantity adjusters" in the sense that they have a safe enough margin of surplus to play the market game to maximise profits ... ' [1985: 12]. These intermediate operators are more self-reliant, but not necessarily in a position to exploit market relations. One might expect to observe defensive market avoidance on the part of the smaller farmers and market participation by the larger [Bharadwaj, 1974b: A-12].

Finally, we have the landless labourers and poor peasants:

> ... the 'chronically deficit' and 'subsistence' households [landless labourers and poor peasants] are involved in exchange compulsively. The very small cultivators and the landless, not possessing adequate resources for a reliable livelihood, have to enter the labour or credit market to incur consumption loans or obtain advances for circulating capital. Under the pressure of immanent cash needs they have to sell outputs, sometimes under prior commitments, even when they have to repurchase them under more adverse terms for their own subsistence [Bharadwaj, 1985: 12–13].

This compulsive market involvement will be reflected in cropping patterns, resource utilisation and a higher degree of monetisation of transactions under distress conditions. Bharadwaj [1974b: A-21] notes that in the West Bengal FMS studies, the farms producing only cash crops were all in the small size groups.

Markets are interlocked through price and non-price links. Such interlocking increases the exploitative power of dominant classes in that they can disperse exploitation over different markets and time periods – thereby circumventing traditional limitations. Exploitation is secured by denying participants in interlinked markets access to any of the individual markets:

> the weaker party in exchange loses the option to exercise choice in other markets due to its commitment in one. For example, the tenant who has committed himself into a land-labour tie (that is, to render free or underpaid labour services on the landlord's land as part of the lease contract) cannot avail himself of opportunities to hire himself out at a higher wage, even when such opportunities present themselves. The producer of a commercial crop who borrows on the commitment of selling his output to the merchant/creditor cannot gain from the higher return otherwise possible as he loses the option of

selling it in the market. Often, unlike pure usurious capital, the merchant/creditor intervenes directly in the production organisation of the debtor, dictating the decisions regarding the crops to be produced [*Bharadwaj*, 1985: 13].

This closing of options cements exploitation since it 'weakens the possibility of the indebted party recovering from a dependency situation, especially when there are no alternative means of livelihood' [*Bharadwaj*, 1985: 13].

Interlinkage further maximises exploitation over time, by the range and depth of control it makes possible:

> The power of the dominant party to exploit in interlinked markets is much more than in markets taken separately. There are conventional limits to exploitation in any one single market. For example, the crop share is conventionally laid down. The division of produce becomes a matter of convention ... There are also limits to exploitation set by the sheer minimum survival needs of the exploited party. With interlinked markets exploitation can be spread over markets (such as intervening in an output market on the basis of a credit tie) and even across generations, when the labour of future generations is committed by the debtor or tenant. Moreover, with options receding for the weaker party, the situation develops as one of dominant control over the entire livelihood of the weaker party. In proportion as the dominant party stretches the domain of exploitation, the weaker party's possibilities of redress diminish [*Bharadwaj*, 1985: 13].

Hossain [1977: 286–87] also finds evidence for this position in rural Bangladesh. Here, the inverse relationship arises due to the existence of a 'pre-capitalist organisation of production, where the market has a limited role and cultivators have differential access to various resources'. The pre-capitalist mode of production dominates the Bangladeshi social formation: private property in land exists but the forces of production are backward (capital plays only a limited role); markets in commodities and means of production are not significantly developed; and barely capitalistic large farms cultivate only a part of their land with hired and family labour and rent out the rest in small plots under sharecropping.

Thus, here we have a very powerful mechanism rooted in the social relations of production of an essentially pre-capitalist mode of production that ensures poor peasants maximise output. The poor peasant maximises output because his/her survival as a peasant depends upon it. It would appear therefore that the factors driving a poor peasant to intensify labour effort are more important than the factors permitting him to do so. The inverse relationship cannot be understood in terms of scale advantages among isolated farms or simply in terms of the poverty and unemployment facing poor peasants. The inverse relationship arises because of factors which are related to farm size, but not because of some independent size effect *per se*. It is thus misguided to treat the inverse relationship as a sign of relative efficiency rather than of distress. Chattopadhyay and Rudra [*1976:* A-115] conclude: 'if the inverse relationship be made the basis of a policy for preserving small farmers as they are, the result would be the destitution and expropriation of poor peasants ... '. At the other end of the class spectrum, rich peasants, who have not yet been transformed into capitalist farmers, use the *same* technology, but with much lower labour intensity, and thus achieve lower yields.

III.3 THE STATIC NATURE OF THE SEN APPROACH AND THE BREAKDOWN OF THE INVERSE RELATIONSHIP IN THE DYNAMIC CONTEXT

We turn now to a further set of considerations that need to be taken into account: the essentially static nature of the Sen approach. The extension of a static result which emerges in a given set of unchanging circumstances to a dynamic context in which the essential circumstances are changing markedly is invalid. The most significant change is likely to be with respect to technology. Chattopadhyay and Rudra [1976: A-115] note:

It is ironical that a static comparative situation between small farms and big farms, allegedly prevailing in the fifties in certain parts of the country – and even that, not at all established beyond doubt – has been the basis of plenty of friends of the rural poor opting for an agrarian policy that is ultimately destined to cause immiserisation of the rural poor. For even if the static comparison is valid in a certain stage of development of agriculture with low technological inputs, it cannot remain so during a period when there is a mounting drive by richer farmers to go in for more and more technological agriculture in search of higher profits'.[6]

In those areas where we find an inverse relationship, it is the case that all farm sizes have access to a more or less similar technology. Large and small farms use the same set of production inputs, and the small farms achieve higher output per acre via far higher cropping intensities which in turn imply higher application of labour effort per acre. With the introduction of a new technology which favours large farms due to its associated economies of scale, then the so-called advantage which the small farms have with respect to labour input intensity, may be matched or more than matched by the new advantages which large farms have with respect to technology. In this situation, we might expect the inverse relationship to break down and eventually disappear, and with it part of the case for redistributive land reform.

In terms of the class-based approach, which is essentially a dynamic theory, what is happening here is that with the development of the forces of production in the form of Green Revolution technology, it is the rich peasants who are better placed to reap the benefits. When the new technology is removed from the laboratory test beds and research stations, and inserted into the wider context of agrarian relations, factors operate to benefit disproportionately the large farmers. Institutional services (extension, credit, input/output prices, information, marketing, and political power) exhibit a strong bias in favour of the large farmer – both cross-sectionally and sequentially, with the large farmers being early adopters and therefore early gainers in terms of high output prices, low subsidised input prices [*Byres*, 1972].

It is the rich peasants who have the resources, which the poor peasants do not have, to gain access to the whole package of new inputs (HYV seeds, chemical fertilisers, plant protection materials). It is the rich peasants who are able to monopolise the available credit necessary to purchase the Green Revolution package. The rich peasants dominate the institutions which supply and distribute the new inputs. While these biochemical inputs may be scale neutral,[7] their adoption steps up pressures for mechanisation which does have associated scale economies. Abhijit Sen [1981: 212–13] notes that with high labour supervision costs on the large farms, this sets a limit to increasing output per acre unless labour-augmenting technology is adopted. Mechanisation can thus be seen as a response to problems of labour supervision on the large farms.[8] This leads to the breakdown of the inverse relation with large capitalist farmers achieving higher yields. Much of this is supported by evidence from the Punjab [*Chadha*, 1978; *Roy*, 1981; *Patnaik*, 1972].

In terms of the other sets of explanations we have looked at, those based on qualitative factor differences and those based on factor scarcities/imperfect markets, being essentially static arguments, have not adequately addressed this question: either the evidence on the breakdown of the inverse relation is denied or ignored and the relationship holds in all places at all times, or it is explained in terms of a U-shaped relation with small farms specialising in labour-intensive production and large farms in capital-intensive production, both sets of farms utilising resources efficiently and achieving high yields. Why such specialisation occurs is only incompletely examined however.

Some neo-classical writers do seem to be aware of the impact of technological change on the inverse relationship however, but have few suggestions as to the mechanism operating.[9] Mellor [1967] writes: 'the two prime inputs of traditional agriculture are land and labour. Capital is not only much less important in quantity, but also is largely a direct embodiment of labour in land improvements, water systems, and simple tools. The level of agricultural production in traditional agriculture is, therefore, limited by the amount and quality of land and by the amount of labour provided by the farmer, directly for production, or indirectly through the formation of capital goods.

> Ghose adds: 'The specific conditions for this superiority [the inverse relationship] appear to be primitive technology and insufficient development of markets ... It seems fairly clear that technological progress involving the introduction of chemical fertilisers, labour-saving machinery (e.g. tractors) and modern irrigation equipment (e.g. tubewells) is likely to erode the basis of superiority of small-scale production' [1979: 42].[10]

Sidhu concludes:

> Thus a major source of greater technical efficiency of smaller farms during the mid-1950s seems to be less important during the late 1960s [1974: 749–50].

The empirical evidence does indeed support the proposition that following the introduction of the Green Revolution technology, the inverse relationship has disappeared, markedly so in those areas where the new technology has penetrated most deeply. Rani [1971: A-89] writes:

> Whatever the situation may have been in the early sixties when the FMS were conducted, the whole controversy loses much of its importance in view of the developments which are taking place in Indian agriculture because, even if the small farmer has certain advantages over small farmers in labour-intensive techniques, these are likely to be wiped out as capital-intensive techniques gain popularity among farmers.[11]

Kahlon and Kapur [1968: 79–80], in an early study,[12] concluded that it was 'apparent that the adoption of yield increasing technology on the large farms in recent years had reversed the trend in yield per acre on large farms'. The trend reversed with technological breakthroughs on the large farms through adoption of improved strains such as hybrid maize, hybrid bajra and Mexican wheat, and intensive use of improved methods and practices. Kahlon and Kapur suggest that it was the higher application of chemical fertilisers that resulted in higher yields on the large farms. While the small farms used higher levels of farmyard manure than the large farms for desi maize, desi cotton and sugarcane, the large farmers used higher doses of calcium ammonium nitrate and superphosphate fertilisers than the small farmers, particularly for hybrid maize and wheat sown after the kharif crops and for irrigated groundnuts.[13] The seed rate per acre was higher on the large farms for almost all crops, especially American cotton and wheat. Rapid technological change and intensive use of non-traditional inputs on the large farms also resulted in higher per acre yields in the Hissar district.[14]

Saini [1971: A-82] however produces some contrary evidence:

> Under the impact of the 'green revolution', one would expect the inverse relationship to undergo a change and to cease to be true at least in the areas which have experienced the 'green revolution'. The data relating to Punjab (Ferozepur) and Uttar Pradesh (Muzaffarnagar), however, do not provide any evidence of such a change. It is perhaps too early to expect a change in the first two or three years of the setting in of the 'green revolution'.

A later study by Bhattacharya and Saini [1972: A-71] shows that for Muzaffarnagar in all years there was a significant inverse relationship, but the evidence was not clear for the Ferozepur district. While they claim that the green revolution had not affected the inverse relation in either region, regressions using gross cropped areas show a shift from negative to positive correlation over time in Muzaffarnagar and from zero to positive in Ferozepur.

In an attempt to study the inverse relationship in an area where the new technology had been widely adopted, Singh and Patel found no variation in yield per acre over farm size and no sign of an inverse relationship: the regression coefficients were all greater than unity, but not statistically significant. They write [1973: 47]: 'it may be concluded that in the context of new technology there is no indication of decrease in output per hectare with an increase in farm size and, therefore, the hypothesis of inverse relationship is rejected in the area under study.'[15]

In a major study of the Punjab, Chadha[16] finds that the inverse relationship ceased to hold in the post-green revolution areas as the resource structure between small and large farms changed. He divides the post Green Revolution Punjab into three agro-economic regions (on the basis of soil conditions, cropping patterns and irrigation systems) with three distinct technological levels: (1) the sub-montane region growing wheat, rice, and maize under rainfed irrigation; (2) a central zone growing maize with tubewell irrigation; and (3) the south-western cotton belt with canal irrigation. The central region was ahead of the other two in terms of irrigation, cropping intensity, HYV use and tractors.

With the introduction of the new technology, high labour/land ratios become less important. The new factors are land saving and capital-absorbing and largely purchased, not produced on-farm so that the on-farm labour content of capital is no longer important. Indeed, the capital/labour ratio becomes as important as the labour/land ratio in traditional agriculture. Investment in machinery was higher in region 2 and on the large farms (the latter invest three times as much per acre as the small farms).[17]

There was a clear relation between levels of irrigation and investment in new technology. Region 2 has a well-developed rental market for tubewell water and machinery. Region 2 was the most modern and region 1 the least modernised in terms of per acre investment in modern machinery.

While small farms show higher per acre investment on traditional items such as hoes, they lose this advantage when improved techniques are taken into account, with large farms showing much higher investment in modern machines such as tractors.[18] In region 2, the small farmers have over 70 per cent of their investment in traditional implements, but large farms have almost completely moved to improved items. On the large farms, the increase in capital inputs outstripped increases in labour input, while the smaller farms experienced a less than proportionate increase in capital input to labour input [Chadha, 1978: A-93, Table 9]. While the small farms could compete with the large farms in terms of HYV seeds and fertilisers, given co-operative services and government aid, they could not compete in terms of machinery [1978: A-95]. Chadha notes [1978: A-87] that while the biochemical innovations are labour-absorbing, land-saving and scale-neutral, the mechanical innovations are labour displacing and biased to scale. Furthermore, both types of innovation call for substantial capital investment.

Region 2 had the highest capital/labour ratios, generating increased output per acre. While the inverse relation still held in region 1, it had broken down in region 2, with region 3 intermediate.

Moving beyond farm size as the stratifying category, Rao and Brahme [1973][19] divided farms into peasant farms and wage labour based farms with the former defined as those where family male labour input was greater than 50 per cent of total male labour input. They conclude: 'the inverse relationship [was] noticeable in the peasant sector, while it [was] not apparent in the capitalist sector' [1973: 15]. On average, the wage labour-based sector registered higher labour input than the family labour-based sector [1973: 22].

Roy also examines evidence from the Punjab to show a significant transition from traditional to modern capitalist agriculture.[20] As in Chadha, Roy divides Punjab into three heterogenous zones: the relatively backward eastern Punjab, the more recently advanced central districts, and the advanced western Punjab [1979: 139]. He notes that the latter region benefited from the existence of British-built canals, it being historically a cotton area with significant market oriented production, and so was most suited to the introduction of the new technology. The central zone also saw recent tubewell expansion in the period 1965–75, thus permitting rapid progress with the green revolution technology. Contrariwise, the eastern submontane region lagged behind in new technology.[21]

The district regressions show a still significant inverse relationship in the eastern zone, insignificant for the central zone (Bhatinda, Jullunder, Kapurthala, Gurdaspur), and in the western Punjab a statistically significant positive relation between output per acre and net cropped area (see Table 16, Appendix A). Using gross cropped area in the regressions revealed that several western and central districts exhibited a positive relation (see Table 17, Appendix A). Roy awards these results some importance, as normally the relationship between output per acre and gross cropped area is neither significantly positive or negative. Since the relationship has turned significantly positive, he suggests that large farmers have attained important scale advantages.

The fact that the inverse relationship disappears despite the still significant inverse relationship between cropping intensity and farm size confirms the importance of crop pattern and the physical yields of individual crops.[22] The regression coefficients for HYV wheat reveal a positive tendency across farm size in three western districts (Ferozepur, Amritsar and Kapurthala) and a significantly positive relation for HYV rice in Amritsar and Kapurthala (see Tables 8–9, Appendix A).

Roy computes two indices of progressivity (see Tables 10–11, Appendix A):[23]

(1) the percentage area irrigated in the 1960s indicates those areas most suited to the introduction of the green revolution technology. Superimposing this pattern on the district maps shows an approximate similarity: the western region with a relatively high percentage area irrigated in the 1960s was the most technologically advanced prior to the green revolution and farmers there were the earliest adopters of the new technology, while the relatively backward eastern belt of districts were poorly irrigated, permitting only limited adoption of the new technology. Roy notes that irrigation differentials between sizes were no longer important in the post-green revolution period.

(2) the percentage of cultivated area under HYVs and American cotton as a proxy for commercialisation (the new seeds and fertilisers have to be purchased in the market rather than be supplied from on-farm production). Again, we find a broad correlation between the spatial pattern of this index and the inverse relationship results. The greater the degree of commercialisation of agriculture, the greater the tendency for the inverse relationship to disappear.

Amritsar and Ferozepur are the most advanced districts of the Punjab in terms of the extent of their adoption of the new technology, and were the most advanced prior to the green revolution. By 1974–75, the Amritsar district had 85.6 per cent of net cropped area cultivated under HYV seeds [1979: 149]. The district experienced a very high growth rate of agricultural output of 8.11 per cent between 1962 and 1973 and a rapid increase in the stock of technology [1979: 148, Table 5.8]. The area under tenancy declined and agricultural labourers as a percentage of the male labour force more than doubled from 9.23 per cent in 1961 to 20.12 per cent in 1971 [1979: 148, Table 5.7]. Ferozepur has a higher than average size of holding (6.32 ha as against 5.0 ha for the state as a whole) and high irrigation ratios. This district specialized in cotton (producing 53.01 per cent of Punjabi cotton in 1967–68) and wheat.

The relationship between farm size and land productivity as indicated by the regression coefficients shows an interesting progression: from a statistically significant -0.17 in 1956–57 to a statistically insignificant -0.03 in 1968–69, and finally to a significant positive coefficient of 2.7415 in 1975–76 [1979: 151, Table 5.9]. Also noteworthy as an indication of changing relations of production in the district is the rapid decline in share tenancy from 33 per cent of the area in 1954–55 to 6.64 per cent in 1969–70 [1979: 152, Table 5.10]. The data also reveal a rapid change in the stock of technology towards chemical fertilisers, tractors, diesel pumps and electric pumps for tubewells [1979: 153, Table 5.11].

The hypothesis supported by Roy is that during the early period of transition, the institutional bias in favour of large farmers ensures that they are the first adopters. Scale advantages become more important in the post adoption period, with large farmers maintaining high investment and growth rates. Thus, rather than the small farmers being able to catch up, the initial advantages captured by the large farmers are further strengthened over time due to intrinsic scale advantages.

Further support for this thesis comes from Pakistan. Khan [1979][24] examines 732 irrigated farms in the Indus basin in 1974. He finds the large farms (those over 25 acres) have land productivity some 9 per cent higher than the small farms (below 25 acres). The land coefficient (which represents the sum of factor elasticities) is 1.0974 which shows increasing returns to scale. Purchased input use (hired labour, machines and chemical fertiliser) increases with size [1979: 72]. With the introduction of the new technology, capital inputs were subsidised and directed towards the larger farmers. Large farms use more chemical fertilisers per acre and a similar bias exists in relation to tubewell technology: the large farmers had more access to credit for investment. All loans from the Agricultural Development Bank of Pakistan went to farms over 25 acres, the ADBP being the main source of finance for tractors and tubewells [1979: 76].

Mahmood and Ul-Haque 1981] dispute some of Khan's findings, using a database for 19 districts in West Punjab provided by the Agricultural Census and Rural Credit Survey of 1972. However, note that Mahmood and Ul-Haque use highly aggregated data, grouped in five size classes over districts [1981: 156]. They produce a U-shaped relation with small farms and large farms having higher productivity levels than medium farms, but no significant difference between small farms and large farms [1981: 161]. Rather than undermining Khan's findings, however, these results tend to confirm them by suggesting an intermediate stage in the introduction of the new technology prior to full-scale mechanisation.

SUMMARY AND CONCLUSIONS

We have seen in this chapter, that the fundamental determinants of factor-use intensities are the nexus of property rights and tenurial conditions that shape market characteristics, resource endowments, and the nature and extent of market participation by different size-holdings. Specific resource constraints affect the bargaining position of farmers in the markets for land, labour, and other inputs. Current and past levels of market participation and the nature of that participation strongly influence production decisions, which in turn affect future resource endowments.

The class-based approach identifies farm size with class position within the context of a relatively backward agriculture. Within the process of peasant differentiation, poor peasants end up with smaller and smaller below-subsistence plots of land, and are forced to intensify land-use and labour input in order to achieve subsistence levels of income. This stratum of poor peasants may also be characterised by compulsive market involvement or 'forced commerce'. Exploitative relations of production and exchange, with landlords, merchants and moneylenders extracting surplus via high rents, usury and price wedges, either singly or conjointly, compel poor peasants to achieve higher than average yields, market a high proportion of high-value cash crops, and sell labour off-farm in order to pay off cash and debt obligations as well as reach subsistence income.

At the other end of the class spectrum, rich peasants accumulate land and do not operate under such subsistence constraints. Through tenurial relationships and moneylending, rich peasants are a part of the exploiting class. They operate on the basis of hired wage labour and market a truly commercial surplus (as opposed to a distress surplus). A middle peasant range is more self-sufficient in terms of labour and consumption/production. This implies lower market participation and they are under no compulsion to intensify labour input.

In those areas where we find an inverse relationship, it is the case that all farm sizes have access to a more or less similar technology. Large and small farms use the same set of production inputs, and the small farms achieve higher output per acre via far higher cropping intensity and application of labour effort per acre. With the introduction of a new technology which favours large farms due to its associated economies of scale, then the so-called advantage which the small farms have with respect to labour input intensity, may be matched or more than matched by the new advantages which large farms have with respect to technology. In this situation, we might expect the inverse relationship to break down and eventually disappear, and with it part of the case for redistributive land reform.

In terms of the class-based approach, which is essentially a dynamic theory, what is happening here is that with the development of the forces of production in the form of Green Revolution technology, it is the rich peasants who are better placed to reap the benefits. They have the resources to gain access to the whole package of new inputs (HYV seeds, chemical fertilizers, plant protection materials). It is the rich peasants who are able to monopolise the available credit necessary to purchase the Green Revolution package. The rich peasants dominate the institutions which supply and distribute the new inputs. While these biochemical inputs may be scale neutral, their adoption steps up pressures for mechanisation which does have associated scale economies. This leads to the breakdown of the inverse relationship with rich peasants/capitalist farmers achieving higher yields.

NOTES

1. T.J. Byres was the first writer to develop a consistent and rigorous class-based approach to the question of the inverse relationship in an unpublished paper presented at the IDS Rupag Seminar Programme in November 1977, and in a modified version at the Institute of Development Studies, The Hague, in April 1979. See also Bharadwaj [1974a; 1974b], and Patnaik [1979; 1987] for complementary inputs to this approach.
2. See Bharadwaj [1974b: A-16]. Punjab, Uttar Pradesh, Bombay, West Bengal and Madras show an inverse relation between cropping intensity and farm size, although it is not significant in all cases.
3. Rudra mentions the wide range of different explanations of the inverse relationship found in the literature, and he recognises the validity of all of them in different combinations in different regions of India.
4. Bharadwaj writes in this context: 'Even when the researcher recognises the inadequacy or irrelevance of some specific assumptions like profit maximization or mobility of resources guided by freely fluctuating prices, he is prone to tinkering with only those specific parts of the competitive model, keeping undisturbed the rest of the framework' [1974b: A-11].
5. Within this literature, both political and neo-classical traditions are represented. For the political economy approach to inter-linked modes of exploitation, which focuses on surplus extraction by dominant classes, see Bharadwaj [1974a; 1979] and [1985]. Other important contributors include Bhaduri [1973] and Srivastava [1989]. The latter includes a useful brief

survey of the literature on interlinkage.

   For the neo-classical approach, which focuses on contractual market relationships and market imperfections, see Srinivasan [1979], Bardhan [1980], and Braverman and Srinivasan [1984].

6. Rao [1968b: 93] writes: 'Even though the application of labour may be higher among smaller farms, they may lag behind the larger ones in regard to the application of technologically new inputs such as fertilizers, improved seeds and insecticides, etc. owing to their low investible surplus.'

7. On the question of scale versus resource neutrality and the pressures for mechanisation see Byres [1972; 1981].

8. Sen [1981: 327] also mentions that sharecropping can be seen as an institutional response by rich farmers to capture some of the 'cheapness' of poor peasant family labour and save on supervision costs.

9. Sidhu [1974: 749–50] mentions the possibility that large farms assimilated the new Mexican wheat strains more rapidly than the small farms due to a 'comparative advantage in research information'.

10. Bardhan points to his Ferozepur results. Over the period 1955–69, the inverse relationship becomes positive. He also points out that the results obtained by Lau and Yotopoulos [1971] pertain to traditional Indian agriculture in the mid-1950s. With the introduction of green revolution technology, land productivity no longer depends on labour input intensity alone, but on the availability of fertilisers, irrigation and so on [1973: 1373].

11. Rani uses disaggregated FMS data for five IADP districts over three years 1962–65. Altogether 1,431 observations. His Chart A [1971: A-86] shows 14 out of 15 negative coefficients indicating an inverse relationship, but only nine significant at the ten per cent level, seven at five per cent and one at the one per cent level: 'Hence one can even conclude that yield per acre remains constant over different size groups of farms' [1971: A-86].

12. The study relates to the Upper Dhaia region of IADP district Ludhiana, the Dehlon Development Block for the year 1965–56. Small farms are classed as those below ten acres and large farms those above 22 acres.

13. In a similarly early study, Sinha and Singh [1966: 19–20] find that per acre maize yields actually increased with size: small farms produced 10.75 maunds per acre, medium-sized farms produced 11.88 maunds, and the large farms 13.40 maunds. They also found that for groundnuts, the small farmers achieved yields a quarter less than the large farmers. This was also true for gram.

14. C.R. Kaushik, 'Farm Adjustments on the Introduction of New Irrigation Facilities in Canal Irrigated Areas of Hissar District', unpublished MSc thesis, 1966, cited in Kahlon and Kapur [1968: 80].

15. A study of 120 farms in four villages in Meerut district, Uttar Pradesh, chosen on the basis of area under Mexican wheat varieties in 1969–70. Land was standardised for soil quality using land revenue.

16 Chadha uses Punjabi data from three sources:

   (1) FMS 1956–57 (two districts: Amritsar and Ferozepur – 200 farms)

   (2) FMS 1969–70 (61 villages over the state (21 patwar circles)-detailed information on 351 farms on the cost-accounting basis collected by the State Statistical Organization).

   (3) Agricultural Census data from 1970–71.

   Small farms were defined as those from 2.5 to 10 acres, medium farms from 10 to 25 acres, and large farms above 25 acres. The 1969-70 data does not include the very small farms (less than 2.5 acres).

17. Compare Table 4 [1978: A-90], for 1969–70, with Table 5 [1978: A-91] for the mid-50s.

18. See Table 6 [1978: A-91] and Table 7 [1978: A-92].

19. The data used is from Amarvati and Akola districts 1956–57 and Ahmednagar district 1967–8.

20. Roy uses disaggregated data from the National Council of Applied Economic Research, Fertilizer Demand Study, Interim Report, Volume 1 – General (mimeo) NCAER New Delhi, February 1978. The results are analysed in his Ph.D. thesis [1979] and in [1981]. Roy

disaggregates household data by district in the years 1975–76 and 1976–77 (that is, in the post-green revolution period). The total sample size was 22,791 across India, with 869 in Punjab (the non-response rate of 5.5 per cent produced a final sample size of 821 for Punjab). The data included area irrigated and detailed information for each crop (for an array of 66 crops), whether they were HYV or traditional varieties, cultivated on irrigated or unirrigated land, and yields. The household level data avoided the biases associated with the use of size class averages as in the FMS studies.

Roy uses a linear regression model for 'simplicity' (he also tried out Rudra's rank correlation tests in the sample cases and found the 'qualitative nature of the relation no different'. The specification for all regressions was $y = a + bx$ where y = output per net cropped area, output per gross cropped area, percentage area irrigated, cropping intensity, and yield per acre of individual crops [1979: 131–4].

21. See tables 5.1–5.7 [1979: 156–62]. See also the maps in diagrams 5.1–5.8 [1979: 141–8] or alternatively [1981].

22 Further, the coefficients on b are both smaller and statistically weaker in the advanced regions than in the more traditional areas (only Amritsar and Gurdaspur show no significant relation).

23 These tables summarise the main findings of Roy noted in the text.

24. Khan fits a Cobb-Douglas production function, running log-log regressions of output on gross cropped area, chemical fertiliser use, the ratio of family top hired labour and expenditure on animals and machinery.

IV

The Evidence for an Inverse Relationship between Farm Size and Productivity in Egypt: A Shadow Debate

INTRODUCTION

In this chapter, we examine the nature and range of evidence for an inverse relationship between farm size and productivity in the Egyptian countryside. In contrast with the extensive Indian literature on the inverse relationship is the rather meagre resonance that the debate has had in Egypt: only half a dozen serious references have surfaced so far (besides a few *en passant* assertions). This relative paucity, however, has not prevented calls by several writers for redistributive land reform in the Egyptian countryside. The Egyptian evidence ranges from simple assertion, by invoking the authority of Berry and Cline [1979], to full-scale field studies. One of these latter we shall subject to detailed scrutiny in Chapter VI.

The studies examined in this chapter present apparently strong, but contradictory evidence on the relationship between farm size and productivity, with some contributors supporting the existence of an inverse relationship while others vehemently deny its existence. However, all the writers below reveal crucial conceptual and methodological flaws in their analyses. It is important to consider these in some detail since they are flaws which recur wherever the inverse relationship has been examined and discussed. We draw heavily on the critical analysis of the debate surrounding the inverse relationship which we have discussed thoroughly in the previous three chapters.

Section IV.1 introduces the main participants in the Egyptian debate on the inverse relationship who suggest that such a relationship exists, and that its existence constitutes a strong case for redistributive land reform in Egypt. All these authors operate at a very high level of aggregation.

In section IV.2, that aggregation problem is addressed in a study by Crouch *et al.* [1983]. They provide rather more inconclusive evidence on the inverse relationship, but while they clearly point out the existence of a macro-level inverse relationship, and its origins in regional land heterogeneity, they fail to proceed beyond that and recognise the distinction that needs to be made between the aggregate level of analysis, and the subject of this thesis, the micro-level inverse relationship.

Finally, in section IV.3, we examine the data and methodology of those researchers who deny the existence of any inverse relationship in the Egyptian context. The writers who fall into this category tend to commit an extrapolative bias, in contradistinction to the writers in the first two sections who suffer from an aggregation bias.

IV.1 SOME EVIDENCE FOR AN INVERSE RELATIONSHIP IN EGYPT: SHEPLEY, RADWAN, WILSON AND MABRO

The assertions include Richards [1982: 177] who, referring to the work of Berry and Cline, mentions 'the very large amount of evidence which shows that small farms are more intensively cultivated and have higher yields per unit area than large farms in the Third World'.

Adams [*1986: 81*] likewise refers to Berry and Cline: 'Experience in [developing] countries demonstrates that not only are small farmers capable of adopting new technological inputs, but that land productivity, labour productivity, and output per hectare are all higher on small farms than on large'.[1] He agrees with Griffin that small land reform peasants use intensive family labour inputs to produce more output per unit of land [1986: 118], and concludes: 'Thus, if the goal is to raise land and labour productivity in peasant agriculture, it would seem necessary for the state to concentrate on the needs and requirements of small farm agriculture.'

Paradoxically, while Adams appears to agree with the theoretical and empirical evidence that land redistribution may result in reduced marketed surplus as peasants consume more of their output on-farm [1986: 126–7], he does not see that the inverse relationship would be similarly affected. If the compulsions which give rise to poor peasants marketing a high proportion of their output are relaxed, on-farm family consumption is likely to increase. Similarly, one would expect to see a relaxation in the intensity of labour effort.

More substantial references include Shepley *et al.* [1985] whose production function analysis of 252 farms in four governorates[2] reveals that 'tillers of smaller plots are economically more efficient [in terms of higher returns] than their counterparts on larger farms' [1985: 29] in rice, cotton [1985: 79], and maise [1985: 91] production. Small farms are defined as those below three feddans, and large farms as those above three feddans – rather large size classes. Their explanation for this finding is that: 'Small farmers are able to coax out high productivities from their land resources because of the concentration of other production inputs on small plots' [1985: 79]. As we have seen with regard to the Indian evidence [*Bharadwaj,*

1974a], if this is true, it probably reflects the indivisibilities associated with animal power or equipment on small farms rather than superior efficiency.

Note too that Shepley et al. are looking at single crop figures (both physical yields and values) for which no inverse relationship might be expected. They show small farm rice yields some 11 per cent higher than large farm yields, with small farms using more labour and machinery per feddan (see Table 12, Appendix A). This is expected, according to the authors as small farmers have a lower risk tolerance than large farmers, and therefore must 'operate more efficiently than larger producers who are able to spread their risks over a broader resource base' [1985: 29]. They also make the interesting observation that the large farmers are operating under a capital constraint, with insufficient machinery and working capital. Furthermore, these large farmers appear to be absentee landlords. The authors, however, do not pursue these interesting points any further. For Shepley et al., the small farm productivity advantage warrants 'an increase in credit facilities and input supply by some 99 per cent' [1985: 31].

The wheat producers in the survey, however, show higher yields per feddan on the large farms, by some ten per cent (see Table 13, Appendix A). This is explained by large farm access to parallel markets for fertiliser. Small farms with a mean area of 0.5 feddan under cotton show a high intensity of cultivation, with higher yields and labour input (see Table 14, Appendix A). Thus, 'small farm resource-use efficiency would warrant larger plots' [1985: 83]. Interestingly, data presented by the authors [1985: 73] show significantly higher labour input intensity on the farms in the above three feddan classes.

A major reference that forms the basis for the next chapter, is that of Samir Radwan in his 1986 book *Agrarian Change in Egypt*.[3] At the end of a section on production conditions, he writes: 'we note that the relationship of farm productivity to farm size follows the inverse relationship that has been frequently observed' [1986: 78].

He produces regression equations (i) to (iii), reproduced in Table 15, Appendix A, which show for the aggregate level, that net farm output and cropping intensity are negatively related to farm sise, as is the input of family labour per unit of land [1986: 79].[4] The inverse relationship holds with a negative regression coefficient significant at the 1 per cent level and where y is net farm output per qirat[5] and x is size of holding.

Radwan goes on to state: 'Thus, in rural Egypt, as is often the case elsewhere in Third World agriculture, resources are used more intensively on small family farms. Therefore, the scope exists, in the sphere of farm production, to raise total output and reduce income inequality through further land redistribution' [1986: 79]. We will examine Radwan's data, methodology and conclusions below in greater detail in Chapter VI. Let us note here however that Radwan employs net farm output (defined as total value of farm output minus input costs, excluding labour costs) in his yield calculations. This methodology introduces a number of distortions and a bias in favour of finding an inverse relationship. Large farms use substantially higher levels of both purchased and own-supplied inputs (seeds, fertilisers, fodder and so on). We need therefore to use the total value of crop output in the yield calculations.[6]

The next reference is that of Rodney Wilson in a 1972 study for the Egyptian National Institute of Planning:[7]

> As it is the smallest holdings which are usually the most intensively cultivated, it seems not unreasonable to believe on a priori grounds that labour requirements per hectare are highest on these smaller holdings also. The absence of data relating agricultural production to farm size in Egypt is an obstacle here. Nevertheless there are strong reasons for believing that the tendency for output per hectare to increase, with decreasing holding sise, which is observed in other developing countries with similar factor endowments, is also found in Egypt' [1972: 2].

His Table 4 (column U') [1972: 8] shows an inverse relationship between labour utilisation per hectare and holding size with man-hours per year declining from 14,348 on farms with less than 0.8 hectares to 2,658 on farms over four hectares.[8] Wilson's Table 5 [1972: 9], reproduced in Table 16, Appendix A, also shows that the tendency for labour utilisation per hectare of cultivated area to decline as holding size increases occurs in Egypt irrespective of the cropping system: 'At least 3 times more labour is utilised per hectare on small holdings under 0.8 hectares, compared with he larger farms surveyed of over 4.0 hectares in sise.'

A possible explanation for this inverse relationship is that:

> Egyptian land-holders do not aim at maximising their farm incomes per hectare, but are satisfied with incomes which cover their families' subsistence, plus some modest household items. In order to attain this target however, those owning very small farms must utilise their land very intensively, which implies high labour inputs per hectare. Those with larger farms in contrast can easily achieve higher income levels, even if they utilise their land much less intensively. Thus income per hectare on the farms below 0.8 hectares surveyed was almost three times that found on farms averaging over 4.0 hectares. On the larger farms, in consequence, the family labour participation may be lower, and few labourers engaged at peak seasons relative to the size of these farms. The general lack of price incentives in Egyptian agriculture

probably discourages the larger farmers from acting in a more ambitious manner [*1972: 14*].

Wilson continues:

> Absentee ownership of the larger farms may provide an additional explanation of this lower land utilisation, and consequent smaller labour absorption relative to farm size ... Land acquired for these motives [prestige, inheritance provision], or for speculative purposes, is seldom developed adequately [1972: 14].

Furthermore, Wilson points out in his Table 7 [*1972: 16*] that labour utilisation per hectare is higher on leased or shared farms than on those which are more than two-thirds owned.[9] He writes: 'leased holdings are farmed more intensively than owner occupied farms. Lessees need to cultivate their land intensively in order to pay their rents ... Landowners, in contrast, may be less aware of the opportunity costs involved in not fully utilizing their land' [1972: 3].

Wilson adduces the following implications for agrarian policy in Egypt:

> The confirmation of the first hypothesis that labour absorption per hectare decreases as farms become larger has important consequences for land tenure policy. It provides an economic justification for Egypt's land reform legislation, which has placed successively lower ceilings on land ownership. A strong case can be argued for tightening the enforcement of the existing legislation, and perhaps applying the 20 hectare ceiling to total family landholding, rather than individual ownership as at present. Pursuance of such a policy would, in the author's view, lead to a more intensive land utilisation, and hence increase rural employment opportunities' [*1972: 18*].

Elsewhere he writes:

> The situation [inegalitarian distribution of ownership] could undoubtedly be improved if the 1969 land reform proposals for lowering the ceiling on individual landownership to 20 hectares were implemented. To date many landowners have avoided having their land expropriated. One means of evasion was by registering land in the names of different members of their usually large families, while still retaining control themselves in practice [1972: 6].

Thus: 'It would therefore appear that land reform [is] socially necessary in the interests of production intensification and employment creation' [1972: 19].

This echoes an earlier reference by Robert Mabro in which he refers to inverse relations between labour intensity and farm size and land productivity and farm size in a study of rural employment problems in Egypt.[10] Mabro writes:

> We have shown that total labour inputs per acre (and ceteris paribus yields) are a function of 'n', the land-to-man ratio. If this ratio increases as the size of holdings decreases, an inverse relationship between labour intensity and size would obtain. Such a relationship is well established empirically and has been discussed at length in the literature [1971: 412].

Mabro's explanation for this inverse relationship in Egypt follows the Sen thesis. He writes [1971: 404]: 'It may be convenient to distinguish two types of farms according to the mode of operation, "capitalist" (sometimes referred to as "large") farms which rely on hired workers and "family" (or "small") farms mainly operated by the members of the household.' The 'capitalist' or wage-labour farms tend to operate according to the postulate of profit-maximisation. In the family sector individuals aim at maximizing their utility when they trade leisure for income (say corn) through their work [1971: 405].[11]
He continues [1971: 408–9]:

> The less well-endowed worker applies more labour inputs per acre than his more fortunate neighbour. Other things being equal, yields will vary inversely with 'n' ... If average incomes are low, peasants may have to apply labour inputs up to the point where the marginal product is not significantly different from zero in order to secure his subsistence.[12]

While noting that his analysis is limited by its exclusion of capital from consideration and that this factor might turn out to be important, especially on the very large farms [1971: 414–15], he concludes that:

> Changes in the structure of land holdings and land ownership may result in a better use of resources. For incomes, yields, and employment are a function of the size of farms. On large estates ... yields are usually low ... On very small farms yields sometimes are significantly higher but the peasant's average income is low and family labour underemployed ... The likely effects of a successful land reform are increased yields (and therefore total production), higher rural incomes, and a fuller utilisation of family labour [1971: 415–16].

IV.2 AGGREGATION AND LAND HETEROGENEITY: CROUCH *ET AL.*

One major problem with the above writers is that they operate at an excessively high level of aggregation which obscures a great deal. Regressing yields on farm size across all rural Egypt eliminates any possibility of regional diversity. Such an exercise not only assumes a homogeneous agriculture throughout rural Egypt, but also confuses two levels of analysis. An important distinction must be made between the 'macro' level size–productivity relationship based on heterogeneous land quality and the 'micro' level relationship (see discussion in Chapters I and II).

Taking rural Egypt as a whole, land is regionally heterogeneous. In some areas, higher soil fertility or land productivity permits a greater population carrying capacity and hence greater population settlement density. This gives rise to a tendency for smaller farm size in those areas, in a situation of limited land. So, at the aggregate level, we have an inverse relation between soil fertility (and hence farm productivity) and farm size, with the direction of causality running from the former to the latter. At the 'micro' level, which may be at the governorate or even village level, it is postulated that the direction of causality is reversed. Farm productivity is seen as being in some way dependent on farm size (see discussion in Chapter I). It is this causal relation that is at the heart of the debate over the inverse relationship.

This problem is recognised, but misunderstood in Crouch *et al.* [1983]. Using data from the 1976 Egyptian FMS (187 farms from 11 villages in the eastern Delta region which covers three governorates: Sharqiya, Daqhaliya and Dumyat), the latter present tables of yields of individual crops in kg per feddan and of per feddan income net of per feddan cash costs for individual crops by farm size which shows 'no clear evidence of any relation between farm size and yield' [1983: 20–21] (see Tables 17 and 18, Appendix A).

However, they also perform linear regressions of (1) physical yield per feddan on farm size and a dummy variable representing Sharqiya governorate; (2) individual crop values per feddan on farm size and the Sharqiya dummy variable; and (3) gross revenue per feddan on farm size and the Sharqiya dummy (see Table 19, Appendix A). They conclude that crop yields are not constant across farm size (a weak inverse relation is indicated in many cases) and that regionality, even within the supposedly homogenous eastern Delta region affects yields. They note that when all crops are taken together, the factor whose influence on revenue per feddan emerges most strongly is the Sharqiya dummy variable: 'The results on the dummy coefficients give strong support to the idea that inter-regional differences in productivity are more important than social class-based differences' [1983: 22–23].[13]

In order to bring out these regionality effects more clearly, Crouch *et al.* carry out regressions of physical yields, values of individual crops and gross revenue per feddan on farm size and five zonal dummies [1983: 24–26] (see Table 20, Appendix (A): whereas when only the Sharqiya dummy was used, the size coefficient was significant for all crops except the aggregate case, with the inclusion of the zonal dummies, the size coefficient is statistically significant in only two cases (and marginal in a third) while the dummy coefficients are almost all statistically significant.

Crouch *et al.* conclude [1983: 26–27]: 'Clearly, regionality is of much more importance than size in explaining yield variations across farms ... Many [studies of agrarian structure in different countries] come to the conclusion that large farm size negatively affects yield, but our results naturally lead to questioning these studies.' They continue [1983: 27]:

> The significance of these regional differences in yields suggest that perhaps the weak relation between size and yield has a causal direction opposite to that normally assumed in studies of agrarian structure. Perhaps in areas where yields are lower, lands are of lesser quality; therefore, farms must be bigger in order to support the same level of monetary output. At the same time, land would be cheaper, so larger farms would be possible. Naturally then, one would expect to see a negative association between farm size and yield, which becomes weaker once one controls for regionality.

Here Crouch *et al.* discover the importance of the distinction that needs to be made between the macro and micro level analyses. But they fail to proceed beyond that recognition to examine the relationship between farm size and productivity at the micro level.

A number of other interesting econometric exercises are carried out [1983: 28–30] (see Table 21, Appendix A). Yields were regressed on a number of factors: farm size, nitrogen fertiliser per feddan, nitrogen fertiliser per feddan squared, labour per feddan, dummies for sharecropping, cash rent and land reform lands, and the share of hired labour in total labour as an index of capitalist social relations. However, these equations explain less yield variation than the equations with the zonal dummies:

(1) the effect of farm size has almost completely dropped out;
(2) nitrogen fertiliser was only marginally important in the maise and rice equations;
(3) labour intensity was only important in the aggregate output case;
(4) cash rentals appeared to be weakly associated with all crop yields (either because farmers are stimulated to attempt higher yields in order to pay cash rents or because cash rents are more common in higher yield zones for unspecified agro-ecologic reasons);[14]
(5) there was a negative relation between yields and the index of capitalist relations (this though they regard as being a statistical artefact generated because capitalist relations are positively associated with farm size which is negatively correlated with yields).[15]

Crouch et al. conclude [1983: 32]:

> If one accounts for regional differences, the influence of farm size on yields becomes fairly small, though still noticeable in some crops. And when one accounts for the influence of physical ... and social ... factors, then farm size is swamped. However, this last result is reasonable given that the per feddan intensity of input use on the larger farms is somewhat less than on the smaller ones. In a nutshell, the hypothesis that farm size affects yields negatively cannot be totally rejected, but we have discovered that the relationship is quite weak statistically and perhaps unimportant economically.[16]

IV.3 THE INVERSE RELATIONSHIP DENIED IN EGYPT: PLATT AND COMMANDER

Finally, a number of references deny the existence of an inverse relationship in Egyptian agriculture. Platt [1970: 16] asserts:

> Figures are not available to show differences in efficiency of production between large and small farms, and between the various forms of tenure at operating level, but a production advantage doubtless went with the larger farms because of their owners' better access to fertiliser supplies, improved seeds, etc., and the production credit needed to utilise them.

A more substantive contribution to this side of the debate however is Simon Commander's study of three Delta villages in Egypt in which he concludes: 'no consistent trend in terms of productivity was found to exist across farm size class ... There was little evidence that any inverse relation between farm size and productivity existed' [1987: 227].

He presents a table (see Table 22, Appendix A) showing crop yields per feddan by farm size which exhibit no one uniform trend for crop production, and a series of regressions for physical yields of individual crops, which all show no significant relation between yield and sise. While wheat yields tend to indicate an inverse relation, this does not hold for cotton and rice yields. For maize, the smallest and largest farm size yields are comparable with medium farm size yields lower [1987: 175]. Regressing physical yield per feddan for individual crops on operated area yielded the expected positive association between operated area and land productivity from the cotton and rice equations, but for the other crops no coherent pattern emerged that was statistically significant. However, when the total value of crop production per feddan was regressed on the operated area (or gross cropped area) in linear form, a coefficient of LE 4.46 per qirat, or LE 107.04 per feddan, was yielded with a constant term of 1,796 and a mean value of LE 2,002 per feddan [1987: 176–8].[17]

The reasons adduced by Commander for this apparent lack of any inverse relationship include the thorough implementation of land reform in the 1950s and 1960s, generally high irrigation ratios, the availability of state subsidised fertilisers and co-operative distribution of other agricultural inputs, and the low variance in production conditions. These all generate a relative homogeneity in cropping patterns and low variance of land productivity across farm size [1987: 175].

None of the familiar factors associated with the inverse relationship appear to be present. There was apparently little variation in cropping intensity across farm size [1987: 178]:

> With cropping intensities varying to a very small extent across farm size this latter factor has limited implications for intra-farm size productivity variation. What proved more significant were differences in cropping pattern. Although virtually all farms had sown the standard crops, the rotational combination was an important factor determining the overall value of crop output when measured over the full agricultural year.'[18]

He notes that the positive association between output per feddan and farm size in the case of cotton and rice is interesting, if only because both crops are the most labour intensive of the core crops sown in the sample catchment area [1987: 178]. There was relatively limited variance in labour inputs committed to crop production across farm size however: 'small farms did not, when estimating labour use over a two-season period, have higher labour commitments to arable farming, even though, as expected, the hired component of that labour time was lower than for the larger farms' [1987: 179].[19]

Commander concludes [1987: 180–81]: 'The relative homogeneity of both material inputs[2] and labour in crop production across farm size clearly shows that no inverse relation between productivity and labour use and farm size is observable in Egypt.' He adds [1987: 178–9]:

> With relatively homogeneous production functions, the idea that small farms devote labour time to crop production without regard for conventional marginal product-wage valuation does not hold. In any event, it is clear that land productivity exhibits no real bias towards the small farms whose labour endowments and scarcity of land assets might, in other circumstances, have been conducive to higher levels of average land productivity.

There are a number of problems with Commander's analysis. Firstly,

Commander's regression equation uses gross cropped area (net sown area adjusted for the multi-cropped area) in the yield calculations. This introduces the opposite bias from those writers above, against finding an inverse relationship. If smaller farms have higher cropping intensities than larger farms (as we shall see they do) then small farm yields will automatically be adjusted downward by using gross cropped area instead of net sown area or farm size (see discussion in Chapter I).[21]

Secondly, Commander produces evidence for the physical yields of individual crops and adduces this as evidence against the presence of an inverse relationship. As we have observed, however, the inverse relationship pertains to total crop value. Here again if small farms have higher cropping intensities than large farms or if the cropping pattern on small farms is different from that on large farms, then even with no relation between the yields of individual crops and farm sise, there can nevertheless be an inverse relationship when we look at yields in total crop value terms (see discussion in Chapter I).

Finally, while Radwan, Mabro and Wilson operate at too high a level of aggregation, Commander commits the opposite fallacy of extrapolating his sample results to all Egypt. Again, any possibility of significant regional diversity is a priori excluded. We may note here that Commander chooses to work in three Delta governorates (Gharbiya, Sharqiya and Daqhaliya) which all manifest high levels of utilisation of modern agricultural technology with some of the highest ratios of tractors, pumps, modern ploughs, pesticide sprayers and threshing machines to land in all of rural Egypt – a fact which, as we have seen, is precisely of extreme importance in the breakdown of the inverse relation (see Table 23, Appendix A).

Indeed, Richards [1989: 58] responds to Commander's results showing the non-existence of the inverse relationship by suggesting that these findings could 'be the result of larger farmers using greater capital inputs per unit land to off-set smaller farmers' higher inputs of labour per unit land'. However, Commander [1987: 178] claims that: 'such yield differences [showing higher land productivity on the large farms] cannot be explained by differences in the availability and utilisation of machinery' because labour-intensive tasks such as cotton picking and rice transplanting were not mechanised. Nevertheless, his data [1987: 292, Table 8C] do show that the mean value of material inputs per feddan increase by farm size for all crops (see Table 24, Appendix A).

With regard to mechanised inputs, Commander's data [1987: 295, Table 9A] show a wide diffusion of machinery in the three governorates, but while governorate mechanisation indices show that Gharbiya and Daqhaliya are more mechanised than Sharqiya, the Commander's own data show that at the village level, Sharqiya is far more mechanised than the other two [1987:

256–7]. Indeed, the Sharqiya village had a machine density four times higher than the governorate average. The machine stock in the Gharbiya village was more restricted and the Daqhaliya village 'was under-mechanised when compared with the other two sampled areas and the governorate as a whole'.[22]

Indeed, perhaps Commander's results have also suffered from too high a level of aggregation. Using his data, we computed output per acre and average farm size for each village. This reveals that whereas an inverse relation appears to hold for the Gharbiya and Daqhaliya villages, it does not exist or has broken down in the Sharqiya village.[23]

SUMMARY AND CONCLUSIONS

In this chapter, we have critically surveyed the contributions to the inverse relationship debate made in the Egyptian context. As we have seen, this literature is rather meagre in comparison to the Indian debate. Certainly, there is no very profound discussion of why such a relationship should arise. A number of propositions echo the Indian debate, ranging from Wilson's satisficing behaviour on the large farms to Mabro's use of the Sen framework.

We have seen, too, that the Egyptian debate exhibits many of the errors and misconceptions we have examined in the previous six chapters. On the one hand, those who have found an inverse relationship tend to be operating at an excessively high level of aggregation which reflects the inverse relationship at the macro-level, as remarked upon by Crouch *et al.* This, however, cannot be used as a rationale for redistributive land reform as most of these authors suggest.

On the other hand, those writers who deny the existence of the inverse relationship in Egyptian agriculture commit the error of extrapolating their small sample results to the Egyptian countryside in general. We have seen, however, that even their use of the micro-level data raises a number of methodological and conceptual problems.

Nevertheless, these inconclusive and partial results do suggest that the inverse relationship may be an important phenomenon in rural Egypt, although not in the way conceived of by the authors looked at in this chapter. In Chapter VI, we will subject the data used by Radwan and Lee to greater scrutiny at a more disaggregated level, and in Chapters VII and VIII, we examine village level data collected by the author from Egypt in 1990. But before turning to the data analysis, we will, in the next chapter, consider the central features of the political economy of agrarian transition in Egypt, features which are of central relevance to our analysis of the fieldwork data in Chapters VII and VIII.

NOTES

1. Adams also refers the reader to Dorner [1972]. Note that Adams is rather confused over the inverse relationship here. Land productivity and output per acre are essentially the same, while the empirical evidence widely shows labour productivity declining with increasing holding sise.
2. Buheira, Gharbiya, Qalubiya and Sharqiya in 1981–82.
3. This study was the result of a 1,000 household survey of rural Egypt undertaken in 1976–77 by the ILO/World Employment Programme.
4. $\log Y =$ 4.016   –   0.5154 $\log X$
            (.0354)
   $r^2 = 0.3637$
   $n = 415$
   where Y is days worked on the family farm divided by the size of holding and X is size of landholding.
5.   1 qirat = 1/24 feddan = 175.03m^2
       1 feddan = 1.038 acres = 4,200.83m^2
   Throughout the text, yield refers to output per feddan.
6. Radwan provides no justification for using this measure of net farm output in his farm productivity computations, but it certainly makes dramatic changes to the results. Such input costs account for 65–66 per cent of crop output on the large farms and only 40 per cent on the small farms. Of course, this does not imply that the small farms are characterised by higher land productivity. What matters here is not the ratio of these input costs to output, but the composition of these inputs.
   In contrast to the small farms, where large farm inputs are land and labour augmenting (and small farm inputs are dominated by fodder), farm productivity will be higher on the large farms. Radwan also includes animal produce in total output. This biases small farm yields upward by some 20 per cent as compared to two to ten per cent on the larger farms. However, large animal/land ratios and animal product/total output ratios on the small farms are not an indication of higher productivity, but rather merely the small size of these farms. The use of Radwan's method on the Qena data below biases large farm yields downward by some 35 per cent in comparison with the small farms.
   Such an approach also faces significant problems relating to the imputation of cost to inputs supplied on-farm. For Radwan's methodology, see pages 17–27 of Radwan and Lee [1986].
7. ILO/INPC Labour Record Survey *Research Report on Employment Problems in Rurual Areas, 6 Governorates*, 1964–65.
8.   size H   U'
       < 0.8 ha   14348 man-hours per yr
       0.8-2   6719
       2-4   4322
       over 4   2658
   Wilson also produces the following regression equation [1972: 9]:
   $\log U' = 1.6174 - 0.6771 H$
   with a correlation coefficient $R_{UH} = -1.00$.
9.   land tenure   U' (labour/ha)
       2/3 owned   5354
       2/3 rented   6408
       2/3 shared   6103
   Wilson explains: 'farmers on leased holdings need to utilise their land intensively, not only to provide for their family needs, but also to pay the rents' [1972: 16]. However, note that these tenure categories include a wide range of farm sises [1972: 15].
10. Robert Mabro, *Employment and Wages in Dual Agriculture*, Oxford Economic Papers, Vol.21, No.3, 1971. This article was based on data collected in *Rural Employment Problems in the UAR*, ILO, 1969, and the UAR/INP/ILO, *Research Report on Employment Problems in Rural Areas* (in ten volumes), Cairo, 1965–68. These are the same data used by Wilson. Mabro writes: 'Labour inputs per unit of land (and sometimes yields) tend to increase as the

size of holdings decrease' [1971: 402]. Mabro also refers the reader to Mazumdar [1965] and Paglin [1965] on the Indian Farm Management Studies.
11. This explicit use of the Sen model by Mabro (and the implicit use by other authors) has been questioned by some writers. Harik [1979: 77], using 1961 census data, estimates the density of workers per feddan on small farms to be only 4.5 times higher than on the large estates with the greatest density on those farms less than two feddans. These estimates are much lower than those given by Mohieddin [1977] who estimates a factor of 11. Harik concludes [1979: 80] that as labour intensity is not marked by extremes, the gap is not wide enough to justify a dual sector model of agriculture with underemployment at the bottom and labour saving at the top.
    Further, Mabro's data [1971: 413, Table II] on the use of hired labour on small farms in Egypt shows that all farm size categories employ wage labour: including 24 per cent of farms below two feddans:

sise	% using wage labour
0.5-2	24 mainly temp
2-5	36
5-10	53
> 10	85

Source: ILO/UAR Report C, p.41.

This evidence would tend to confirm that even in 1961 there existed a highly developed labour market in the rural areas, reflecting a considerable degree of inter-farm labour mobility. Therefore we are not speaking of highly immobile family labour here.
12. Mabro notes here that: 'There is no choice between goods and leisure at a level of income near subsistence' [1971: 409, fn. 1].
13. The authors do note however that 'smaller farms grow somewhat more high value crops (but not much)' [1983: 23].
14. Their own data are however unclear on this. There appears to be no clear association between areas of high land productivity and areas where cash cropping is predominant [*Crouch et al.*, 1983: 30–31].
15. Although farm size and the hired labour index are positively correlated, Crouch *et al.* are aware of the elision made by Sen and Mabro: 'while it may be true that capitalist farms are in general larger than peasant farms, it should not be assumed that "large" and "capitalist" are equivalent' [1983: 16].
    In an attempt to go beyond farm sise, Crouch et al. perform an interesting exercise by clustering farms into socio-economic groups: [7] small peasants with little marketed surplus and using little hired labour, [3] small farms using more hired labour and marketing a higher proportion of total output, [5] small capitalist farmers with 8–12 feddans using mostly hired labour, [2] large capitalist farmers, and [6] land rented out by large landlords under sharecropping. This shows that for wheat, group 7 has higher yields than groups 5, 3 and 6; for cotton, groups 3, 5 and 7 have higher yields than group 2. They conclude: 'Thus, we confirm earlier results about the importance of size and capitalist relations when regionality is not taken into account' [1983: 31].
16. Regressions of factor input intensity on size and on size with zonal dummies show that:

   (1)   'farm size certainly does influence factor use intensities. There is no doubt that larger farms use less of every input per feddan, except for chemical nitrogen fertiliser, and manure. In all crops larger farms use less human and animal labour per feddan, and in cotton, rice, and wheat they also use less mechanical power. This holds in spite of the fact that we have controlled for regional variability and the impact of possible bad measurement on in the small farms by providing dummy variables. Of course, these results simply confirm our previous result that there is a definite but weak tendency for bigger farms to have smaller yields'; and

   (2)   'there are clear regional differences in intensity of factor use. In fact, in almost all cases, regionality seems to be just as important a variable as farm size in explaining variability

in per feddan input use. However, it is not altogether clear that the zones using less inputs are the same as those achieving less yields' [Crouch et al., 1983: 37–8].

17. Commander [1987: 173–9; 178, fn.3]. His regressions of crop value per feddan on operated area show:

$$\text{linear:} \qquad y = 1795.749 + 4.464\ x \qquad r^2 = 0.31$$
$$\qquad\qquad (60.821)\ (0.888)*$$
$$\text{log-linear:} \qquad y = 2.979 + 0.198\ x \qquad r^2 = 0.24$$
$$\qquad\qquad (0.042)\ (0.027)*$$

* = significant at the 1% level

where y is total value of crop production and x is gross cropped area, which shows a significant positive relation at the one per cent confidence level.

Commander exhibits some confusion over his regression results. He writes [1987: 178]: 'The positive sign for the constant [sic] indicated that the crop value per operated area tended to decline [sic] with area operated. This was confirmed when the regression was run in log-linear form where the coefficient was significantly below one.' The fact that the coefficient on the independent variable is positive would suggest that output per acre increases with farms sise. The coefficient in the log-linear case simply shows that yields increase, but less than proportionately with sise.

These regression results are confirmed by Table 8D [1987: 292, Appendix]:

average crop value per feddan per annum, 1984

farm sise	mean(LE)	index
0-1	1665	100
1-3	2176	131
3-5	2203	132
5-10	2634	158
> 10	2499	150

He adds [1987: 178]: 'crop values per feddan do indeed rise for farms of up to ten feddans but fall off for the larger units. Nevertheless, the value differential between the smallest farms and those with the highest per unit values – the 5-10 feddan holdings – exceeded 50 per cent. This may be partly due to soil quality differences. In particular, it is likely to reflect the level of investment in drainage on farm, as well as the relative accessibility of irrigation.'

18. Commander also mentions land quality as an important factor. While there was no attempt to grade land quality, land values showed a positive relation with farm size [1987: 177, Table 8.3]. Large farm land values were a third higher than those of small farms. Fallow was non-existent and the reference period covered a two crop cycle.

19. However, Commander's data [1987: 65, Table 4.4] show that his Sharqiya village does exhibit higher labour intensity on the smaller farms even though the aggregate results reveal little variation:

average labour inputs per feddan in crop production for 1983–84
(standardised man-hours)

sise	Sharqiya	Gharbiya	Daqhaliya	all	all(man-days)
0-1	2214	961	1378	1384	261
1-3	1745	1073	1668	1566	295
3-5	1395	988	1808	1557	294
5-10	1039	1112	1815	1434	270
> 10	1302	–	2027	1544	291

Wheat yields (y) regressed on the ratio of hired to total labour time in crop production (x) actually revealed a negative association:

$$y = 10.051 - 3.280\ x \qquad r^2 = 0.21$$
$$\qquad (.3566)\ (.5737)* \qquad F = 32.7$$
$$\qquad\qquad n = 126$$

*significant at the 1% level.

Commander suggests that for this crop, family labour may put in greater effort or sustain a higher quality of work, but the result did not hold for other crops [1987: 179; fn.4]. Why this should be the case for wheat and not for other crops is not revealed.

He adds that, although small farms have higher available labour per feddan, and there was a clear positive association between farm size and labour productivity (with rice, for example, labour productivity was 45 per cent higher on the large farms), the availability of off-farm work opportunities implied no compulsion to intensify labour effort on the small farms [1987: 181].

20. The regression of crop values (y) on material inputs which included seeds, fertilisers, and pesticides (x) showed a positive association:

$$y = \quad 1526.763 \quad + \quad 1.845 \quad r^2 = 0.24$$
$$\quad (77.397) \quad \quad (0.252)* \quad F = 53.4$$
$$\quad n = 171$$

* = significant at the 1% level

Even at the level of individual crops, there was a positive relation between crop value and material inputs [1987: 180; fn. 5]

21. Commander provides no explicit justification for using gross cropped area in his yield calculations. However, he does claim [1987: 178] that he finds little variation in cropping intensity across farm sise. He does not provide any figures to substantiate this claim.

22. In 1984, the Sharqiya village had 36 tractors and 15 threshers, as well as 6 large sprayers, 31 small sprayers and ten trucks. The nearby Mechanisation Centre had an additional 16 tractors available. The Gharbiya village had only five tractors and 3 threshers, and no co-operative or machine centre. The Daqhaliya village had 18 tractors and seven pumps (below the norm) and no co-operative or machine centre [Commander, 1987: 257].

23. The data were derived from Commander [1987: 53, Table 3.3] which provides average class farm size and [1987: 293, Table 8F].

TABLE 3.3

(EXCERPT) DISTRIBUTION OF LANDHOLDINGS, 1984 SAMPLE VILLAGES

	Sharqiya		Daqhaliya		Gharbiya	
farm size	units	area	units	area	units	area
0-1	721	405.22	592	264.19	158	79.09
1-3	487	891.05	288	457.09	59	88.19
3-5	43	143.19	28	99.19	4	13.17
5-10	34	236.09	11	65.18	3	21.04
> 10	12	174.11	2	24.22	–	–

Source: Village Agricultural Co-operatives.

TABLE 8F

AVERAGE VALUE OF CROP OUTPUT (PER FARM), 1984

farm size (feddans)

village	0-1	1-3	3-5	5-10	> 10
Sharqiya	757.6	1658.4	2752.9	6505.5	19941.5
Daqhaliya	496.8	1204.5	2295.7	4571.6	8729.0
Gharbiya	457.6	1144.7	2441.8	3514.0	–

Source: ODI/Zagazig Survey, 1984.

Combining the data in the two tables and computing average output per feddan for each size class in the three villages gives (rounded to the nearest whole number):

village	0-1	1-3	3-5	5-10	> 10
Sharqiya	1348	906	827	937	1374
Daqhaliya	1113	759	648	772	721
Gharbiya	914	766	742	501	–

Notice the strong inverse relationship in Daqhaliya and Gharbiya. But in the Sharqiya village, the large farms have higher productivity than the smaller size classes. This would seem to tie in with the evidence on machine use, supporting the hypothesis that advanced levels of technology are associated with the disappearance of the inverse relationship.

V

The Political Economy of the
Contemporary Egyptian Countryside

INTRODUCTION

In this chapter, we shall consider some of the central features of the political economy of the Egyptian countryside, which have been identified by other researchers (most notably Mahmoud Abdel-Fadil)[1] and which are central to our own analysis. In other words, we shall here survey the evidence with respect to the mechanisms and institutions which have been central to the emergence of rich peasant dominance in contemporary Egypt. This is an important prelude to the treatment of the ILO data and the author's study villages in the following chapters. As we shall see, the influences identified in this chapter were crucial in the study villages, both with respect to the causal factors behind the inverse relationship and its disappearance.

In section V.1, we examine how the Egyptian agrarian reform, begun in 1952, and subsequent legislation, enhanced and consolidated the position of the rich peasantry, particularly those owning over ten feddans of land. The following two sections explore the institutional structure of rural Egypt, and how the agrarian elite were able to exercise their power through the co-operative system (section V.2) and rural credit system (section V.3).

Section V.4 examines the implications of rich peasant domination of these institutions for the diffusion of modern technology which, as we have seen, is a crucial element in the breakdown of the inverse relationship. Finally, section V.5 shows how that rural dominance has been extended to the national policy-making level and the implications this has had for agrarian transition in Egypt.

V.1 AGRARIAN REFORM AND THE CONSOLIDATION OF THE RICH PEASANTRY

Prior to 1952, some 2,000 landlords (the pashas),[2] representing 0.01 per cent of all landholders, owned 20 per cent of the land, and some six per cent of landholders owned 65 per cent of the land [*Ikram*, 1980: 213]. The agrarian reform of 1952 led to the redistribution of land held by individual landlords over 200 feddans, and in 1961, the permissible ceiling fell to 100 feddans. Later, in 1969, ceilings were reduced to 50 feddans.

Land was redistributed in plots of two to five feddans (depending on soil quality and family size). Rents were to be controlled at seven times the basic land tax, but this condition often seems to have been evaded in practice however [Ikram, 1980: 212]. There were a variety of ways of evading the land reform regulations: land retained for self-cultivation, false registrations, and open flouting of the ceilings legislation. Although the pashas were weakened, they were not eliminated as a class in the Egyptian social formation, and many have since made a comeback under the Infitah regime.[3] In the non-land reform areas, landlords could easily evade the laws or could shift to direct exploitation using wage labour.

Thus, initially the reform was limited in its impact. A generous ownership ceiling was set originally, thus confining the number of affected landowners to only 1,768 out of a total of more than 2,800,000, or about 6/100 of one per cent [Platt, 1970: 63]. Only 12.5 per cent of the cultivated area was directly affected with 341,982 families receiving land, and this was restricted to ex-tenants with the landless receiving nothing [Abdel-Fadil, 1975; Richards, 1982].

Except on expropriated land, tenure structure remained essentially unchanged: landlords retained most of their lands up to the legal maximum (and beyond) and even 18 years after land reform it was still the case that land was cultivated predominantly by sharecroppers and tenants [Platt, 1970: 44].

While initially large landlords observed rent ceilings as they felt vulnerable to exposure, the smaller landlords 'used their local prestige to force higher rents, being supported, in cases of complaint, by the local courts set up to settle rent disputes' [Platt, 1970: 45]. Saab [1967: 145] mentions the considerable rental rate abuse that followed the 1956 law allowing landlords to withdraw half their formerly rented lands from tenancy. A common practice was to sign leases calling for the legal rent, but compel the tenant to sign separate bills of exchange for extra amounts. Adams [1986: 90] provides an example of land reform law circumvention from el-Diblah: 'The concept of renting land with a [written] contract died here 30 years ago, right after 1952. The only land that is rented out now is rented out on an oral basis, for a crop or two at a time.' Many poor peasants fear the rich peasant: 'many ... still "forfeit" their legal rights out of fear, ignorance and an abiding reluctance to antagonise "those who matter" in the village' [1986: 92]. Hopkins [1987: 185] notes that 'free market' rents are usually on a seasonal basis and several times higher than legal rents.

The land reform process, including distress sales to the rich peasantry, reduced the large landholdings from 1,177,000 feddans to 354,000 feddans to only six per cent, or 30 per cent of the original level. Some 659,000 feddans were distributed to farmers with less than five feddans [Abdel-Fadil, 1975: 11, Table 1.6] (see Tables 25 and 26, Appendix A). But the main beneficiaries of the land reform process were the stratum of rich peasants who acquired land via crash or distress sales. Land was sold directly by landlords in larger sizes to rich peasants [Platt, 1970: 45]. Some 164,000 feddans were transferred via distress sales to those with between 20 and 50 feddans (Abdel-Fadil's 'rich peasants'). The 5–20 feddan category of middle peasants remained more or less the same.

Abdel-Fadil stresses that even by 1970, land ownership remained highly skewed and the main trend was the 'steady improvement in the relative position (increase in numbers and acreage) of the medium-sised properties, and in particular owners of 20 to 50 feddans' [1975: 23] representing some five per cent of landholders with 30 per cent of the total cultivated area. This compares to one per cent of landholders and 11 per cent of the land in 1952. Thus, the consolidation of the rich peasants' position in the countryside was perhaps the most important aspect of the reform. Their purchases of land in distress sales by larger landlords, the elimination of the pashas, and the absence of mobilisation of the poor and landless peasants made them the dominant force in the countryside [Richards, 1982: 179].

Nasser bolstered the legitimacy of his regime by avoiding the expropriation of rich and middle peasant holdings. By not seizing the medium-sised properties, the reforms avoided alienating the much needed 'passive support' of the rich peasantry. Even when ceilings were lowered and all peasants compelled to join co-operatives, the rich peasants continued to control their villages, just as they had always done, as mediators between the peasantry and the government [Richards, 1982: 177].

Over the first decade of land reform then, land and income was redistributed away from the large landlords, and moved towards the rich and middle peasantry operating 5–50 feddans. Abdel-Fadil estimates that the share of agricultural income of peasants owning more than five feddans rose from 25 per cent in 1950 to 32 per cent in 1961 [1975: 60]. The structure of initial asset endowments markedly skewed income distribution.

It is interesting to note that in Egypt widespread inequalities of land holdings tend to persist after tenancy arrangements are made notwithstanding the fact that some 47 per cent of the cultivated area is leased in various ways [Mabro, 1971: 405].

The ILO survey income data [Radwan and Lee, 1986: 33] appear to show that the size of the rental market in land is relatively small: only 18 per cent of landowning households rented out land and such households comprised only six per cent of the sample. This was explained by the low levels of rent (LE 1.56 per qirat or 2.7 per cent of the average value of land) brought about by rent controls reducing the attractiveness of renting out land.

However, tenancy data from the same survey [1986: 66–8] show that the land rental market is far more significant than the income data would suggest: 47 per cent of total land area operated in the sample was rented and almost 20 per cent of total land owned was let. Some 72 per cent of all households owning land rented some land, with almost half the tenancies supplied by absentee landlords living outside the village (57 per cent of rented land was from this source).

Of the tenancies supplied by resident landlords, 45 per cent are under one feddan, whereas only 24 per cent of absentee landlord tenancies are under one feddan. The dominant type of tenancy is cash rental (92 per cent of tenancies and 89 per cent of rented land) while sharecropping (on a 50–50 basis) accounted for only seven per cent of tenancies. The average area rented did not vary between cash and share tenancies. However, the cost of renting under a sharecropping arrangement is on average 80 per cent higher than for cash rents [1986: 69]. The strong bargaining position of the landlords results in exorbitant rental values and insecurity of tenants.

Most (94.5 per cent) registered farms are below five feddans in size but only 83.4 per cent of operated holdings. Nevertheless, it is the case that the overwhelming proportion of the 2 million Egyptian farmers work units less than three feddans. The average plot size is generally small and has been falling over time. At present, there is not more than 0.3 feddans of land for every rural resident and no more than 0.15 for every Egyptian: at this rate, a rural family of six persons would only have 1.8 feddans to support it which is less than the amount of land considered necessary to keep a family at subsistence level [*Harik*, 1979: 128]. Mare'i [1954: 145–6] suggests that five feddans are considered adequate for a peasant household since it would produce LE 128 in the average year (enough to support an average family of 8). A figure of three feddans is however supported by more recent data.[4]

In fact, the degree of land concentration is probably understated in the official records. Rich farmer circumvention of agrarian reform laws continues today. Adams [1986: 89] gives the example of one rich farmer who owns 200 feddans but is registered at the co-operative as having only 30 feddans. Commander [1987: 55] mentions one farm of 400–475 feddans comprising 22–26 per cent of total land in the village: thus, despite the legal ceiling of 50 feddans, registration of land in the names of family members can circumvent these restrictions – the farm functions as a consolidated entity. Indeed, it is often the case that several families (say, several married brothers) operate several plots together as *one* business, in spite of having the plots registered as different farms in the official records [*Crouch et al.,* 1983: 61].[5]

V.2 THE AGRARIAN ELITE AND THE CO-OPERATIVE SYSTEM

The 70,000 farmers with more than ten feddans form an agrarian elite with an important role in national and local politics, and are relatively autonomous from direct government action in the countryside. They are descended from around 300 prominent clans that have dominated Egyptian politics over this century and controlled all major political offices outside the major cities: 71 per cent of seats on provincial councils and 55 per cent of district offices. They supply the vast majority of 'umdas (village headmen). When the co-operative system was set up, they were able to circumvent the laws on co-operative board membership by planting poorer members of their clans on the boards [*Sadowski, 1991*: 77–8].

The idea of co-operatives was not new to Egypt in 1952: as early as 1908 Lutfi, a private philanthropist, had introduced rural credit; then in 1923 national legislation set up agricultural co-operatives. However, throughout the 1930s, these co-operatives were no more than credit facilities catering to the needs of the wealthy classes [*Rochin and Grossman, 1985*: 16]. By 1952, there were around 1,700 co-operatives with half a million members. The large landlords dominated at both local and national level, and thus the impact on small farmers was relatively insignificant. Credit, for example, was only extended to those with over 25 feddans of land [*Mayfield, 1974*: 23-4] 'who borrowed most of the funds for their own use or for sub-lending to their tenants at exorbitant rates' [*Platt, 1970*: 40].

After 1952, all land reform recipients had to join the co-operative system. At first, the co-operative system was confined to land reform areas; then later (after Law 317 of 1956) extended to non-land reform areas by 1963. The co-operatives specified the crop rotation to be followed locally and took control of crop marketing and highly subsidised input supplies. They also attempted to consolidate blocks of cultivated land. The Department of Co-operatives came under the umbrella of the Ministry of Agriculture. At the national level there were four main groupings: (1) the General Agricultural Co-operative Society (grouping multi-purpose co-operatives); (2) the General Society for Agrarian Reform; (3) the General Society for Land Reclamation; and (4) the Co-operative Society (for special crops), all grouped under the Central Agricultural Co-operative Union (CACU). There are then strata at *muhafidhah* (governorate) and *markaz* (district) levels, and finally at the bottom, village co-operatives with a minimum membership of 20, run by an elected board of 5 to 11 persons and managed by a *mushrif* (supervisor) appointed by the Ministry of Agriculture who is assisted by an accountant from the Village Bank. By the 1980s, there were over 5,000 agricultural co-operatives covering approximately three million farm families [*Rochin and Grossman, 1985*: 10].

There is every reason to believe that such a system has favoured the rich peasants: this emerging class of relatively well-to-do peasants replaced the pre-revolutionary wealthy landlord class. Due to an inadequate supply of personnel necessary to supervise the co-operative system, the government relied heavily on this new elite who in turn, in many cases, exploited the co-operative system to their personal benefit. These land reform beneficiaries quickly gained control of the boards of directors of the co-operatives [*Rochin and Grossman,* 1985: 25].[6]

The pre-reform institutional lines and rankings still persisted, with the Land Reform agent at the top of the order in lieu of the landlord, the landless labourer still at the bottom, and the steps between dependent on relative prosperity. Richards [1982: 182] writes: 'it is clear that the rich peasants dominated the co-operatives, especially those set up in non-land reform areas after 1963. The government simply did not have the cadre to carry out such a massive extension without relying extensively on the local power structure.' This is supported by Baker: 'The attitude of these more prosperous peasants toward the co-operative movement has been not so much one of opposition but one of subverting the service offered by the co-operative to their own exclusive use' [1978: 205].

However, even in the land reform areas, the rich peasants exerted considerable influence. The mushrif or co-operative supervisor was often the same person as the former landlord's agent. Concerned more with debt collection, he had a short term view that did not encompass modernisation programmes [*Platt,* 1970: 55–6]. Further, the managerial personnel, usually from the stratum of rich peasants, continued to act as representatives of the government, just as they had done for the absentee landlords. Even when qualified government personnel appeared in the land reform areas, these men were themselves often of rural middle-class origins; their origins, training, and inclinations (as well as their low pay and lack of incentives) often led them to rely on the more successful local farmers for guidance [*Richards,* 1982: 181].

There is little doubt that rich peasants controlled the board of co-operatives. Before 1969, 80 per cent of board members were supposed to be small farmers with less than five feddans, but the latter were easily manipulated by the rich peasants, being 'highly vulnerable to rich farmer pressure and bribery' [*Adams,* 1986: 69]. Small farmers depend on rich peasants for land, labour, input purchases, crop sales, cash loans, and intercession with government authorities. Adams [*1986:* 136–44] suggests that the success of all four survival strategies for the poor peasant household (agricultural wage labour, animal raising or intensification of cropping, having a large family or labour migration) is linked to rich peasant patronage. These 'ties of dependence mean that the bulk of poor peasants ...

have been "captured" – not by the state – but by rich peasants (that is, farmers having access to over ten feddans of land)' [1986: 80]. In 1969, the ceiling for co-operative board membership was raised to 15 feddans and illiterates were excluded: this guaranteed rich peasant dominance.

Adams [1986: 105] writes that the leaders of four large extended families dominate economic, social and political life in his survey village of El-Diblah: 'In El-Diblah the small peasants elected to co-operative boards generally own such minuscule plots of land that they are either economically dependent (in the form of wage labour and loans) or materially vulnerable (in the form of bribes) to rich peasants.' [1986: 84] One fellah told him: 'There is only one *ragul* in this village: the *umda*. Everyone else looks to him for work, loans, and brokerage services with the government' [1986: 129].[7]

Rich peasants were able to use their direct or indirect control of co-operative boards to help themselves to co-operative supplies and monopolise tractors and other mechanised inputs [*Adams, 1986: 85–6*]. Richards [1982: 182–3] states that the co-operative allocation 'mechanism excluded the poor as systematically as a price system in an environment of unequal resource endowments would have done'. The rich peasants were first in line for inputs while the poor peasants were locked into a consolidated crop rotation directed by the co-operative: this increased need for credit which the rich peasants supplied. Adams [1986: 62] records one peasant:

> It is a well-known fact here that only the *umda* and certain rich farmers can use the co-operative tractor. No one else here has the connections within the co-operative to reserve the tractor. And few of us have the money needed to buy cigarettes and tea for the driver and his helper.

Only those owning five work animals could participate in animal insurance schemes and therefore qualify for 150 kg of forage at subsidised prices, and only those with 15 feddans could acquire selected seeds [*Richards, 1982: 183*]. Poor peasants with less than five feddans were prohibited from planting highly profitable fruit trees, while rich peasants with over ten feddans could avoid planting regulations on price-controlled crops by obtaining permission to opt out of the official crop rotation in cotton regions, shifting into more profitable crops such as fruit and vegetables [*Adams, 1986: 69*].

An extensive black market emerged on which small farmers sold their quotas of fertiliser to rich peasants [*Richards, 1982: 182*]. Some 10–20 per cent of the total value of fertiliser distributed via co-operatives wound up being sold on black markets at mark-ups of 150 per cent in Lower Egypt and

300 per cent in Upper Egypt [*Sadowski*, 1991: 75]. Mayfield [1974: 130] provides an example from Gharbiya where a peasant obtains two bags of fertiliser from the co-operative for each feddan owned; half gets sold on the black market to a larger owner in order to make quick cash; but after harvest, the yields are too low and the farmer finds that he cannot cover his production costs.

V.3 RICH PEASANTS AND CO-OPERATIVE CREDIT

Similar diversions affected the subsidised credit programmes as well: most peasants did not gain access to medium and long-term loans as the co-operatives employed the same kind of criteria as used formerly by the Agricultural Credit Bank. The critical investment loans for livestock and machinery remained predicated on property with machinery loans requiring a minimum of ten feddans [*Sadowski*, 1991: 75–6], producing what Adams calls a 'large farmer bias in the provision of credit' [1986: 57].

In 1957, the Agricultural Credit Bank was required to deal only with co-operatives and not directly with individual farmers, and the credit system was used to expand the co-operative system in the 1960s. The Egyptian experience with co-operative credit has a longer history however. According to Saab:

> During the first two decades of the twentieth century, ample long-term credit had been made available for agriculture through the Agricultural Credit Bank, but most of it had been appropriated by the large landowning class who either diverted the funds borrowed to consumption purposes or utilised them for the purchase or enlargement of agricultural estates ... [1967: 7].

The Agricultural Credit Bank failed to carry out its mandate, as few loans were granted to small farmers. Meanwhile large landowners established a powerful economic and social base, upon which the smaller landholders and landless masses became dependent. Unable to gain credit from the banks, small farmers were forced to turn to village moneylenders – often the same large landholders – who charged high interest rates. Thus a relatively few large landowners were able to dominate credit facilities by borrowing more in total than many small farmers, at considerably lower interest rates, and move to a position of economic control. With the economic crisis of 1907, however, loans to small farmers all but ceased [*Rochin and Grossman*, 1985: 14]. The Agricultural Reserve Fund advanced loans to small farmers in 1929, but these were limited to export crop producers [*Ministry of Agriculture*, 1989: 35].

Rural credit has unduly benefited the large farmers. By advancing loans to all farmers on the basis of the size of their cultivated crop, the Egyptian government has actually engaged in the unequal subsidisation of large farmers [Adams, 1986: 59–60]. Large farmers with more than 25 feddans who represent about one percent of all Egyptian farmers received 19 per cent of all rural credit in 1963–64 and seven per cent in 1972–73.[8] Small peasants, who represent the majority of debtors (83–85 per cent) and the most needy, get half the credit advanced by the co-operative system, while the medium and large landowners get the other half. When the government tried to check this trend by imposing a rate of interest of four per cent on loans advanced to holders of ten feddans and more, many large landowners reacted by dividing their holdings into plots of less than ten feddans to benefit from the exemption from interest [Radwan, 1977: 69]. As of 1978, 2.6 million peasants owning less than five feddans were receiving LE 71 million in government loans, or 56 per cent of total available credits. But 195,000 farmers with over five feddans collected LE 55 million or 44 per cent of the total [Sadowski, 1991: 76].

The loans from the village banks are given at high rates of interest (relative to small farmers' ability to repay) and with strict rules regarding loan security. Consequently, only a small proportion of poor peasants have been able to benefit from these loans [Harik, 1979: 137]. Nadim's study of village banks found that 'the small farmer, who really needs the support of the Bank, usually cannot meet the requirements for a loan'. While bank managers claimed that the Bank did not favour the large farmers, they admitted that the reliable farmers are the rich ones. In general, small farmers rented land and did not therefore qualify for loan eligibility [1979: 33].

Only three per cent of the sample took medium term loans from the bank. The percentage of those who received loans increases with holding size, but stops beyond a certain point as very large farmers did not borrow from the bank. Small owners and renters obtain loans from relatives, while larger owners borrow from the bank [Nadim, 1979: 41]. The farmers who sought loans unsuccessfully believed they were turned down because their holdings were too small [Nadim, 1979: 18]. In Qalubiya, one fellah remarked: 'if a hiyazah is small, the farmer is not entitled to credit' [Nadim, 1979: 30]. In both villages, the bank required that the borrower own ten feddans in order to qualify for a loan to buy a tractor or plough, five feddans for an irrigation pump, and one feddan for a six month loan to buy cows [Nadim, 1979: 22]. Complaints about the bank included abuses by employees, the bribes required of farmers, delays in granting loans, the favouring of friends and acquaintances, and the neglect of small farmers [Nadim, 1979: 24]. Nadim [1979: 32] mentions one case where a bank employee forged a farmer's signature and took rations of seed and fertiliser and sold it on black market.

Only in 1980, did the Principal Bank for Development and Agricultural Credit (PBDAC) begin to recognise that its main orientation in agricultural development gave more weight to the large farmers. They also noted that during the period 1968–77, loans were directed almost completely to short term loans, and that debts borne by farmers were accumulating rapidly [*Ministry of Agriculture*, 1989: 12–13].[9] Only one per cent of total credit volume is for medium term loans (for orchards and purchase of cattle and machinery) [*Dethier*, 1981: 44]. This recognition led to the establishment of the Small Farmer Project, but only in trial form in only 21 villages in three governorates.

As in the past therefore, poorer peasants continued to secure loans from the wealthier farmers. Dethier [1981: 44] notes that 'the existence of usury and of private moneylenders has not been eradicated from the countryside'. Indeed, Adams [1986: 57–8] suggests that the state supply of rural credit has 'actually strengthened the importance of local moneylenders'. He explains:

> In the absence of any government credit for the main food crops grown in the area (maise, wheat), small peasants must still frequently turn to village moneylenders. For example, a small farmer wishing to plant wheat in November may well have to mortgage off part of his future crop at high rates of interest (exceeding 110 per cent per annum) in order to obtain the requisite working capital.

This would suggest that 'usury has not been eliminated ... in rural Egypt. The state has only partially, and not completely, assumed the functions of local moneylenders' [1986: 57].

It is difficult in the small farm context to separate production from consumption credit: the economic situation of many small *fellahin* is so precarious that when a harvest falls short of family subsistence needs, they are forced to seek consumption loans to survive. Since the latter are not available from the co-operatives, and since credit from relatives and friends is generally very short term, peasants are forced to resort to more onerous informal credit sources such as moneylenders.

Nadim [1979: 19] mentions the presence of usurers in his Qalubiya village where interest rates reached 50 per cent. Currently there are few such persons, but more people in Minya borrowed from other farmers at high rates of interest and 'judging from the high interest rates reported, usury is still present'. He states [1979: 20] that private lenders of interest-bearing loans are regarded as 'thieves and embezzlers, and thus have very poor reputations in the village'. Some 36 per cent of the Minya sample of peasants pay interest rates above 25 per cent, some reaching as high as 75 per cent.

Marketing is also available as a means of surplus extraction with prices set by centralizing merchants who can store crops until prices are right, whereas small peasants want to sell for cash immediately after harvest [*Hopkins, 1987:* 186]. In pre-land reform Egypt, the first obligation of the tenant in disposing of his crop was to pay the rent (often 75 per cent of net income [*Platt, 1970:* 15]). If there were subsistence or other debts to merchants or moneylenders, these must be paid. If the lender was also a grain or cotton dealer -a usual combination – he commonly required payment in kind, setting the price well below free market value. The tight grip of the local merchants is indicated by the fact that 23 years after the co-operative law was passed there were only five marketing co-operativess in existence [*Platt, 1970:* 22]. Nadim's study [1979: 19] mentions three cases of peasants taking advances from merchants to whom they sell produce. Another common borrowing practice is to mortgage a piece of land until its produce is sold.

V.4 IMPLICATIONS WITH RESPECT TO THE DIFFUSION OF MODERN TECHNOLOGY OF RICH PEASANT BIAS IN CREDIT

This rich peasant bias in access to co-operative and village bank credit resources has had important implications for the pattern of diffusion of modern technology in Egyptian agriculture. On the basis of extra-economic considerations large farms are able to obtain inputs before other farm households, the timely supply of such inputs constituting a major bottleneck and a condition of high productivity. This is central to one of the arguments of this thesis, already identified and pursued further in the following chapters.[10]

Ownership of tractors, and other modern farm equipment such as irrigation technology, is strongly correlated with farm size. Commander's 1984 survey shows 60 per cent of the tractors and a third of irrigation pumps owned by farms over five feddans [1987: 240].[11] Hopkins [1982: 168] points out that these machine owners are the large farmers over five feddans who are also most likely to have bought or sold land in the last five years.[12] In his later study of the village of Musha, he discovered that the seven largest farmers who farm 20 per cent of the village land own 27 per cent of the tractors and share ownership of 46 per cent of the irrigation pumps. One of these families with about 300 feddans owned three tractors, nine others owned two each and six out of those nine are from families owning 50 feddans or more [1987: 106].[13]

In the 1976 ILO study, only 16 per cent of sample households owned any machines. Tractors are too expensive and indivisible an investment for small farmers. The strict policy of PBDAC lending helps to restrict the diffusion of mechanised equipment to small farmers. Tractor loans require collateral of five feddans and a 25 per cent down payment [*Commander,* 1987: 246] and water pumps require a collateral of three feddans [*Greenberg,* 1985: 10]. Besides interest payments on the loan, the cost of borrowing is augmented by bank commission surcharges. Indeed, only 40–45 per cent of tractor purchases were financed by PBDAC loans or dealership agreements, with over half being financed by private saving or borrowing [*Commander,* 1987: 246]. Hopkins[14] found that 65 per cent of the farmers in his study felt that they would not qualify for a loan to purchase agricultural machinery, while half the respondents felt the government was doing nothing to help them in mechanisation [1982: 115–16].[15]

Use of tractors via the rental market was more widespread (63 per cent of respondents had an entry for operating costs of machinery). While the proportion of farms using machines increases with size, even tiny farms less than a quarter of a feddan use some machinery and 60 per cent of farms less than one feddan use machinery [*Radwan,* 1986: 78].[16]

Most farmers have to rent tractors and pumps from private owners rather than the co-operative [*Hopkins,* 1982: 93]. The 1976–77 FMS showed 86 per cent of tractor horsepower provided by co-operatives, but current evidence suggests over 90 per cent of mechanical power is owned and provided by the private sector.[17] Private farmers have been in the lead in mechanisation with most tractors owned by rich peasants [*Richards,* 1982: 218]. Hopkins [1987: 185] notes that machine rental has become increasingly important as a mode of surplus extraction: those who own machinery rent to others on a piecemeal basis in return for cash or crop share.[18] The profitability of such operations is enhanced by subsidised fuel, oil and machine purchase. Further, rental prices are set fairly high through tacit collusion between machine owners. Co-operative tractors, when they are available, are rented for 15 piastres per qirat: 'far cheaper than renting a tractor from another farmer (25 piasters per qirat)' [*Nadim,* 1979: 23].

In the 1980s, the emphasis has been on machine accumulation rather than land accumulation: 'Thus the relationship of the larger farmers to the smaller farmers around them was mediated through their control of the access to machinery more than through control of the access to land' [*Adams,* 1986: 189]. Thus, questions of cost, payment schedules and tips become important [*Hopkins et al.,* 1982: 93]. Hopkins *et al.* [1982: 242] found machine owners were reticent to talk about their relations with machine renters. The relationship between machine owner and farmer is critical for the organisation of production [1982: 93]. Mechanisation has increased the division of labour with the pattern being set by the rich peasants and capitalist farmers [*Hopkins,* 1987: 25]. In the past, reciprocal labour exchange between small peasant farms solved labour availability problems at peak periods, but mechanisation and monetisation have produced a pattern of hired labour with a high correlation between degree of mechanisation and hired labour use [Hopkins et al., 1982: 236–7]. As tractor density increases, it is possible that owners attempt to tie farmers to them [1982: 242].

Hopkins notes that the machine owners are strongly differentiated from most farmers by virtue of the size of their own farming operation. While most of the machine owners have farms of five feddans or more, they represent a very small percentage of the farmers in general. This evidence thus supports the contention that the present pattern of agricultural mechanisation in Egypt tends to reinforce or even accentuate the distinction between large and small farmers. It gives an additional advantage to the large farmers, and creates a very different pattern of social relationships between the machine owners and the others: 'It is probable that mechanisation is also to the advantage of the small farmer ... but the point here is that relatively speaking it is *more* to the advantage of the machine owner' [Hopkins et al., 1982: 238]. The mechanisation process reinforces the power and position of large farmers and the choice of technology reflects the perceived interests of large farmers.

This process has been of immense importance in accelerating peasant differentiation in rural Egypt, and as we shall see in the following chapters, has had important implications for the inverse relationship between farm size and productivity.

V.5 THE DOMINANCE OF THE RICH PEASANTRY AND THE
    POLITICAL SPHERE

This dominance of the rich peasantry extends to the political sphere at both local and national levels. In the smaller villages, with less than 10,000 people, the social structure is more likely to be shaped or influenced by a limited number of families. These family relationships are extremely crucial in local institutions [Mayfield, 1974: 115]. The village council chairman's authority and influence rest on his association with the leading families and informal village leaders [Mayfield, 1974: 92].

Mayfield [1974: 111] found that many village councils do not function as intended because the traditional families still dominate:

The popular powers in the villages have no strength within the ASU (Arab Socialist Union) because the *umdah* and the *shaykhs* in the village dominate the village and the agricultural labourers ... They did not organise themselves together into an Agricultural Workers' Union because of the *umdah* and the large families and thus they continue to accept ten piastres a day ... The *umdah* is the real head of the village's administrative machinery ... His family controls over 800 feddans either by owning or leasing, and the members of the village council are all from his family ...

Adams [1986: 152] describes how rich peasants distribute vote money among their client *'umdas* who control the small peasant vote for National Assembly elections. At the national level rich peasant power is clearly visible. Agrarian policy itself was heavily influenced by the rich peasantry. Sayyid Mar'ei (a former large landlord) consolidated and enlarged various supervisory agencies into his own personal fiefdom: the Higher Committee of Agrarian Reform. This latter took control of the Agricultural Credit and Co-operative Bank in November 1955. In 1957, he became Minister of Agriculture and in 1960, the entire co-operative system was transferred to the Ministry [Sadowski, 1991: 60].

Sadat himself was from a rich peasant background in Minufiya. His policies consolidated rich peasant power in the rural administration: minimum property requirements were decreed for village mayoral elections, and the number of poor peasants serving on co-operative boards declined throughout the 1970s. Ever since 1952, rich peasants had been assured of at least half the seats in the National Assembly, simply by defining peasants as those with less than 25 feddans. In 1974, this was further diluted by raising the ceiling on this definition to those cultivating up to 50 feddans. Indeed, members of the agrarian elite were soon to form one of the largest and most important blocs in Parliament [Sadowski, 1991: 81].[19]

In the 1970s, the main spokesman for the rich peasantry was Ahmed Yunis, head of the CACU. He had established a vast patronage network which was able to influence the top political elite and a third of the parliamentary deputies. This developed into a power struggle between Sadat's Misr party and the CACU, the latter attempting to secure greater co-operative independence while the government tried to expand its control. Sadat disbanded the CACU in 1976 under Law 824 and transferred its functions to PBDAC based in Cairo and its network of village banks. In fact however, the village banks catered even more narrowly to the rich peasants because of property qualifications [*Sadowski,* 1991: 82], and the latter were able to dominate the shift of PBDAC towards medium and long term loans [*Sadowski,* 1991: 202]. By 1980, CACU had been reactivated with the *mushrifs* elected locally.[20]

These developments and the power of the rich peasantry in the Egyptian countryside have, however, been uneven. This heterogeneity has had profound implications for agrarian transition in Eypt. Hopkins [1987: 4] delineates two paths of agrarian transition in Egypt: a capitalist path (using hired wage labour and machinery) and a path dominated by petty commodity production with small farmers producing for the market and agriculture becoming increasingly marginalised. The paths are manifested in variant forms of village development. He provides [1987: 55] a typology of villages reflecting these different paths of agrarian transition in Egypt: (1) land reform or resettlement villages which have moved in the direction of intensification of petty commodity production; and (2) villages in which capitalist agriculture and the emergence of capitalist relations of production around wage labour have appeared.[21]

The land reform villages are dominated by family farms of three to five feddans dependent on the use of intensive family labour. The intent here is to maintain the 'traditional' family farm as the unit of production and link it to the market through co-operatives [*Hopkins*, 1981: 56–7]. These small farms are not fully commercialised and operate with different decision variables from the large farms: small farms allocate land first to food and fodder crops, secondly to co-operative quotas and areas (in order to get input supplies), and only market if there is a surplus [*Ikram*, 1980: 197]. Hopkins states however, that 'up to a point, larger farmers are not qualitatively different from smaller farmers, just quantitatively' [1981: 48].

These villages, characterised by small scattered land possessions prohibit the application of modern technology and lead to the fragile formation of capitalism. Fragmentation weakens their ability to adopt new agricultural methods, representing the intensification of capital utilisation [*Ministry of Agriculture, 1989: 79*].

In the land reform village of Zeer, in Adams' study, where a more thoroughgoing land reform took place, less social differentiation and elite land accumulation occurred. Indeed, in the 30 years since land reform, out of 1,500 beneficiaries in Zeer, only 11 bought mechanised farm inputs, only 22 bought private land, and four of those had owned private land prior to land reform but had concealed it [1986: 106]. Thus, land reform had actually had the effect of slowing down capital accumulation: it 'actually accelerated the rate at which farm units are unable to save and invest' [1986: 128].

In contradistinction, 'direct government influence was certainly much stronger in the land reform areas than elsewhere ... In the other villages the co-operatives were easily dominated by the rich peasants and the village headmen' [*Richards*, 1982: 179]. Villages in which large farmers have been able to accumulate land and other means of production such as machinery have exhibited a different outcome with increased social differentiation and the potential disappearance of the small farmer rather than his survival.

The capitalist villages appear to have relatively greater concentration of land, larger area and population, and higher levels of mechanisation. Such villages also benefited from development efforts in the form of loans for machinery and other modern inputs. The mode of production changes because capital has penetrated the village and changes the system of production instead of being merely externally imposed via market relations [*Hopkins*, 1987: 5–6]. The family farm gives way to larger enterprises organised by the family, but based on wage labour and the intensive use of machine inputs [*Hopkins and Mehanna*, 1981: 59]. As we shall see in the following chapters, these distinctions and classifications are echoed throughout the survey data, and provide the political economy foundation for understanding the dynamics behind the inverse relationship and its breakdown.

SUMMARY AND CONCLUSIONS

In this chapter, we have established the political economy parameters of the framework within which to analyse the inverse relationship at the micro level in the Egyptian countryside. We have seen that despite significant land reform measures, important elements of semi-feudal agriculture remain strong: sharecropping tenancy, personalised oral contracts, and debt. Access to land and resources lies through the patronage of the rich peasants and those landlords who managed to evade land reform legislation. This is the environment, the matrix of exploitative relationships, in which the inverse relationship flourishes.

Our hypothesis is however, that in the early stages of transition, institutional biases act strongly in favour of the larger farmers – often the legacy of previously existing systems continuing to operate where political power and status determine access to the resources which make up the package of technological change in agriculture.

Several studies, as we have seen in this chapter, show that the main beneficiaries of the land reform legislation, and subsequently, the co-operative and rural credit system in Egypt were the rich farmers. The control of the latter by the rich peasantry, those owning over five or ten feddans of land, ensured their dominance with respect to the diffusion of the new technology. While at an earlier stage, intrinsic advantages of scale are not unimportant, these become increasingly significant over time, enabling the large farmers to maintain relatively high investment and growth rates. In this two stage process, the first impact of agrarian transition is the weakening and disappearance of the inverse relationship. Later, when scale advantages operate for a substantial length of time the relation turns significantly positive.

In the next chapter, we subject the data used by Radwan and Lee in their 1986 study to much closer examination, in order to discover the nature and extent of the inverse relationship in the Egyptian countryside, and its relationship to technological change. This will provide a stronger empirical support for our hypotheses. Then, in the following chapters, we can explore, at the more disaggregated level of individual villages, just why such an inverse relationship exists, where it exists, and how it is changing.

NOTES

1. See Abdel-Fadil's 1975 work, *Development, Income Distribution and Social Change in Rural Egypt 1952–1970*, which establishes the central thesis of this chapter: the dominance of the rich peasantry in rural Egypt. While we can agree with Abdel-Fadil in his masterful analysis of the increasing domination of the Egyptian countryside by a rich peasantry, we must, however, following Byres [1977b: 268], question his assumption that the rich peasantry are necessarily capitalist farmers. As we have seen in Chapter III, this assumption has been the source of somewhat premature judgements concerning the development of capitalist agriculture and the resolution of the agrarian question in particular countries. There are indeed hints in Abdel-Fadil [1975: 46–8] that significant elements of semi-feudal structures remain prominent in Egyptian agriculture.
2. These actors were large absentee landlords.
3. Infitah (=opening) is the process of market liberalisation initiated by Sadat in 1974. A more apposite name might be Inghirab (=turning West).
4. This figure was provided by interviewees in the author's survey villages. See Chapters VII and VIII.
5. Ansari mentions one notable who owned 477 feddans and who kept his holding intact by parcelling out titles among five grandsons and eight female relatives [1968: 131]. The operation of several officially registered landholdings as one unit can also be seen in the ten feddan farm in the author's 1990 survey of Shubak al-Sharqi in Giza. See Chapter VII.
6. The literature on rich peasant domination of co-operatives includes Kamal [1968]; Dumont [1968]; USDA [1977]; and Baker [1978].
7. The word *ragul* is used in the sense of 'big man'.
8. See Adams, [1986: 60, Table 3.3].
9. See Ministry of Agriculture [*1989: 56-8*]. The duration of short term loans does not exceed 14 months and repayment is linked to crop maturity and marketing dates. The duration of medium-term loans is never less than 14 months and not more than five years. The long term loan period is 5–15 years and is lent for land reclamation or building which requires real estate pledges

   By 1985–86, loans in kind still constituted more than 50 per cent of total short term loans: 54.1 per cent in 1985–86 [1989: 62, Table 5], and PBDAC medium and long-term loans accounted for 50 per cent of advances [1989: 66, Table 7]. The majority of investment loans go for animals, followed by agricultural equipment [1989: 69, Table 9]. The development of loans for agricultural machinery shows increasing values over the period 1975–88 [1989: 76, Table 11].
10. Abdel-Fadil [1975: 31–34] stresses mechanisation in the process of peasant differentiation and the development of a capitalist farmer stratum in a permissive sense: only the rich peasantry had the necessary investible surpluses to invest in improved machinery. Byres [1977b: 265] asks why this should necessarily be so given the plentiful supply of underemployed and unemployed rural labour. The answer possibly lies in the accelerating process of international labour migration to Libya, Iraq and the Gulf states during the 1970s. This comprised both direct and indirect effects: rural labour moved not only to the labour-importing countries, but to replace urban construction sector workers within Egypt. This produced temporary labour shortages in Egyptian agriculture during this period [*Richards,* 1989; *Richards and Martin,* 1983; *and Birks and Sinclair,* 1980].

11. See Commander [1987: 244, Table 9.5] which shows machine ownership by type and farm size in 1982 (taken from *Hopkins et al.*, [1982: 169]). The distribution of machine ownership shows a clear large farm bias.
12. See Hopkins *et al.* [1982: 169, Table 7]: 48 out of 83 tractors and 49 out of 112 irrigation pumps are owned by farmers with more than five feddans of operated area.
13. Other studies tell the same story. The ERA 2000 report [1979: 8.6] found that of the 158 farmers in the survey, only seven owned tractors – all of them large; 31 owned pumps, five owned sprayers and four owned threshers. The majority of these are in the hands of the farmers who hold between five and 24 feddans. The larger the farm holdings, the greater the proportion of farmers who are highly mechanised.
    Nadim [1979: 46] also finds machine ownership increasing with farm sise: the single owner who had machines in all categories was the largest landowner in the village (with over 20 feddans). In Minya, no-one with less than three feddans owned an irrigation pump, although access was available through rental markets.
14. A survey of 1,000 farms and 170 machine owners in ten villages across four governorates in 1981–82.
15. The ERA 2000 study supports this finding. It finds that farmers were unable to adopt machines because they had 'no money for down payment' (53 per cent) or because it was 'too hard to get credit' (29 per cent) [1979: 8.16].
16. The use of tractors (a) and mechanical threshers (b) has increased markedly over time [*Commander*, 1987: 255]:

	(a)	(b)
mid60s	6%	9%
1970	25	32
1975	66	81

Data source: El-Kholy and Abbas, [1982: 61–66].

Commander [1987: 255] also cites a nine village survey in Qalubiya, Sharqiya and Minya which shows low levels of machine ownership, but a highly developed rental market [*Goueli et al.,* 1980: Tables 5 and 8].
    See also Commander [1987: 259, Table 9.9] which shows the use of machinery by operation and farm size for 1984. For all operations, the percentage of farm households using machines increases with farm sise. And Commander [1987: 265, Table 9.11] shows increasing irrigation technology by farm size in terms of the percentage of farm households using pumps in 1984.
17. See Commander [1987: 255] who cites Hopkins *et al.* [1982: 158 ff.] and Reiss *et al.* [1983: 31 ff.]. Table 9E [1987: 298] shows a massive increase in the growth of private machine ownership.
18. Radwan and Lee [1986: 39–40] show that farm household income from the rental of equipment (and livestock) features only in the upper income classes [Table 3.7]:

LE	income	no/HH	income/HH
0-300	0	0	0
300-600	130	6	21.66
600-1000	201	4	50.25
1000-1400	1326	6	221.0
1400-2000	1280	4	320.0
gt 2000	400	1	400.0

19. One of the effects of this has been that taxation of the agricultural sector has been a neglected issue in Egypt. In 1973, the Egyptian government proposed exempting small peasants with less than three feddans from a series of taxes and duties, but rich peasants managed to get this extended to all farmers regardless of size [*Sadowski*, 1991: 82].
    Similarly with the intersectoral terms of trade. Abdel Fadil [1975: 100, Table 5.8] has shown that these have moved in favour of the agricultural sector, with the prices of manufactured inputs being heavily subsidised and crop output prices being increased.

Radwan [1977] has calculated two separate terms of trade indices for rich and poor farmers in which the former increased more than the latter. The income terms of trade also moved relatively more favourably for the rich peasantry. Abdel-Fadil [1975] has demonstrated that the share of agricultural income of farmers with over 5 feddans increased from 25 per cent in 1950 to 32 per cent in 1961.

TERMS OF TRADE INDICES FOR THE AGRICULTURAL SECTOR
1960–75 (1960=100)

year	all farmers			poor farmers			rich farmers		
	(1)	(2)	(3)	(1)	(2)	(3)	(1)	(2)	(3)
1960	100	100	100	100	100	100	100	100	100
1965	85	88	79	86	88	79	92	85	86
1970	98	98	101	99	98	104	111	111	111
1975	102	97	120	102	96	124	127	122	146

(1) overall terms of trade index between agricultural output and all manufactured commodities.
(2) terms of trade between agricultural output and manufactured consumer goods.
(3) terms of trade between agricultural output and manufactured inputs.

20. Recent policy developments have also allowed the former landlords to re-enter the rural power structure. In the early 1970s, Sadat packed Parliament with rural notables in order to pass legislation restoring land titles to formerly sequestered owners, and in 1975 this led to Law 67 which strengthened the hand of large landlords by adjusting tax assessments to give owners the ability to raise rents. This new legislation (which was passed after only six hours of debate) enhanced the power of landowners at the expense of sharecroppers and tenants: rent contracts could be cancelled at the behest of the landowner and rent disputes were to be settled at the local level [Sadowski, 1991: 293–5].

Shortly afterwards, these land owners were pressing for more radical legislation, their proposals including: an increase in rents from seven to ten times the value of land tax, the legal right to unilateral rental contract termination, the eviction of tenants who were late rent payers, and a reversion of cash rents to sharecropping [Sadowski, 1991: 295]. These measure would have permitted evictions on 90 per cent of the cultivated area by allowing landlords to re-register plots in smaller parcels in order to evict tenants.

In 1982, landlords and rich peasants who formed a siseable proportion of NDP membership (Mubarak's own party) lobbied to make the right of eviction and landlord resumption of land a centrepiece of their agrarian policy. When the New Wafdists won 58 seats in the 1984 elections, Mubarak conceded, but the proposals proved too radical and unpopular, and large popular opposition led by the Tagammu'a party prevented these proposals from becoming law.

Regardless, the landlords took the law into own hands: half refused to give tenants a written contract, only oral agreements which could easily be revised or single season contracts which were exempt from the rent laws. One method of land resumption was to bribe the tenant to leave the land. The result was massive resumption of own cultivation and tenancy agreements declined. Ownership increased from 25 per cent in 1952 to 58 per cent in 1983, with rich peasants increasing their share of land from 13 per cent in 1977 to 18 per cent in 1982 and large landowners enlarging holdings from 20 to 25 per cent [Rochin and Grossman, 1985: 300].

21. Hopkins also mentions a third type of village which is dependent on migrant remittances or off-farm employment, and is mainly non-agricultural.

VI

A Disaggregated Analysis of the ILO Data: Technical Change and the Inverse Relationship in Egypt

INTRODUCTION

The survey carried out by Samir Radwan and Eddy Lee in February 1977 within the framework of the ILO World Employment Programme provides an opportunity to test the relation between farm size and productivity.[1] The main focus of the ILO survey was on rural poverty, income and asset distribution, and employment, but it also includes information on production conditions with most of the variables necessary for our own purposes.

The principal arguments are, as we have seen in previous chapters that, at a high level of aggregation, an inverse relationship between farm size and farm productivity will be manifested, with its origins in land heterogeneity and long-run processes of population settlement. However, at a more disaggregated level, we may find a very different type of relationship and one that exhibits greater pattern variability. In regions of relatively backward agriculture, we have hypothesised that an inverse relationship will be found. In more advanced regions, however, that relationship may weaken or even cease to be negative with the transformation of existing production conditions from backward agriculture to a system employing modern technology – both biochemical and mechanical.

In section VI.1, we present the methodology and characteristics of the ILO survey. Section VI.2 recapitulates Radwan's analysis and results and the problems associated with his approach. Then, in sections VI.3 and VI.4, we present our results from a more detailed and disaggregated analysis of the ILO data. Section VI.3 presents a contextual account of technological change in Egyptian agriculture, showing the degree of unequal development and regional heterogeneity; while section VI.4 shows how the ILO data reflects this, and its implications for the inverse relationship at a more disaggregated level. This exercise represents a preliminary empirical analysis of agrarian technical change in Egypt before we come to the more in depth study of two of the villages in the ILO survey in the final two chapters.

VI.1 THE ILO SURVEY AND ITS CHARACTERISTICS

The ILO data possess a number of advantages in comparison to much of the data used in earlier debates. First, since the data were collected at household level there is no need to rely on averaged data according to size-groups. Any level of disaggregation is possible. However, given the small sample size of some of the villages, it was thought that a governorate-wise level of disaggregation would be adequate for our purpose. Secondly, the period in which the data was collected provides a sufficient elapse of time since the major agrarian changes of the 1950s and 1960s – land reform and technological innovations. Finally, the data allow us to examine the size-productivity relation in conjunction with other important variables.

This study is based on the results of a sample survey carried out in 1977. A random sample of 1,000 households in 18 villages was drawn using the 1966 and 1976 Population Censuses as a frame. The sample size was partly dictated by considerations of comparability with the country's Household Budget surveys, which usually cover the same number of households in each of their four rounds. The sample was selected through a multi-stage sampling procedure.

First, the country was divided into strata according to *muhafidha* (governorate or administrative region) boundaries. Seven of the 25 governorates were excluded because of their atypical features (being exclusively urban such as Cairo and Alexandria, or desert such as Sinai). From the list of the remaining 18 governorates a random sample of three was chosen from each of the two major agro-ecological zones, Upper and Lower Egypt. These were: Dumyat, Gharbiya, Menufiya, Giza, Beni Suef and Qena.

Second, the total number of households in the sample was distributed among the six governorates in proportion to their share of the total rural population of those governorates. The definition of rural used here is that of the Population Census, where the breakdown between rural and urban is based on administrative distinction: the urban population includes all people counted in the major urban governorates, capitals of all other governorates and capitals of markazes (administrative districts).

Third, a stratified sample of 18 villages was chosen in such a way as to allow large and small villages to be represented in proportion to their respective shares in the six governorates combined. A population of 5,000 in the 1966 Census was taken as the dividing line (the cut-off point of 5,000 inhabitants in distinguishing between large and small villages is the criterion used by the Egyptian Family Budget Surveys). According to this criterion, one-third of the villages were large and two-thirds small in 1966. Thus, six large and 12 small villages were drawn at random from the six governorates according to these governorates' shares of large and small villages. The principle chosen was the following: if governorate i had x per cent of the total number of large villages in the six governorates then we select at random 1/100.x.6 large villages from that governorate. For small villages, the formula similarly was 1/100.x.12 where x was the percentage share of i in the total number of small villages in the six governorates. Since whole villages (and not fractions) were to be chosen and since the total numbers chosen were small, the rounding error was large. According to the above criteria the numbers of large and small villages selected from each of the six governorates were as follows.

Finally, the number of households to be drawn from each village was obtained by distributing the number of households to be drawn from each governorate among the selected villages of the governorate according to the relative population of these villages. From each selected village in the governorate ij a sample of rij households was randomly drawn according to the following formula:

$$r_{ij} = [\ P_{ij}/N_i . \text{SUM}\ P_{ij}]\ S_i \ (i=1....6)$$

where: S_i=number of sample households in governorate i
           P_{ij}=population of village j in governorate i
           N_i=number of sample villages in governorate i

Of the 1,000 households, 586 were to be drawn from the six large villages and 414 from the 12 small villages. A random sample corresponding to these numbers was drawn using the lists of the 1976 Population and Housing Census as a frame. The 1966 Population Census was used as a frame in drawing the governorate and village samples and, as the 1976 Population and Housing Census became available just on the eve of the survey, it was used to draw the household sample. Since the household sample was drawn from a frame different from that of the governorate and village samples, a number of checks were performed to ensure consistency such as relative sizes of governorates, numbers of villages and average size of households within the villages of the sample. No serious inconsistencies were found. Tables 27 to 29 provide a summary of the sample distribution.

The sample's representativeness of Egyptian rural society can be seen by comparing the survey results to national data. The geographical spread of the 18 villages in the sample was such that it ranged from the tip of the Delta (Meet al-Shiukh in Dumyat) to the south of the Nile Valley (al-Amiria in Qena). The villages represented a wide variety of rural economies with those that are purely agricultural (Tilwana in Menufiya), those that can be considered extensions to urban centres (Shubak al-Sharki in Giza), those with traditional handicrafts (head-cover making in Atf Abu Gindi in Gharbiya), and those near a large industrial centre (Kamalia in Gharbiya). Finally, some of the main characteristics of the household sample, such as the age and sex structure, employment patterns and income per capita were not significantly different from the national data. In one aspect, the sample was different from rural Egypt: the distribution of landholding. A comparison of the survey results with the 1976 statistics on landholding shows that the sample may have failed to capture the upper end of the distribution. The analysis of the sample results should therefore be interpreted with this bias in mind.

VI.2 ANALYSIS AND RESULTS: (I) THE RADWAN REGRESSION AND ITS QUESTIONABLE NATURE – THE NEED FOR A MORE DISAGGREGATED APPROACH

Given the relatively profound technical changes experienced by Egyptian agriculture, the results obtained by Radwan's regression of net farm output on farm size might seem somewhat surprising. Radwan finds the following relationship to hold:

$$\log y = 2.6517 - 0.2559 \log x$$
$$(0.0363)$$

$R^2 = 0.1075$

$N = 425$

where y is net farm output per qirat and x is size of landholding.

Radwan argues that this result is consistent with the large amount of evidence which shows that small farms are more intensive cultivators and have higher yields per unit area than large farms in the Third World and provides scope for further land redistribution in order to raise total output and reduce income inequalities.

However, Radwan's approach is questionable with regard to two points: first his use of net farm output may seriously bias the results in favour of finding an inverse relationship. Using imputed values both on the output and input sides as well as excluding labour costs on the small farms, as Radwan does, can easily produce substantial bias against the larger farms since an important cost element for the smaller farms is ignored. However, we have retained net farm output in our yield calculations below as well as running regressions on yields using total crop values; and secondly, we must relate the results of these regressions to other factors, such as cropping patterns, cropping intensities, labour input intensities, and levels of technological development and commercialisation. Running regressions for all the variables cited, we arrived at the results for all Egypt presented in Table 30, Appendix A.

These mixed results are very similar to those observed repeatedly for areas of traditional agriculture. The relationship between farm size and output per net cropped area is significantly negative for the three alternative versions of the latter. Cropping intensity shows, as expected, a strong inverse relationship with operated area. We get mixed results for the relationship between farm size and output per gross cropped area: using net farm output we get a strong inverse relationship; using Radwan's total crop value figures we get a negative relationship significant at the five per cent level; and using the corrected figures for total crop value, we get a positive but insignificant relationship. For individual crop yields we find significantly negative results for winter wheat, birseem, and cotton, while that for maize is negative only at the ten per cent level. For rice, however we find a statistically insignificant positive relationship.

These regression results would, if our hypothesis is correct, appear to suggest either that Egyptian agriculture has not yet undergone as thorough a transformation as is suggested in the literature, or that the regressions which have been carried out at the all Egypt level are excessively aggregated and providing us with misleading results. Both explanations are partially correct and their joint operation can be seen when we turn to the regression at a more suitably disaggregated level.

VI.3 AND RESULTS: (II) A DIGRESSION ON TECHNOLOGICAL CHANGE IN EGYPTIAN AGRICULTURE, UNEVEN DEVELOPMENT AND REGIONAL HETEROGENEITY

While scientist man-years devoted to agricultural research and expenditure on agricultural research both doubled in the period 1959–74 [*Antle and Aitah*, 1982: 57], Richards was able to write in 1982: 'The Green Revolution has had only a limited impact so far on Egyptian agriculture' [1982: 215–16]. Similarly, Antle and Aitah [1982: 35] write: 'The preliminary evidence reported here suggests that there has not been the substantial technical change in Egyptian agriculture needed to generate long-run productivity growth.'

However, it is not agricultural pricing policies that have played the major role in the stagnation of aggregate output, but the deficiency of investment in agriculture which has had a significantly adverse impact on the aggregate growth rate of the sector [*Esfahani*, 1988: 135–6]. The shift from public to private investment in Egyptian agriculture in the mid-1970s meant that most of it would have to come from large farmers who were able to expand production through more flexible combinations of crops [*Esfahani*, 1988: 217].

In general, there have been low rates of HYV dissemination in Egypt, despite generous seed subsidies. Less than one per cent of the total rice area in Egypt was planted under HYVs in the early 1980s [*Adams*, 1985: 714].

The expansion of Mexican wheat varieties was quite rapid in the early 1970s: from 0.3 per cent of the area in 1972 to 37 per cent in 1974, but this declined steeply to 12.9 per cent in 1976 (this compares with 76 per cent in India and 84 per cent for Pakistan) [Ikram, 1980: 189–90].

Improved maize varieties have been introduced since the 1940s but have had only limited impact on yields. Indeed there is little in the way of genetically improved maize varieties actually used by the Egyptian farmer: about 80 per cent of the total area under maize is grown in local varieties from farm-supplied seeds. One 'hybrid' (American Early) is now probably more local than improved by current standards. It is also probable that many of the varieties identified as hybrid are in reality seed which has been derived from hybrids rather than true hybrids [Fitch, 1983: 13–14; Basheer, 1981: 5].

In general, farmers do not have adequate knowledge of what seed is available from the co-operatives. Morsi [1982: 242, Tables 6–19 and 20] reports that the proportion of small farmers with information on modern technology, but who were unable to adopt were 13–22 per cent of his sample and the small farmers who had tried modern technology were only 17–20 per cent of the sample. Hopkins et al. [1982: 113–14] report that less than 15 per cent of respondents in their study had heard of the Soil Improvement Organisation and a quarter of those did not think it did any useful work. The extension worker fared even worse: 87 per cent of farmers felt that he had given no information to them.

The reasons advanced for the low adoption rates for HYVs include the fact that these require heavier doses of other inputs such as fertiliser, irrigation water, and more careful handling, but the supply of fertiliser and seeds has been insufficient. While the gross returns are higher for the new varieties, the net returns are less than for the traditional local varieties. Harvest timing is more critical with greater potential losses. Ikram [1980: 225] states: 'family settlements in the new lands failed because the technology developed was not suitable for small farmers'.

Production of HYVs was confined to large farms and areas cultivated under the Land Reform administration [Morsi, 1982: 52]. Fitch [1983: 64] reports that trials tend to be held on larger farms and therefore may not be representative of typical farming conditions:

> The fact that trial farms tend to be larger, and trial farmers better educated than the average, suggest that they may enjoy certain advantages which others do not. In addition to having better access to tractors for ploughing, trial farmers may also have advantages in the acquiring of seed and fertiliser; the fact that they are more timely in their application of nitrogen may reflect that supplies at the co-operatives are more available to them.

Similarly with livestock feed subsidies which primarily accrue to large private producers and to the public sector, not to the small farmers who own 80-90 per cent of the country's livestock [*Richards*, 1989: 4].

Antle and Aitah [1982: 71, Table 2-1] show substantial growth in the local production of nitrogen and phosphate fertilisers in Egypt in the period 1965-78. In 1982-83, nitrogen fertiliser production capacity was 727,000 tons per annum with actual production of 666,000 tons produced by four local companies. Phosphate fertilisers are produced by three companies in Egypt with 1982-83 production reaching 127,000 tons [*Kaldas*, 1984: 2-3].

With the massive increase in fertiliser subsidies over the 1970s [*Antle, 1982: 78*, Table 2-8], fertiliser consumption in Egypt grew rapidly.[2] The growth of fertiliser consumption decelerated in the 1980s but remained at high levels: indeed Egypt uses more fertiliser per cultivated acre than any other country except Japan – so high that the ecological sustainability of such practices is being increasingly questioned [*Richards*, 1989: 12]. However, while Egypt has very high rates of fertiliser consumption, the figures on annual fertiliser consumption do not indicate actual patterns of fertiliser use. Adams shows that small peasants facing a shortage of liquid resources regularly sell co-operative-supplied fertiliser to rich peasants for cash instead of using it themselves [1986: 51-2].

Egypt is mainly dependent on imported pesticides with domestic production limited to one government owned plant [*Schutz*, 1987: 4]. Use is not widespread as the expense of unsubsidised pesticides discourages small peasants from using them. Rich peasants growing fruit and vegetables however, do use them [*Adams*, 1986: 225].

Mechanisation is the most obvious example of an increase in the level of the productive forces, together with new crops and techniques such as pesticides and fertiliser use. It has clear implications for the penetration of capitalist relations into rural areas in terms of the participation of the village in the market and in terms of the organisation of productive labour within the village framework. Hopkins and Mehanna write: 'There is certainly a sense in which one can say that mechanisation of agriculture is the "locomotive" of changes in the Egyptian countryside' [1981: 45].

The diffusion of farm mechanisation in Egypt has followed the typical sequence found throughout the developing world, in which power intensive operations are mechanised first. Egyptian mechanisation basically means ownership or use of an irrigation pump and tractor with ploughing and threshing being the operations most likely to be mechanised [*Hopkins et al., 1982: 93-4*].[3] Most mechanisation has been tractorisation, but use of grain threshers and irrigation pumps has become increasingly common [*Richards, 1989: 63; Imam, 1983: 2*]. Mechanisation spread rapidly in the 1970s with the stock of tractors growing at 7.8 per cent per year, then decelerating to

2.8 per cent per year during the 1980s.[4] Tractor production began in Egypt in 1961 in a joint venture with Yugoslavia (which was halted during 1970–74) and then Romania from 1972 and later Canada [*Khalil*, 1981: 12]. But the industrial capacity for domestic manufacture of modern farming equipment remains limited in relation to imported units, some financed by aid [*El Sahrigi and Shepley*, 1984: 12].[5]

As we saw in Chapter IV, Commander's Sharqiya village was characterised by an abundance of agricultural machinery and mechanical energy widely diffused for power-intensive activities [1987: 55–56]. But the diffusion of mechanisation throughout Egypt has been very uneven. The level of mechanisation varies considerably even from one village to the next [*Hopkins et al.*, 1982: 93]. While some 66 per cent of the cultivated area is ploughed by tractors, mechanised seedbed preparation has reached less than half of the area on farms less than one feddan [*Imam*, 1983: 3].

The benefits of tractorisation can be seen in terms of increasing cropping intensity and yields, providing more flexibility in the cropping pattern, timeliness, and cost savings. In the early 1980s, Richards [1981: 414–15] did not see much scope for mechanisation increasing cropping intensity in Egypt, but did admit that: 'Perhaps mechanisation will increase the cropping intensity of rich farmers. These crop less intensively than their smaller neighbours because of the problems of supervising and controlling a large hired labour force.' This is precisely what brings about the breakdown in the inverse relationship.

Yields have also been improved by mechanisation. Hopkins *et al.* [1982: 131] found in their study that the Gharbiya and Qalubiya villages reported higher yields than those in Buheira and Minya: 'In general this pattern corresponds to the pattern of highly and poorly mechanised villages.' Of course, what is important are the factors which led to the differences in mechanisation levels in the first place. Indeed, they found that the variation in levels of mechanisation between villages was much more significant than the variation between crops and higher mechanisation associated with higher yields [1982: 235].

El Sahrigi and Shepley [1984: 8, Table 2] show substantial net benefits per feddan from mechanisation in terms of animal loss recovery, labour cost savings and increased production. They found a wide range of modern farm equipment was associated with net benefits: mower binders [1985: 33] reduced labour costs and increased timeliness of operation, and mechanised threshers also [1985: 40]. Seed drills produced yield increases [1985: 49] and increased seed loss recovery while reducing labour costs [1985: 52]. Mechanical irrigation pumps released animal power to increase milk and meat yields and also helped large farmers to avoid labour supervision problems in *saqiya*[6] rings [1985: 59]. Mechanical tillage led to yield increases and savings in labour time in cotton cultivation [1985: 69], and Imam [1983: 15] reports improved yields for mechanised tillage in Upper Egypt for maize and for cotton. Scale economies were also important factors, with large pumps above 7.5 hp more economical to use than small five hp pumps [*El Sahrigi and Shepley*, 1985: 64], while combine harvester use produced losses on small farms, but were feasible on large farms over five feddans [1985: 28–31].

Thus, in this section, we have seen evidence of considerable technological change in Egyptian agriculture, but this change has been uneven both regionally, and in terms of control and diffusion of benefits which have been skewed towards the large farmers. These benefits have been real and positive, and may have allowed the larger farmers to reap significant productivity advantages. We shall see in the next section how this is reflected in the data through a heterogeneous pattern with respect to the inverse relationship.

VI.4 ANALYSIS AND RESULTS: (III) A DISAGGREGATED ANALYSIS AND EVIDENCE OF TRANSITION

It remains to choose an appropriate technique to test the relationship between farm size and the other dependent variables. For parametric tests the choice of regression specification lies between the conventional linear, log-linear and semi-log and so on. As there is no a priori reason to select any particular specification, we employed the same technique as Radwan – the log-linear regression. The specification of the regression equations is the same in all cases: $\log y = \log a + b \log x$ where (x) is always operated area and (y) is the indicated dependent variable.

When running regressions at the governorate level, we first notice the heterogeneity of rural Egypt in terms of production conditions: cropping patterns, levels of commercialisation and mechanisation. The results are presented in Table 31 in Appendix A. The governorate-wise analysis of the relation between farm size and output per net cropped area reveals that Egypt is undergoing a process of transition. For net yields (y1), based on total crop values, we find that a significant inverse relationship exists only for two governorates: Menufiya and Giza. Negative but insignificant relationships exist in Beni Suef, Dumyat and Gharbiya, but in Qena the relationship is positive. Even for net yields (y4), based on net farm output, we find that while the relationship is negative for all governorates, those for Qena and Beni Suef are statistically insignificant. Again, using corrected net yields (y6), we find that the inverse relationship is significant only for Giza while the other governorates are only weakly negative and that for Qena is actually positive.

This pattern is more sharply brought out by regressing output per gross cropped area on farm size. For gross yields (y2), based on total crop values, we find weak inverse relationships only for three governorates: Dumyat, Giza and Beni Suef, while for Qena governorate the relationship has become significantly positive at the one per cent level. Gharbiya and Menufiya show weak positive relationships. For gross yields (y5), based on net farm output, we find significant negative coefficients for Gharbiya, Dumyat and Menufiya, but for Beni Suef and Giza only statistically insignificant negative coefficients, and for Qena the regression coefficient is positive. Regressing corrected net yields (y7) on operated area we find only one significant result: a positive coefficient for Qena governorate. Gharbiya and Menufiya have statistically insignificant positive coefficients while the other three have weak negative ones.

These results show a clear and important departure from the results obtained by Radwan and others. While it is common to find neither significantly positive nor negative signs in the relation between farm size and output per gross cropped area, the fact that we have obtained significant positive coefficients means that either due to cropping patterns or yields of individual crops, large farmers have achieved important advantages. Since the use of gross cropped area tends to eliminate differences in cropping intensity it would be interesting to see whether small farmers have retained their traditional superiority with higher cropping intensities than large farmers. Regressing y3 (cropping intensity, equal to the ratio of gross cropped area to net cropped area) we do find that the traditional pattern has been retained. Regression coefficients for all governorates are highly negative.

For Dumyat, there was no variation across farm size with the cropping intensity two for all 15 farms. However, the fact that the inverse relationship between farm size and productivity has in many cases disappeared, despite greater cropping intensities on the smaller farms, tends to confirm the importance of cropping patterns and yields for individual crops. It should further be emphasised that cropping intensity remains an inadequate measure of land utilisation. The possibility that large farmers choose a cropping pattern with longer average growth periods, and that the inverse relationship associated with cropping intensity neglects these differences in cropping patterns cannot be ruled out.

As far as yields for individual crops are concerned, we ran regressions for winter wheat and clover, cotton, maize, rice and sugarcane separately (these crops account for over nine tenths of crop production in Egypt). For wheat (y8), we find a significant inverse relationship (at the ten per cent level) only for Giza, while in Qena we find a significant positive relationship. All the remaining governorates have insignificant coefficients.

Birseem yields (y9) exhibit a significant inverse relationship for Dumyat, Menufiya, and Giza (again at the ten per cent level) while the relationship is statistically insignificant for the other governorates. For cotton (y10), there is no clear relationship: yields vary inversely with farm size in Beni Suef and in Gharbiya, but the relationship is only significant at the ten per cent level, while there is no variation across farm size in Menufiya. None of the sample farms in Dumyat, Qena or Giza plant cotton during the summer season. Summer maize yields (y11) show no significant relationship across farm size, although the coefficient for Qena is positive. For rice (y12), the coefficients are all positive, but insignificant. In our sample, only Qena has land under sugarcane (a Sa'idi crop and one typically grown on large farms with an annual cropping cycle) and yields (y13) exhibit a significant positive relationship with farm size.[7]

On the whole, the governorate regressions indicate a more heterogeneous pattern of the relationship between farm size and productivity, possibly reflecting the process of change that the national all-Egypt regressions do not reflect. Ranking the governorates from those with the strongest positive relationship between farm size and productivity to those with the strongest negative relationships we find the following order: Qena, Menufiya, Gharbiya, Giza, Beni Suef, and Dumyat. We must now attempt to relate these findings to other factors in the process of agrarian transformation in Egypt. We have calculated several alternative indices of relative levels of 'progressiveness' ranged in Table 32, Appendix A.

In these tables, Qena which as we saw exhibited positive regression coefficients for the relationship between farm size and productivity is ranked consistently highly for all four indices, which reflect the level of use of both Green Revolution inputs and total purchased inputs. The same holds true for Minufiya, whereas Dumyat with strong negative coefficients in the regressions is here ranked consistently at a low level. The other three governorate rankings vary according to whether we use indices based on total crop values or on net farm output.

For the ratios of purchased to own produced inputs we find again that Qena is ranked consistently highly. High fertiliser use is closely correlated with the cultivation of HYV crops. Fertiliser use is high in Beni Suef also, reflecting the traditional variation in the use of fertiliser for cotton (use of fertiliser for cotton increases from north to south with good yield responses due to higher temperatures and better drainage). The high seed ratios for Giza can be explained by its location in the Cairo vegetable zone in which market gardening is the predominant activity. We can see that for all governorates, birseem purchases are only a fraction of self-cultivated fodder, but again Qena shows the highest level of purchase of this input.

Turning to the mechanisation indices, we find that the governorates of

Dumyat and Giza are ranked bottom while Gharbiya is at the top. Qena and Menufiya are also ranked in the top three positions. In Tables 23 and 32, which present figures for tractors and other agricultural equipment by governorate, we can see that Qena and Gharbiya are ranked highest for tractors, ploughs and trailers while Qena has by far the highest level of mechanical power for irrigation. By contrast, Beni Suef fares consistently badly as far as these tables are concerned.

Thus, the results of the regression exercises on the sample households reveal a more regionally differentiated pattern of the relationship between farm size and productivity, which when compared with the indices of progressivity, appear to reflect a more heterogeneous process of transition taking place. In those areas of progressive agriculture, such as Qena, with high levels of technology use, we find that the inverse relationship has turned positive while for regions where the impact of the new technology has been limited, such as Beni Suef and Dumyat, the inverse relationship remains negative and significant. The other governorates present an intermediate picture, with Menufiya and Gharbiya tending, on the whole, to show a high level of progress and weakly positive coefficients on the size-productivity relation, while Giza tends to reveal signs of backward agriculture still predominating and a strong inverse relationship.

SUMMARY AND CONCLUSIONS

Thus, on the basis of the evidence in this chapter, we might suggest a plausible hypothesis for the impact of agrarian transformation on the relation between farm size and productivity. We have found in the Egyptian rural sector striking parallels with the process of agrarian transition in India, with regard to the technological factors. The heterogeneous pattern of technological change in Egyptian agriculture is mirrored by the pattern of occurrence of an inverse relationship between farm size and productivity. Where technical change in agriculture is at a relatively undeveloped stage, we appear to have evidence of a significant inverse relationship. In those regions where technical change is relatively more advanced, the inverse relationship is absent. We can advance the hypothesis, on the basis of the evidence in previous chapters, that technical change in these latter regions has led to the breakdown of a previously existent inverse relationship.

The 'traverse' from Giza to Qena, representing a development of the forces of production both determines and is determined by the development of the relations of production. In particular, rich peasants, either as proto- or fully-developed capitalist farmers monopolise productive resources and dominate access to the new technology through their control of the co-operative and rural credit systems. The utilisation of this new technology accelerates rich peasant accumulation and deepens the process of social differentiation. The productivity advantages thus gained lead to a structural reversal in the size–productivity relationship characteristic of a relatively backward agriculture.

However, there is little more we can say on these political economy aspects at such a relatively high level of aggregation (governorates are certainly a more reasonable level of aggregation than Egypt as a whole, but still exhibit significant heterogeneity with respect to both soil quality and technical and social change). In order to explore these aspects in greater detail, we carried out fieldwork in two of the villages contained in the ILO study in the summer of 1990. The results of this analysis are presented in the following two chapters.

NOTES

1. I am greatly indebted to Samir Radwan, Chief, Rural Employment Policies Branch, Employment and Development Department, International Labour Office, in Geneva, for providing me with the original data on which his joint study with Eddy Lee on the anatomy of rural poverty in Egypt was based. Many thanks are also due to his colleagues Albert Wagner and Patrick Cornu for preparing the SPSS-X tape files and instructions. I appreciate immensely the enabling help of Ajit Ghose, formerly at the ILO and Ruchira Chatterji, formerly in the Faculty of Economics and Politics, Centre of South Asian Studies, Cambridge University.
2. See Richards [1989: 63, Appendix, Tables 6A and 6B] who shows the intensity of chemical fertiliser use and growth rates between 1972 and 1988: the nitrogen use index rises from 100 to 493; and the phosphate index rises from 100 to 384. In the 1970s, fertiliser prices were only between 41 and 61 per cent of world market prices [Adams, 1986: 53].
3. See Richards [1989: 63, Appendix, table 15] who presents details of the spread of mechanisation by agricultural operation in 1982: 90 per cent of ploughing and 62 per cent of irrigation activities are mechanisd. See also ERA 2000 [1979: 8.5, Table 8.1] which shows machine use by operation.
4. See Richards [1989: 63, Appendix, Table 14] who presents figures for the growth in the Egyptian tractor park and combine harvesters over the period 1971–86: the tractor park increases from 17,556 to 44,000; and the number of combine harvesters rises from 1,750 to 2,250.
5. See Khalil [1981: 14, Table 3] who presents figures for domestic tractor production, reaching only 306 for the Yugoslav model and only 160 of the Romanian type in 1978–79. These were swamped by imports of 6,061 tractors in 1977 [1981: 16, Table 3-2]. Khalil [1981: 10] gives details of aid funds for mechanisation in the early 1980s: $32 million from the IBRD, $1.7 million from USAID and $5 million from Japanese AID.
6. This is a traditional form of waterwheel irrigation operated by a group of farmers.
7. The regression equation for sugarcane yields (y13) was:

$$\log y13 = 0.915 + 0.049 \qquad R^2 = 0.029$$
$$n = 63$$
$$t = 1.35*$$

VII

A Closer Look at the Inverse Relationship in the Context of Agrarian Transition: Evidence from Fieldwork in Rural Egypt

INTRODUCTION

In order to test the various hypotheses associated with the inverse relationship in the context of agrarian transition, further fieldwork was required at a more disaggregated level than the ILO data permit. Two village surveys were carried out in the summer of 1990. On the basis of the results from the ILO data, a village was chosen from Qena governorate which was expected to show a positive relationship between farm size and productivity. A second village was chosen from Giza governorate which was expected to shed light on the inverse relationship.

Section VII.1 describes how the fieldwork villages were selected, the survey methodology employed and some of the problems associated with the data. Section VII.2 analyses the data for the Giza village, and section VII.3 shows how and why an inverse relationship arises in that village.

VII.1 FIELDWORK METHODOLOGY AND PROBLEMS

The first task was to select the appropriate villages from the ILO survey for further analysis. Clearly, on the basis of the results in the previous chapter, Giza governorate presented the strongest evidence for an inverse relationship between total crop output per net cropped area and farm size. This governorate also showed a weak, but statistically insignificant negative relationship when crop output per gross cropped area was used in the yield calculations. We have also seen that Giza ranked consistently low in the tables for indices of 'progressivity', particularly in terms of new technology use and mechanisation.

Qena governorate, on the other hand, provided clear and strong indications of a positive relationship between farm size and productivity: a positive, but statistically insignificant regression coefficient using net yields, and a much stronger and statistically significant positive coefficient when gross yields were used. This governorate ranked consistently high on the indices of 'progressivity', particularly with regard to machine use. These two governorates then would be the starting point.

It was possible to disaggregate the ILO data one further stage, down to village level. At the village level though, sample size was too small in most cases to be a reliable indicator of the strength and direction of any relationship between farm size and productivity. Thus, attention was directed only to those village samples of adequate size. The two largest samples were from the village of Shubak al-Sharqi in Giza governorate (151 households, 68 of them with an operated area) and the village of Higaza in Qena governorate (129 sample households, 38 of them with operated holdings). The disaggregated ILO data is presented in Table 33, Appendix A.

The village of Shubak al-Sharqi revealed a statistically significant inverse relationship when net yields were regressed on farm size, and a statistically significant inverse relationship between cropping intensity and farm size. The three villages in Qena governorate all show no relation between farm size and output per acre, although it may be significant that the strength of the positive relationship increases as we move from net yields to gross yields, despite significantly higher cropping intensity on the small farms. Note that the Al-Amiriya results differ, but the sample size is too small to really tell us very much. Higaza, with the largest sample size provides the most robust results. Therefore, the two villages Shubak al-Sharqi in Giza and Higaza in Qena governorate were selected for more detailed fieldwork, the former expected on the basis of the ILO results to be an inverse relationship village, and the latter one in which the inverse relationship had broken down.

Both villages had the additional advantage that they were more suitable logistically in terms of access. The fact that Shubak was only an hour's drive from Giza, and Higaza an hour and a half from Luxor greatly facilitated the fieldwork in terms of accommodation and transport. The Giza governorate Ministry of Agriculture on the Pyramids road was some 30 minutes taxi drive from Cairo. From Giza, the ministry vehicle took us down the east bank of the Nile past the pyramids at Saqqara on the desert horizon. Some 30 kilometres further south we turned off through a date palm grove at Shubak al-Gharbi to cross the cantilever bridge into Tabbin on the east bank. The village of Shubak al-Sharqi lies just to the south of Tabbin.

The journey to Higaza was rather more complicated. From the main bus station in Luxor (721 km south of Cairo and 14 hours by train), a minibus travels north for 90 minutes to the district centre of Qus, where the district Ministry of Agriculture and research station is located. From there a 25-minute ride on the back of a motorbike brought us to the village of Higaza, some 15 km to the south-east.

The survey method comprised both formal questionnaire and informal interview, as well as limited access to the records compiled by the village co-operative and district Ministry of Agriculture. A formal structured questionnaire was necessitated by the impossibility of actually living in the survey villages. It was only possible to visit the villages on a daily basis. The local ministries and village co-operative officials frowned on any suggestion of staying in the villages for any length of time, as the political situation at the time of the visit to Egypt was somewhat dangerous, particularly in Upper Egypt.

The surveys were conducted between June and September 1990 with the help of two assistants loaned by the local ministries of agriculture.[1] The questionnaire was conducted in Arabic, as were the interviews.[2] Each questionnaire interview took an average of an hour to complete. The informal interviews were taped and lasted from one hour to 90 minutes. These covered a variety of qualitative indications of the circumstances of the village, village history, locations, amenities, and the dynamics of the villages.

Each questionnaire consisted of 15 pages. There were several sections to the questionnaire which was based on the original ILO format. The first section covered basic demographic details of the household members: age, gender, marital status, relationship to head of household, principal and secondary occupations, and educational attainment. The second section covered household labour: each working member's on-farm work in each season (winter, summer and nili) in standardised days, permanent and or casual work off-farm, but within agriculture, again for each season, and the wage earnings for work off-farm and outside agriculture both inside and outside the village.

The third section covered land ownership and operated area of the household: land owned, land rented in, land rented out, and estimated land value. Respondents were asked to give details of the terms and conditions under which land was rented in or out (for example, whether it was sharecropped land, the level of share, and whether cash or kind payments were made). This section also included information on the expansion or diminution of land over the previous year, over a five-year period and over the lifetime of the current head of household, either by inheritance, purchase, gift or mortgage.

The fourth section covered the ownership of agricultural machinery and equipment: whether fully owned or shared, their going market value (on the basis of new for old), and recent additions to the machine stock, while the fifth section dealt with ownership of animals: whether fully owned or shared, their market value and recent additions or sales. The sixth section asked about the ownership of other assets such as vehicles, non-agricultural machinery, artisanal tools or non-residential buildings, and the income earned from their use. The seventh section covered the house itself: type (mud brick or red brick) and value, facilities such as electricity, running water, sanitation, and building extensions to the house in the recent period. The eighth section covered credit transactions: savings and loans, and their terms and sources.

The ninth section gathered information on the crop production of the household: crop grown, type, season, output, area sown, quantity consumed on-farm, and quantity marketed with unit price. The tenth section covered other income from production: land rental income, dairy and poultry produce, including on-farm consumption and market sales. The eleventh section covered production inputs: land rental cost, fodder, machine rental, fuel and maintenance, the quantities and prices of chemical and organic fertilisers, insecticides and pesticides, seeds, and labour costs for hired labour for each season, with days worked and wages. The final section covered input purchases and credit from the co-operative system, as distinct from the total inputs in the previous section.

Problems of data collection besides the impossibility of living in the village to carry out participant observation, included the impossibility of collecting data on the labour input of female members of the household. Although women are to be plainly seen working in the fields, tending to plants or collecting animal fodder, almost all respondents claimed that women do not work in the Sa'id (Upper Egypt). For female household members to work in the field would have been *a'eb* (disgraceful). Some information on child labour was forthcoming, not by the respondents themselves, but from some large labour hirers in informal interviews (see below).

Another problem was the inability to get good information on savings and loans. No respondent would admit to having savings. And although information on bank or co-operative loans was readily forthcoming, and one or two of the larger farmers gave me details of their private borrowing, smaller farmers were extremely reluctant to give me any information on borrowing from informal sources. The financial status of households has therefore had to be deduced from the cash flow of the household and the sustainability of their declared incomes and expenses.

Finally, we need to pursue the important matter of size classification. Indeed, the question of size as the relevant stratifying variable is to some extent raised by the Giza data. This will be discussed below in section 10.2 within the full analysis of that data. Here we limit the discussion to the question of stratification. Abdel Fadil presents the following stratification schema [1975: 41]:

(1) landless peasants;[3]

(2) poor peasants with less than two feddans;
(3) small peasants with two to five feddans;
(4) middle peasants with 5–20 feddans;
(5) rich peasants/capitalist farmers with more than 20 feddans.

This schema he compares with that presented by Samir Amin [*1964*]:

(1) landless peasants
(2) poor peasants with less than one feddan;
(3) middle peasants with one to five feddans;
(4) rich farmers with 5–20 feddans;
(5) rural capitalists with more than 20 feddans.

Abdel-Fadil's classification schema can be questioned on a number of points. Byres [1977b: 266] suggests that the cut-off point for the poor peasantry should be two feddans, as suggested by the land reform legislation's redistribution of land in plots of not less than two feddans. However, the distribution of plots in this manner was dependent on family size and soil quality. Two-feddan plots would have been characterised by either better soil quality or by their distribution to farm households with less than the average number of persons. Most respondents in informal interviews with the author however were certain that three feddans was the minimum size of farm to sustain the average farm household. I have further subdivided the class of farms below three feddans into those below one feddan, which for all intents and purposes are extremely marginal farms, operated by practically landless labourers, and those above one feddan but less than three who can be classed as the poor peasantry proper. Interestingly, as the results show below, while we have high productivity on farms from one to three feddans, productivity actually falls off below one feddan. These latter farms are just too small and marginal to sustain high productivity farming.

Abdel-Fadil's category of small peasants is problematic. These he describes [1975: 41–2] thus: 'They usually operate on a family basis, and in most cases manage to raise most of their subsistence food requirements. In other words, they are under somewhat less pressure to resort to "consumption loans", and hence are less indebted to money-lenders.' However, as Byres [1977b: 267] points out, these are surely the middle peasants identified in the classification schemas of Lenin and Mao, as well as those of Alavi and Wolf. We have classified the farms between three and five feddans as middle peasants.

Finally, Abdel-Fadil's middle peasantry with 5–20 feddans:

Having somewhat larger holdings than that of the 'small peasantry', this group is usually more prosperous and employs permanent wage labourers to some extent. These peasants produce mainly for the market and their crop-mixes normally cover a wider and more profitable variety of crops (i.e. cash crops and vegetables). In general, their holdings are 'technically' more efficient in terms of the use of better irrigation facilities, improved seeds and more intensive use of bullock labour and farm equipment.

They generally enjoy a surplus over and above their consumption requirements after meeting other fixed money obligations. Often these 'middle peasants' are also engaged in other gainful activities such as retail trade and money-lending. In other words, these farmers have a fallback source of income in case of low yields [1975: 42].

As Byres states [1977b: 267]: these appear to be full-blooded, archetypal rich peasants, the same stratum as Abdel-Fadil's rich peasants with identical class interests. Indeed Abdel-Fadil's mispecifications, as pointed out by Byres, may be structured around the mis-identification of rich peasants as capitalist farmers. As we have seen in our discussion of the Indian mode of production debate, rich peasants are not the same as capitalist farmers, although the transformation of such a class into a capitalist class is a central process of a successful transition to agrarian capitalism. But that transformation has to be demonstrated and not simply asserted.

A central hypothesis of this thesis is that within the uneven development of the Egyptian countryside, these rich peasants are in many cases not 'technically more efficient' based on their use of modern technology. On the contrary, in those areas of relatively backward agriculture, rich peasants are using essentially the same traditional technology as the poor and middle peasants, thus generating the circumstances under which an inverse relationship arises. Only in those areas where the rich peasantry have transformed themselves into a class of capitalist farmers will they be more efficient, and produce the conditions for a breakdown in the inverse relationship.

VII.2 AN INVERSE RELATIONSHIP VILLAGE IN GIZA

Giza is a large governorate west and south of Cairo, with an estimated 1990 population of 4.265 million and covering an area of 85,153 square kilometres. The northern part is a sprawling suburb of Cairo, but rural Giza stretches some 750 km down the Nile valley. The village chosen was Shubak al-Sharqi in al-Saff district, around 35 km south of Cairo (and some 12 km south of the Hilwan industrial complex on the east bank of the Nile. To the west of the village is the Nile and the main road to Giza and Cairo (on the west bank). On the east is the Saff-Cairo road. Al-Tabbin, the nearest town, is five km to the north, and to the south is the Minya-Shubak road.

The total village population is around 50,000. Shubak comprises 711 *ha'izeen* (farm holdings). About half the population are landless, and the number working in farming has decreased in recent years. Many work in the local cement factories and foundries which surround the area, while others with greater means run private businesses. The *mushrif zira'i* (agricultural supervisor) estimates the proportion of village population who actually own and operate land at 15 per cent, based on an average of 9.5 persons per holding. This of course does not include landless agricultural labour.

Many people work full-time in the local factories. A floor cleaner can earn LE 40–50 a month. The mushrif was of the opinion that a person without land is better off with a factory job because they pay regularly, but the agricultural work is seasonal, and there are long periods when the farm labourer does not work. Some villagers have gone for work abroad in the Gulf, most of them aged under 40.[4] Those with artisanal skills, such as plasterers or coppersmiths, tend to commute and work in Cairo.

There is a *suq* (market) in the village every Thursday for animals, vegetables, and fruit. There are around 500 shops in Shubak. There are further trade relations between the local villages. Every group of villages in the locality has a market with one in al-Minya and Shurafa every Sunday. Ikhsas and Ghamaza villages hold a joint market south of Shubak. On the average, there is one *suq* for every two or three villages. A large number of people from Shubak own land in other villages. Some rent tractors to farmers in other villages.

The local institutional infrastructure in Shubak includes an *i'timan* (credit) co-operative or village bank. There are currently only two co-operative staff members, one having died recently. The director is located in al-Saff, the district centre, some 25 km further south. There is a local government unit in the village, headed by an engineer, and there is also a local council, elected to serve Shubak and Minya. The Minya unit is fairly large, but the *zimam* (cultivated area) is smaller than that of Shubak, and most of the land there is unsuitable for cultivation due to sewage outflow. There is a veterinary clinic in the co-operative building, but no government machine centre. There is one at Saff, and the engineers are located there. The irrigation system is supervised by the department in Hilwan.

There is a medical clinic in the village and a hospital in al-Saff. Education is catered for by one primary school and one intermediate school, and there is a religious college attached to al-Azhar. There is no secondary school in the village, but there is one in Ikhsas and in Saff. Most of the houses have electricity, and 60–70 per cent have piped drinking water. The rest have to use the village pump.

The *mushrif* explained that the village population were originally bedouin migrating from the Hijaz in Saudi Arabia. Prior to the 1952 revolution, the land used to belong to a small elite of feudal landlords in large *'azab* (estates). One large landlord used to own over 300 feddans, for example. In 1952, the land was divided up into smaller plots and distributed to smallholders who bought land.

There are still important families in the village of long standing, such as the Dawud, Azzam, Maliji and Zeid clans. The Dawuds and Azzams were large landowners prior to the revolution, and many members of these families hold prominent positions locally. Of the co-operative officials in Shubak, one is from the Azzam family (the *mushrif* himself) and the other is from Cairo. The director of the local council is Dr Mohsein Azzam, and includes members of the other families.

The village *zimam* (cultivated area) is just over 1,185 feddans, out of a total village land area of around 2,100 feddans. The non-cultivated area is accounted for by factory sites and the rest of the area is covered by the mudbrick and breeze block houses of the village population. A main road runs down through the centre of the village which for the most part is unsurfaced and turns into a muddy concourse in the rain.

The village exhibits the size-class land distribution shown in Table 34, Appendix A. This compares well with the governorate level distribution shown in Table 35. As can be seen from the table, over 92 per cent of the farms (658 out of 711) are less than three feddans. Three feddans is generally regarded as constituting the minimum feasible size in terms of subsistence income. Of these, 263 or 40 per cent are less than one feddan. Over 76 per cent of the small farms are owner operated (503 farms), and 155 are rented. The former account for 77 per cent of the operated area (917 feddans out of 1,185). The three to five feddan farms or middle peasant farms account for just over 6 per cent of the holdings (44 out of 711 with 36 or 82 per cent of them owner operated). These account for 189 feddans or 16 per cent of the operated area, of which 81 per cent is owner operated. The farms above five feddans or rich peasant farms are nine in number or 1.26 per cent of the total farms. These farms account for nearly seven per cent of operated area. Note the difference between those five to ten feddan farms and the one farm above ten feddans. Of the former, half are owned and half are rented, with just under half the operated area rented in. The 15 feddan farm is wholly owned.

Note that this 15-feddan farm, which belongs to the village *shaykh*, the most important village notable, is not the farm used in the regression equations or data survey. Unfortunately, the *shaykh* had been hospitalised for some time before the survey period and was unavailable for interview. A close family member did provide some approximate indications of farm size and output over the year, but was unable to provide any details of input costs or other expenses. These indications pointed to relatively high output per acre, but as the figures were only indicative, and not significantly robust, it was decided to exclude them from the survey. The ten-feddan farm included in the survey is not officially registered as ten feddans. It belongs to an important family in the village consisting of two brothers and a sister. The land is thus registered in three parcels, but it is operated as a single and contiguous production unit, with the respondent in overall control.

The cropping pattern in Shubak prior to the revolution was dominated by cotton, but 25 years ago after construction of the High Dam, the village moved to the current cropping pattern. The predominant cropping pattern in the village is three season. The winter season (November–February) cropped area is almost entirely accounted for by birseem (54 per cent), potatoes (30 per cent), and vegetables (14 per cent) including tomatoes, eggplants and haricot beans.[5] The summer crops (March–August) include maize (60 per cent) and vegetables (26 per cent), mostly tomatoes. The short nili season[6] (September–October) is devoted to millet which is cut green for animal fodder (89 per cent). Only 60 per cent of the net sown area is planted in the nili season, predominantly small farms producing their own fodder. Birseem is an important animal fodder crop. Poor farmers prefer to grow their own birseem as purchased fodder is very expensive.

One group of farmers grow potatoes both in summer and winter. The summer potatoes are put in the cold store and planted four months later. Summer potatoes have to be bought in from outside. If potatoes were not cultivated in the previous year, the farmer cannot get seed potatoes on credit. Those who do not grow summer potatoes can obtain seed potatoes only from other farmers who have extra bought from the cold store. They cost LE 600–700 per ton, while the normal price for harvested potatoes is only LE 100–200 per ton. A small group of farmers prefer the purchase of improved seeds from outside which give better yields than the normal red potatoes. These are the yellow Diamond variety potatoes. Small farmers do not have enough land or enough capital to cultivate potatoes in this way.

With help from the officials in the village co-operative, a stratified sample of 69 farm households was drawn, based on the size distribution given in the 1981 Agricultural Census for Saff district in Giza governorate. This represents approximately a ten per cent sample. The district distribution was a close fit to the village distribution which was not available at the beginning of the survey. The sample was not random, in the sense that landless households were excluded unless they were renting in some operated area. The sample was limited to those heads of household whose principal occupation was *fellah* (peasant) or *muzari'a* (farmer). Furthermore, care was taken to avoid farms with significantly below or above average soil fertility. We discuss this below when we come to the question of soil quality in the village.[7]

OLS regression of net yields on farm size, without logarithmic transformation, for all 69 farms in the sample shows no clear relation across farm size. However, following Rudra and Patnaik, it is important to examine the data graphically, that is, in scatterplot form, in order to present the underlying pattern of the data visually. This indicates a kinked U-shaped average curve, with the small farms between one and three feddans and the one large ten-feddan farm exhibiting high yields.

Seven outliers were excluded from the subsequent regression exercises. These were identified on the scatterplot of net yields against farm size. Detailed examination of the residuals and computation of Mahalanobis and Cook statistics confirmed that these observations unduly distorted the underlying pattern.[8] The outliers included the ten feddan farm (see below for a fuller discussion of this exceptional case), two farms which lost their entire tomato crop due to pollution from a nearby cement factory, and four highly capitalised farms growing two improved variety potato crops per year. Their cropping pattern was significantly different from the rest of the sample, with very high yields. Their inclusion would have unduly strengthened the inverse relationship. Thirty farms in the sample grew a winter potato crop, but only 14 grew a summer crop, 13 of which grew both a winter and a summer crop. Four of these used improved Diamond varieties rather than the normal red potatoes.

Thus, only 62 of the farms surveyed were included in the regression exercises. Exclusion of the ten-feddan farm was based on the grounds that it is a single observation, it is significantly different in terms of soil quality, and, looking more closely at the data, is a very different type of farm, highly capitalised and commercialised. This is also true of four of the farms which grow two Diamond potato crops which have very high yields and are highly capitalised. Exclusion of these outliers produces a scatterplot displaying a quasi-rectangular hyperbolic curve, similar to an isoquant, with many of the observations lying in towards the origin. This suggests some form of target revenue curve.

We also tested for any disjunction between farm size categories and those relating to economic scale which, according to Patnaik, are better proxies for class location. We computed Spearman rank correlation coefficients (rs) between farm size and gross annual output, total annual income, total capital assets, machine stock and stock of all productive assets as various indicators of economic scale.[9] The results obtained show that despite the existence of a small group of highly capitalised farms which would tend to support the Patnaik argument, farm size and economic scale are closely correlated for all definitions of economic scale, as far as the village samples are concerned. Thus, we continue to use farm size as the relevant stratifying variable in our analysis.

OLS regression equation R.1, Table 36, again without any logarithmic transformation of the data, but excluding the outliers identified above, shows a significant inverse relation between net yields (total value of crop output per net cropped area) as the dependent variable and farm size.[10] The relation is significant at the five per cent level of confidence. Net yields on the five to ten feddan farms are less than two-thirds those on the smaller farms. This result confirms prior expectations. Regressing gross yields (total value of crop output per gross cropped area) on farm size, the relationship is insignificant as expected, suggesting higher cropping intensities on the smaller size farms (see equation R.2, Table 36. This is further supported by the regressions of physical yields for individual crops on farm size. Equation R.3 for winter potatoes shows no relationship between yields (measured in qantars per feddan)[11] and farm size for the 26 farms which cultivate this crop. Likewise, summer maize (ardebs per feddan)[12] and summer potatoes (qantars per feddan) show no relation across farm size in regression equations R.4 and R.5. Only nili maize (ardebs per feddan) in equation R.6 shows a significant inverse relationship (within the ten per cent level) between physical yield and farm size, but given the use of this crop as animal feed on the small farms, such productivity comparisons are misleading. However, cultivation of a nili crop has significant implications for the inverse relationship as we shall see below.

The regression of cropping intensity (the ratio of gross cropped area to net sown area) on farm size in equation R.7, Table 36, shows clearly that small farms do have significantly higher cropping intensities than large farms in Shubak, falling from an average of 2.72 on the smallest farms and 2.44 on the farms between one and three feddans to 1.59 on the five to ten feddan farms (see Table 37, Appendix A). There is also some evidence of greater land-use intensity during particular seasons (see Table 38). The smaller farms have a stronger tendency to triple crop and intercrop summer and winter vegetables. The results confirm the existence of a significant inverse relationship between farm size and productivity in terms of crop output, the proximate cause being significantly higher cropping intensities on the smaller farms.

VII.3 THE ROOTS OF THE INVERSE RELATIONSHIP IN SHUBAK

But what factors explain the higher cropping intensities on the small farms? To begin with, we can dispense with the arguments relating higher cropping intensities to higher irrigation ratios on the smaller farms. While this factor may be important in the Indian context, it is irrelevant in rural Egypt. All arable land in Egypt has been characterised by 100 per cent irrigation ratios since the shift to perennial irrigation with an extensive network of canals and tanks from basin irrigation after the completion of the High Dam at Aswan in the 1960s. Shubak al-Sharqi has historically had access to perennial irrigation, and there is a well developed hire market for irrigation pumps in both survey villages.[13]

There is no evidence to support the variant hypotheses that small farms have better soil quality or that small farmers possess inherently superior management abilities. Soil type does indeed differ between the different *ahwad* (basins).[14] The best soil is in Hawd al-Gezira, situated west of the Nile, an area of about 400 feddans. The land on the eastern outskirts of the village and near the factories is poor. Poor land is used for birseem and good land for potatoes. On the east bank, there are three poor *ahwad* due to their elevation, and yields are weak. Some of the land is near the cement factory, and the dust from the plant affects the vegetable crops. For two seasons, tomato yields have been poor. A qirat of good land can be bought for 3,500 pounds. Saline or weak land would only cost LE 600.

However, care was taken to exclude land which was characterised by very low or very high fertility from the regression equations, in order to isolate this effect. We wanted to compare small and large farmers on the same quality of land. Regression equation R.8, Table 36, and Table 37 show no relationship between land value per feddan (as a proxy for land quality) and farm size. Neither is there any relation between family members per feddan and land value per feddan as one might expect to find if Sen's demographic scenario were operative at the micro level. Despite the existence of partible inheritance, families tend to operate plots as a single farm, as is the case with the ten feddan farm in the sample. The results show that there is no clear pattern of land fragmentation over farm size. More significant however than the number of fragments per farm is the intensity of fragmentation or fragments per feddan. This decreases steeply as farm size increases which invalidates this as a causal factor behind the inverse relation (see Table 37). Further, if small farmers did have better land quality, this would be expected to show up in the physical yields of individual crops. As we have seen, this is clearly not the case.[15]

The same finding undermines the hypothesis that small farmers possess inherently superior managerial aptitudes. If this was the case, we would expect to see higher physical yields of individual crops. Questions of scale, complexity of organisation, and supervision costs do not really enter the picture here given the relatively small range in farm sizes. There do not appear to be any hidden transactions costs involved in hiring or supervising labourers, given the control of the farmer over the labour force. Generally the winter and summer seasons are the busiest for wage labour, particularly

September when preparation for potato planting takes place. The majority of wage labourers are from the village. They are supervised directly by the landowners. One large farmer interviewed said:

> Every week I hire 3 or 4 kids (less than 12 years old). They pick the vegetables: beans, aubergines, tomatoes. But for the main work on the land I hire adults. Children's wages are around 2 or 3 pounds. In the potato season they might get paid in kind: 10 kg of potatoes at the end of the day. Adults are paid 6–7 pounds a day, 5 for shorter days. Many people are available for work. The men who work are in need of money. They work in factories, but work extra time in the fields. I get in touch with the workers the night before. I know them, so I go to their homes and ask them if they can make it. They are not relatives or friends. Some change from year to year. As people get older I have their sons. If they are busy I go to others until I have enough.

Clearly, then, we can say that the suggested qualitative differences in factor endowments do not appear to have much explanatory power with regard to the inverse relationship between farm-size and productivity. The small farms do not appear to possess land with better soil quality, nor are they blessed with superior management aptitude. At the other end of the scale, large farmers do not appear to suffer from diseconomies in terms of farm management or problems associated with labour recruitment and supervision.

The higher cropping intensities on the small farms do appear to be associated however with the intensive application of labour inputs on the smaller size-holdings.[16] Regression equation R.9, Table 36, and the figures in Table 37 show a highly significant inverse relation between labour input intensity (standardised man-days per feddan per year) and farm size. Labour input intensity falls from 369 man-days per feddan per year on farms less than one feddan to 116 on the five to ten feddan farms. These results would appear to present clear evidence for a labour-based explanation of the inverse relationship: higher labour input intensity on the small farms leads both to higher cropping intensities and higher net yields.

However, while we have found strong inverse relationships between output per feddan, cropping intensity, labour input intensity and farm size, the relationship between labour input intensity and output per feddan is positive, but statistically insignificant. There is a much stronger positive relationship between cropping intensity and output per feddan (see regression equations 7 and 8 in Table 38, Appendix A).

The Sen hypothesis which rests upon cheap family labour is not supported by the data. Small farm labour supply is 96 per cent family labour as opposed to only 17 per cent on the largest farm which depends for 83 per cent of its labour supply on hired labour (see Table 36, Appendix A).

However, note the relatively narrow range of variation between farms of less than one feddan and five to ten feddan farms with respect to labour use. Although there is a clear difference in terms of the nature of labour utilisation between the small farms and large farms, as can be seen in Table 36 with regard to the use of family and hired labour, in fact, there is no relationship at all between family labour input over the year, the ratio of family labour to total labour, or family labour intensity and output per feddan (see Table 38, regression equations 9, 10 and 11).

If we disaggregate crop output on a seasonal basis, we find that for winter and summer crops, there is no statistically significant relationship between yields and size, nor between yields and labour intensity (see Table 38, regression exercises 1 to 6). In other words, despite the higher land use and application of labour by the small farmers during the winter and summer seasons, these farms do not achieve higher output per feddan. This would tend to suggest that these farmers are in fact rather inefficient.

The reason we have then higher output per feddan on the small farms is because these latter overwhelmingly utilise the land to squeeze in a third seasonal crop, during the nili season. It is cropping intensity that determines labour use and higher output per acre.

It might be argued, at one remove, that the additional cropping season is a manifestation of the availability of cheap family labour on the small farms, but this would be to obscure the strong economic compulsions which force these poor peasants to intensify cropping and produce an extra nili crop in a struggle for income. As can be seen from Tables 39 and 40, Appendix A, the very marginal economic circumstances of poverty and debt compel poor peasants to intensify cropping intensity and therefore labour use. In Table 39, net income (the difference between income earned from all sources, including total farm output, wage earnings and other income, and paid-out costs) rises from an average of LE 1,786 on the farms below one feddan to well over LE 14,000 on the large farm over ten feddans. The increase on a per capita basis is even steeper, rising from only LE 227 on the smallest size class to over LE 2,000 on the ten feddan farm. The deficit or surplus is calculated in relation to the World Bank poverty line for rural Egypt of LE 365. We see that the poor and marginal farmers operate, on average, deficit farms, whereas middle peasants and rich farmers enjoy a surplus. Farms below one feddan are too small to support a family, and these farms show a much higher proportion of income earned off-farm (43 per cent), either in agricultural labour or in a factory job, as opposed to the rich peasants who earn only four per cent of their income off-farm (see Table 40).

Turning to Table 41 on average levels of farm debt, the average size of loan borrowed on the smallest size class is around LE 1,000 for one year. This represents 50 per cent of income and 75 per cent of net income. Note that the ten feddan farm actually has a longer term, three year loan, so that on an annualised basis, the loan represents only 19 per cent of income and 37 per cent of net income. As we can see from the last two columns, the smallest farm size and the largest have very similar levels of debt to asset ratios and debt per feddan, the difference being of course that the larger farmer has a higher and more consistent capacity to repay.

Clearly, the levels of absolute poverty and debt in which the poor peasants exist compel them to intensify cropping intensity and labour use. But there are also indications in the data of other forces at work. Table 42, Appendix A, presents data on levels of rent paid. Thirty of the 69 farms rent in land. The data show that small peasants on average rent in about half an acre or 80 per cent of their operated area. Notice, however, that rents per feddan are significantly higher on the smaller farms than on the larger. The official land rental price is around LE 180 per feddan which is what the rich farmer actually pays. The small farmers are forced into the illegal private land rental market at much higher levels of rent. A feddan for tomatoes, for example, can cost between LE 500 and LE 1,000. Animals can also be rented on a seasonal basis. A farmer with many animals might rent a piece of land to grow birseem, the rent varying with the price of birseem. The rental contract is an oral agreement between the owner and the tenant. The co-operative would not be informed. Again the need to pay that rent, either in cash or in kind as in sharecropping, forces the poor peasant to intensify land use and labour intensity.

The fieldwork data are somewhat atypical in that they under-represent sharecropping arrangements. There are only four farms involved out of 69 in the sample, but one respondent confirmed in an interview that sharecropping arrangements were a common feature of land rental transactions:

> If I rent land to someone, I would do it under the sharecropping system. The returns are higher. If the tenant pays money then he might claim rights to the land under the land reform laws. But under sharecropping you can get your land back easily. I can change the sharecropper from year to year depending on the output per feddan. If we share half-half, we share half the costs and half the returns. With vegetables or tomatoes though, seasonal rent might be used because of the high returns, compared to wheat. I need to be with the sharecropper in everything. I can't leave him on his own. I supervise every stage: ploughing, fertilising, and I work with him to harvest the crops (to avoid cheating). The sharecropper will accept such deals because he doesn't own any land of his own. Even somebody with three feddans with many children will go in for sharecropping. I decide all the steps. I supervise. I bring the fertilisers, not him.

Land rents on sharecropped land do indeed offer high returns to the landowner. In Shubak, one middle peasant, owning 3.25 feddans, rented out one feddan for LE 300 for the year. At the other end of the scale, one poor peasant operating 23 qirats or 0.96 feddan was paying the equivalent of LE 495 for half a feddan. Another, operating 0.66 feddan, and renting half of that on a sharecropping basis for about LE 140, was thus paying LE 420 per feddan. These compare to cash rentals of somewhere between LE 180 and LE 300.[17]

Finally, we also have some evidence, presented in Table 43, Appendix A, of forced commerce and market domination by merchants. In terms of the marketed output data, we can see that the farms in the smallest size class are marketing a larger proportion of their crop output, and total output which includes animal products, than the next two size classes, and almost as much as the rich peasants above five feddans. Clearly the ten-feddan farm is highly commercialised, marketing some 94 per cent of output.

One respondent explained in an interview:

> Generally the smaller farmers will see a trader who will take the crops from them. Many merchants come here every year. For transport to market, after harvest, the merchant will come with big sacks to collect them, and camels take them to the main road. Then vans take them to market. For farmers growing potatoes, the merchant will come and check the quality of the crops. Sometimes though, a farmer keeps crops at home, for crisis situations. In a crisis he can sell it. But when they sell it quickly, the price certainly drops. If I have 100 ardebs of wheat, and the market price is LE 80, I would go to the merchant who would take it for probably LE 70. A small farmer in crisis will even sell an animal.

There also appears to be a flourishing parallel market in co-operative-supplied inputs such as seeds, fertilisers and fodder which the large farmers can take advantage of. The same respondent explained:

> The co-operative will distribute improved seeds. Sometimes its obligatory to plant them, but we don't always do so. Small farmers in bad financial conditions, might sell them on the black market for need of money. If a farmer doesn't have enough seeds or fertiliser he would buy from the black market. The prices are very high. For example, a bag of fertiliser is LE 8 at the co-operative, but 16 outside. Fodder is about LE 300–400, but 500–600 outside.

Another explained:

> There are farmers who buy from the co-op and then sell privately. The

same for insecticides. It is more expensive outside. Farmers if they need money can get insecticides from the co-op and then sell them. We get forage through the co-operative. I might buy 30–40 bags. If someone has a goat I sell him two or three bags for cash. Big traders can buy in bulk and charge extra on the price.

Clearly, then, the poor peasant is suffering not only deep poverty, living at or below subsistence levels, but is also subject to heavy indebtedness. He is often further locked into exploitative relationships with landlords, moneylenders and merchants. Given then these economic compulsions, the poor farmers intensify land use and labour input in order to achieve a minimum subsistence income and to pay back cash obligations.

The fact that the inverse relationship is evident, means that the larger farmers have not yet achieved higher yields through the application of modern technology. There is no clear relationship between HYV seed use and farm size[18] nor between the use of machinery (owned and hired)[19] and farm size (see Table 37, Appendix A). The five to ten feddan farms have a very low percentage of gross cropped area under HYV, but there is no systematic variation across farm size overall. While the ten-feddan farm does have significantly higher machinery inputs, again there is very little variation across farm size. The main implements used in agricultural production on all farm sizes are the *fa's* (hoe) and *sharshara* (sickle). The *fa's* is used for a variety of cultivation tasks such as bunding and furrowing. They cost around LE 15 in the village, about the same as a sickle. Every year the farmer will buy new ones. The traditional plough which can last up to ten years is also very common, particularly for potatoes. It costs LE 100–150. A local carpenter fits the ploughshare to the wood.

Twenty-five years ago, irrigation was carried out using the *tunbur* (Archimedean screw), but is nowadays overwhelmingly carried out using diesel irrigation pumps. There are 79 irrigation pumps in the village (32 fixed and 43 mobile), all of them 7.5 hp, and all privately owned. Only ten fixed pumps existed prior to 1960, eight were bought between 1960 and 1965, 12 between 1965 and 1970, another 15 between 1970 and 1975, and 34 since then.

There is a lifting station from the Nile and it flushes the water through the branch canals. The water level is kept high throughout the year. The fixed lifting pumps are in Hawd al-Gezira. The others are mobile, serving small areas. The landowners, both large and small, own the fixed pumps, but the large have more. In Gezira, the farms are better-off, owning the machines than rather than renting them. The owners control the use of the pumps, and will rent them out to smaller neighbours with ¼ or ½ feddan. The big fixed pumps that feed the canals control the irrigation, not the private pumps.

Locally, there are only eight Romanian-made tractors, two of them 65 hp and five of them between 70 and 100 hp. One was purchased prior to 1970, two between 1970 and 1975, and five were bought since 1975. The *mushrif zira'i* explained:

> Tractor rental is through the Qabdshiya service station as the Hawd al-Gezira is nearer than the Saff centre. Tractors are rented by feddan: LE 30 per feddan from private families, but from the service station it is only LE 20. The tractor comes with a plough. The difference in price is due to the fact that, certainly for the families, they intend to make more money which is not the case for the government which intends to help the farmer.

One farmer explained that he rents a tractor once a year, from local people who own it. The owner supervises the tractor, and drives it and maintains it. He pays LE 1.5 per qirat or LE 36 per feddan for ploughing and LE 8 per qirat for cutting up the earth, as it takes longer. He stated that he would not hire the government tractor: 'It's not cheaper and it makes for better relations if I hire locally from individuals.' He also hires once a week a medium size irrigation pump at LE 2–3 per hour for six to eight hours.

SUMMARY AND CONCLUSIONS

The above data suggest that all farm size classes are utilising essentially the same techniques of production, and thus the large farms in the middle and lower rich ranges have not been able to capture any productivity advantages from the use of new technology. Further, as we shall see in the next chapter, Higaza al-Qibli, where no inverse relationship is present, has significantly higher levels of such input use than Shubak, particularly as far as the top two size classes (five to ten and over ten feddans) are concerned.

NOTES

1. The Egyptian Ministry of Agriculture was very helpful. One assistant was from the Giza Ministry of Agriculture, Statistics Division, and the second, an extension worker from Qus district Ministry of Agriculture. The Village Co-operative and Bank staff were also of immense help. I was present at over 60 per cent of the interviews in Shubak al-Sharqi and 34 per cent of the interviews in Higaza al-Qibli.
2. A trial run was conducted in Shubak before the start of the survey proper in order to sort out bugs in the questionnaire and train the research assistants in obtaining robust responses. Numerous cross-checks were required in different parts of the questionnaire, particularly in the sections on production for both output and inputs. For the section on labour inputs, a negotiated response was often required, given the difficulties associated with the respondent's memory and the concept of 'standardised work days'. The formal questionnaire sessions were conducted with the head of household, sometimes with other family members present. Most of

the Shubak sessions took place at or near the village co-operative building. No co-operative staff were present during these sessions. The sessions in Higaza were either conducted in the household itself or in the field under a tree. Again no co-operative staff were present.

3. Given the main aim of our survey to examine the inverse relationship, we excluded landless labourer households from our survey sample.

4. Return migrants use their savings to build a house or purchase land. The returnee has also earned the financil status to marry. The average bride price locally is around LE 4–5,000.

5. While vegetable cultivation is not subject to price controls with payments direct to the grower, it does suffer from high price instability and crop wastage [Harik, 1979: 193].

6. The nili season was historically the Nile flood period. Since the introduction of perennial irrigation, many farmers, particularly the small farmers, now use this period to cultivate extra animal fodder crops. This is of immense importance for the inverse relationship as can be seen below.

7. In fact three such farms crept into the sample and were excluded from the regression equations. See the details of these farms in the text.

8. Cases that have unusually large residuals or atypical values of the independent variable can have a substantial impact on the regression results and need to be identified. Studentised residuals allow identification of outliers. The Mahalanobis distance is a measure of the deviation of cases from average values of the independent variable. Even when a residual is not particularly large, certain observations can influence the regression parameters. Cook's D identifies an influential point by considering changes in residuals when the suspected case is omitted.

9. We computed Spearman rank correlation coefficients to compare ranking of farm size and a set of other variables suggested as being closer proxies for class location: total output, total income, total capital assets, machine stock and total stock of productive assets. This was done for both village samples.

The Spearman rank correlation coefficient (r_s) is computed in the following way: $r_s = 1 - [6.\Sigma d^2]/[n(n^2 - 1)]$, where d is the difference between the ranks assigned to the variable observations being compared, and n is the number of pairs of observations. The values of rs range from -1 to +1. A value of +1 indicates a perfect association between the variable rankings. If r_s is close to zero, we would conclude that the variables are uncorrelated.

The following results were obtained for both sample villages:

farm size and:	Shubak (r_s)	Higaza (r_s)
1) output	0.89	0.94
2) income	0.77	0.91
3) assets	0.61	0.84
4) machinery	0.64	0.80
5) productive assetts	0.71	0.68

10. All the regression results mentioned in the text are presented in Table 36, Appendix A. Size class averages in Shubak al-Sharqi for all the variables used can be found in Table 37, Appendix A.

Crop values are expressed in Egyptian pounds (LE) per feddan. During the survey period the Egyptian pound fluctuated between a rate of LE 4-5 to the pound Sterling.

11. 1 metric qantar = 157.5kg = 308.5lb.

12. 1 ardeb (maize) = 140kg = 308.4 lb
1 ardeb (wheat) = 150kg = 330.4 lb.

13. Irrigation pumps are hired by the hour. The hourly rate is LE 1.5-2. One feddan takes six to seven hours. The average per feddan cost is then LE 14. In summer, irrigation takes place every five to seven days, and in winter, every 10–12 days. Maintenance and fuel costs are the owner's responsibility and the owner will supervise its use.

14. The cultivated areas (zimam) in Egyptian villages are still divided by name into the traditional flood irrigation basins (hawd, pl. ahwad) used prior to the introduction of perennial irrigation.

15. Rochin and Grossman [1985: 19] mention that land was distributed to small farmers in plots

of two to five feddans depending on family size and productivity of the land. However, given the relatively small impact of land redistribution in terms of the cultivated area actually affected (around 12.5 per cent) this will not have resulted in a strong correlation between small farm size and higher quality soil. In fact, the largest farm in the sample with ten feddans has the best quality land in Shubak. The owner is also a university-trained agricultural engineer.

16. Labour intensity was computed by summing the total male labour input for each season and dividing by cultivated area. These figures of course understate the total labour force and therefore labour input intensity, possibly considerably, as they do not take into account female and child labour force participation. Richards [1989: 19] estimates, based on rural labour force surveys, that approximately a third of all crop labour is done by women. Harik [1979: 67] estimates that unpaid family labour (women and children) constitute a third of the rural labour force in size and anything from 10–50 per cent of labour time by children and 33 per cent by women. Mayfield [1974: 32] writes that average annual working days per man was 286 per year in 1966 (with 188 for women and 159 for children). Other surveys however, (for example, Shepley et al. [1985]) have found rather lower percentages: around ten per cent for female crop labour. Women in Upper Egypt have very low participation ratios, and Harik [1979: 83] mentions that female workers have a tendency to drop out of the ranks of field workers before they reach the age of 20.

    However, for our purposes, what is important is not the exact number of labour-days per feddan per year, but the general trend of labour input intensity across farm size. Indeed it is likely that the under-reporting of female and child labour force participation would tend to bias the figures against an inverse relationship between labour input per feddan and farm size as the actual participation rates are higher on the small farms than the large farms. On the former, women and children may be compelled to work in the fields, whereas on the rich peasant farms, female members of the household are able to withdraw from the labour force.

17. The rich peasantry had originally supported the rent control components of the agrarian reform: after all, they rented more land than other any other group, usually from poor peasants with less than three feddans. Land reform changed their situation from net renters to owners and as land values and incomes rose during the 1970s because of the injection of oil remittances, rent became a smaller proportion of peasant income and rich peasants turned against rent controls which stood in the way of either raising rents or reclaiming plots for sale.

18. There is a generally high level of purchased seed inputs in all size classes. Adams [1986: 51] explains that small farms do not normally use own-produced seed anyway: it is too expensive in opportunity cost terms because of their need to use land for fodder crops rather than producing a seed crop.

    This is also true for birseem, the main animal fodder crop. Dr Ahmed Rammah, a forage agronomist at the Agricultural Research Centre in Giza, informed me that 1989 and 1990 marked the beginning of field trials for improved varieties of birseem: Giza 6, Giza 10, Giza 15, Sakha 3 and Sakha 4. These produce yields some 30 per cent above those of baladi (traditional) varieties. But only the large farmers with over ten feddans are willing to grow seed crops. For the small farmers, a birseem seed crop would use land cutting into the summer cropped area. This is even the case when the Research Centre supplies new seeds free of charge.

19. HYV seed use was computed by taking the percentage of gross cropped area under HYV crops. The indices of machinery use are the value of rented machinery (pumps, tractors and ploughs) plus ten percent of the value of owned machinery per feddan.

VIII

A Positive Relationship Village in Qena and the Emerging Comparative Picture in the Context of Egyptian Agrarian Transition

INTRODUCTION

In the previous chapter, we have seen how and why an inverse relationship between farm size and land productivity arises in the Giza village. In this chapter, we turn to the second village in our survey, Higaza al-Qibli in Qena governorate, in Upper Egypt, where we have identified a positive relationship between farm size and land productivity.

The first section VIII.1, analyses the data for the Qena village, showing how the inverse relationship has broken down there. Then, in section VIII.2, we compare the results in the two villages, within the wider context of the political economy of the Egyptian countryside.

VIII.1 A POSITIVE RELATIONSHIP VILLAGE IN QENA

The evidence from Higaza al-Qibli in Qena governorate presents a striking difference. Qena governorate, in which the second village survey was undertaken, lies some 700 km south of Cairo in Upper Egypt. Qena is a narrow ribbon of fertile land running down both sides of the Nile from Nag Hammadi in the north to Esna in the south, a distance of about 200 km. It supports an estimated 1990 population of 2.5 million and covers an area of 1,851 square kilometres. The village chosen on the basis of the ILO survey was Higaza al-Qibli in Qus district, halfway between Qena town and Luxor. Higaza is situated about 14 km east of the Nile near to the desert plateau. There are nearly 14,000 households in the village. Higaza is a narrow village which runs for 1.5 km along the lower edge of the plateau. It is around 40 km from Luxor and 12 km from Qus.

The total village population is approximately 60,000. Some 60 per cent of the households are landless, and around 80 per cent of the latter are wage labourers. The *mushrif* explained that most of the young people work outside the village. Agricultural work by itself would not be sufficient to buy certain expensive commodities. In the 1970s, many people went to Iraq or the Gulf to work, and labour shortages occurred during that period. Labour hirers had to book labour up to one month in advance. Nowadays, however, landless labourers queue up for work.

The local institutional structure is dominated by the co-operative. It supplies both agricultural inputs and credit, and is responsible for the village and its surrounding area. The Qus district centre manages 24 co-operatives, including Higaza (there were 28 co-operatives four years ago). Each co-operative centre is headed by a director, and a number of agricultural supervisors. Higaza has three supervisors, one supervisor for each 1,200 feddans. Other smaller co-operatives would normally have one supervisor for each 300 feddans. There is a general veterinary centre and three machinery workshops for repairs. The latter are all privately owned. A workshop attached to the co-operative centre is under construction which will cover the whole area. The irrigation department is in Qus.

Each village, including Higaza, has one small medical unit. There are some 20 primary schools, two intermediate and one secondary school. Drinking water is available to every house. The pipe system was put in by the government. Electrical power comes from the High Dam, and is regarded as being the most important development in the village. The main market is held every Saturday at Higaza. Traders arrive from all the surrounding villages with their merchandise. There are around one-and-a-half thousand shops, around 600 of them licensed.

The history of Higaza goes back some 400 years when people arrived from Hijaz (in Arabia) where they were facing starvation. The tribes first arrived at Be'ess. They had problems with the local people, and so they moved nearer to the edge of the plateau, which was unpopulated. The Harb and Jouheinah families came from Arabia. The Christian families are much older. In the nineteenth century, during Muhammed Ali's period, the local bedouin settled down.

The structure of landholdings was feudal. The whole district of Qus was owned by only four families. One of them was Christian and they owned around half of all the land. In 1952, some land was distributed under the reform legislation, with a ceiling of 500 feddans, and later 100 feddans for individual landowners. The largest family are the Al Esheish. This family still owns around 2,000 feddans. The 'umda (village headman) is a member of this family and a member of the majlis al-shaab (People's Assembly). There are three other important families. The large Christian landlords sold their land to the Al Esheish. They bought estates in Cairo and moved there. The major families tie together some 15 villages in the area, and many own land in more than one village.

The important actors in the village are the 'umda and the member of the majlis al-shaab who is the uncle of the Higaza co-operative supervisor. The latter is a farmer. There is one member of the family in the *majlis al-shaab* and one member in the *majlis al-shura* (local consultative council). Ten people are elected to the local *majlis*, one from each family.

Higaza comprises some 2,080 registered operational holdings, but these are actually owned by some 1,650 *ha'izeen*. The operated holdings have a size-class distribution of land much more skewed toward the larger farms than in Shubak (see Table 44, Appendix A). As can be seen from the table, 84 per cent of the farms are below three feddans, farming 55 per cent of the *zimam* (cultivated area). Again as in Giza, three feddans are regarded as the minimum feasible size of farm. Nearly half of the holdings (43 per cent) under one feddan are rented on a cash basis. The middle peasant category operates 181 farms (nine per cent) accounting for 18 per cent of the cultivated area. The rich peasants operate 141 farms (seven per cent), 16 of which are above ten feddans, and account for 27 per cent of the land. Note that the distribution of land is further skewed by the fact that the rich peasants actually farm a proportion of the small rented plots in the table. As this distribution was unavailable at the start of the survey, we used the statistically similar distribution of operated area in Qus district in order to draw our sample.

A stratified sample of 71 farms was selected (or a four per cent sample of the 1,650 ha'izeen) on the basis of the farm land distribution given in the 1981 Agricultural Census for Qena governorate (see Table 45). This distribution is more heavily skewed towards the larger farmers. Three outliers were identified in the survey returns and 68 entered in the regression exercises. One of these outliers was a small farmer with 0.67 feddan whose land was right in amongst the residential area of the village and suffered from particularly low fertility. The two others (0.67 and 2.25 feddans) had responses that were clearly well outside the range of possible yields, but we were unable to return to the respondents for correction.

The cropping pattern in Higaza is essentially two season, but with a very short nili season overlapping the end of summer and beginning of winter. Given summer temperatures of 40–50 degrees celsius, the cropping pattern is dominated by sugarcane cultivation which is grown on 42 per cent of gross cropped area all year round (in fact a 13-month crop cycle). Wheat and birseem account for 84 per cent of gross cropped area (not under sugarcane) in the winter season, while maize and millet or sorghum account for 87 per cent of summer gross cropped area. The short nili season is again devoted to coarse grain cultivation and cut green for fodder.

Sugarcane is grown on a four to five year cycle. There is spring sugarcane which takes 14 months, and summer cane that takes only 12 and which is in the ground from the end of March to the beginning of April in the following year. A summer crop is cultivated from March and a nili crop in October. The land does not get rested. With fallow, sugarcane yields can increase to around 80 tons. But normally yields are around 50 tons maximum. With copious use of fertilisers, yields can be substantially maintained at high levels.

Note that the returns to sugarcane are longer term, more so than vegetables, for example, which have quick returns. Thus small farmers do not grow sugarcane because they need fast returns, and cannot afford the high levels of fertiliser input. A specialist in sugarcane production at the Cairo Museum of Agriculture also explained that poor peasants do not prepare the sugarcane tops properly in terms of the required washing and coating, and thus suffer lower physical yields. Intercropping takes place on all farm sizes with spring vegetables.

Table 46 and regression equation R.10 in Table 36 show that net yields per feddan increase markedly with farm size. The relation is statistically significant at the one per cent level. Net yields are more than a third higher on the large farms than on the small. There has been a clear strengthening of the trend towards higher yields on the large farms. As we saw above, the relationship between farm size and yields was positive, but not statistiscally different from zero in the 1976 ILO survey. In other words, there appeared to be no relation across farm size for the 1976 ILO data. That the relationship has become significantly positive between 1976 and 1990, would lend to support to our thesis that in the dynamic context, the large farmers' access to credit and new technology has allowed them to capture significant economies of scale. We explore this further below.

Gross yields in equation R.11, Table 36, confirm the evidence for a positive relation and suggest the continuing presence of higher cropping intensities on the smaller farms. Table 46 presents figures on cropping intensities and labour input intensities which confirms that these are indeed characteristically higher on the smaller farms, but note that there is a much narrower range of cropping intensities than in the Giza sample. That the large farms do have higher net yields despite the higher cropping intensities and labour intensities on the small farms provides clear evidence that the large farms have achieved important scale advantages of some sort.

Again, there is no variation across farm size with respect to value per feddan which points to relatively homogeneous land quality in the village (see Table 46). The majority of the soil in Higaza, around 3,000 to 4,000 feddans, is *tina safra* (sandy clay). The soil nearer Qus is better quality. The *ahwad* around Higaza are poor because the soil is sandy and takes a lot of water. The *ahwad* nearest to the village have the best soil. All the respondents were selected from *ahwad* within walking distance of the village centre, thus assuring that soil quality was fairly homogeneous in the sample. While fragmentation appears higher than in the Giza village, with generally higher numbers of plots per farm and higher intensities of fragmentation, this could be rather misleading. Plots tend to be contiguous and the cropping pattern has a significant influence. Whereas in Shubak, vegetable and cereal intercropping produces a patchwork effect of tiny plots, in Higaza the cropped area is dominated by vast stretches of land under sugarcane and coarse grains. In Qena, land is cultivated in a consolidated fashion.

Regression equations R.12 and R.13 in Table 36, show results for physical yields of individual crops, respectively wheat and sugarcane. Wheat yields (in ardebs) show no trend across farm size, but interestingly, sugarcane shows a strong positive relationship between yields and farm size. This is highly significant – unlike Giza, where all size classes have a similar cropping pattern, in Qena there is a noticeable skew towards sugarcane cultivation on the larger farms (above two to three feddans). We find the same relationship between farm size and the use of family or hired labour as in Shubak, but Higaza shows much higher levels of wage labour utilisation, indicating a more dynamic labour market (see Table 46).

A large farmer explained the system of labour hiring:

> We hire workers through an agent. We make a deal for cutting and taking the crop away. The poor work as labourers. Sixty per cent of the villagers have no land and 80 per cent of them work in agriculture. They work temporarily for me, not continuously through the year. They work until I tell them they are not needed any more. They get paid by the day. They start around 7.30 or 8.00am until 2.00pm. I never pay them more or less than the going rate. The workers are not happy with LE 5. They say LE 5 doesn't bring them anything. But when they work from 8.00am to 2.00pm with a half hour break, LE 5 is not so bad. They bring their own lunch. I tell them when to take a break and when to have lunch. I don't use migrant labour.

> If someone has many children he takes them to work with him. Children work on stripping the sugarcane, cutting birseem, light jobs. They age between 11 and 15 years. They get LE 3 for stripping sugarcane. Two pounds for normal days. They work the same hours as the adults and work alongside them. The adults cut the sugarcane and the kids strip it down. Loading the rail trucks takes two kids. The chopper takes one with two to feed it. Two people will be cutting and four stripping. One feddan would need four trucks, with seven adults, giving in total 28 men per feddan and 16 children.

The construction of the High Dam at Aswan had a major impact on agricultural production in the Qena governorate. The *mushrif zira'i* explained:

Before the High Dam, land used to be planted with wheat in winter after flooding. No canals existed then and flood irrigation used to take place from August to September. No reforms happened before the High Dam. But afterwards, we were able to cultivate the land three times a year. We can irrigate any time. Each village has a set period for irrigation.

The main Qalbiyah canal arrives from Aswan irrigating all the regions. Each region is fed by secondary canal branches, irrigating all the villages. Each of the secondary canals has doors which open in turns. The water is high for 40 days in the year (during winter). Higaza is fed by four canals from the Nile, with two filled with water every other week.

Also of importance is that while HYV use and machinery use do not vary significantly across farm size in the Giza village, the large farms in Higaza (the top two size classes five to ten and over ten feddans) use significantly higher applications of HYV seeds and significantly higher machinery inputs than the small farms (and also higher levels than similar large farms in Giza, as comparison of the data in Tables 37 and 46 shows). The large farms have between 51 per cent and 64 per cent of gross cropped area under HYV as compared to around a third for the smaller farm sizes. This compares with 13 per cent and 39 per cent for the top two size classes in Shubak.

The sample data indicate that whereas in Shubak the use of modern agricultural machinery varies little over farm size classes, except for the ten feddan farm, there is a clear positive relationship between machine use and size in Higaza, and overall a higher degree of machine use (see Table 46). Machine use is particularly heavy on the rich peasant farms above 5 feddans. Machine use on the farms above ten-feddans is nearly 18 times the level on the smallest farms. And on the farms between five and ten feddans, machine use is over six times that on the farms below one feddan. These ratios can be compared to those in Shubak of 2.5 and 0.9 (see Table 37).

Note that in Shubak the evidence would suggest that whereas the above ten feddan farm can be classed as a capitalist farmer (given the indications on labour hire, accumulation and investment in modern equipment, and level of commercial participation) the farms in the five to ten feddan class are not qualitatively different from the smaller farm sizes. In fact they have practically the same levels of technology use as the small farms. They have remained rich peasants rather than developing into capitalist farmers. The contrast with the Higaza sample is clear. There, both the farms above ten feddans and those above five feddans have high technology utilisation, and in combination with the other indicators, would seem to have become capitalist farmers, earning high returns.

In fact, figures obtained from the village co-operatives show that Higaza does have a significantly higher level of technological development than Shubak in Giza. Whereas Higaza is roughly twice the size of Shubak, it has 65 tractors, 225 irrigation pumps and 25 mechanical threshers as opposed to Shubak's eight tractors, 79 pumps and no threshers. Of the 225 irrigation pumps, the majority are mobile (213 as against 12 fixed). The 12 fixed pumps are all between 25 and 45 hp. Most (160) of the diesel pumps are less than 10 hp, while 38 are between 10 and 12 hp, and 15 are greater than 12 hp. Prior to 1960, only the 12 fixed pumps were in existence. The first eight diesel pumps appeared in the village in the 1965–70 period, and 80 were bought in the 1970–75 period. The bulk of the diesel pumps (125) have been introduced since 1975. The majority of irrigation pumps are owned by the large farmers. Twelve of the more powerful pumps are owned by farmers with more than 15 feddans, and 213 others are owned by farmers with five to ten feddans.

The 65 tractors in existence comprise 45 Romanian, 12 Russian and seven other makes. Only one is between 35 and 50 hp, 40 are between 50 and 70 hp, and 24 above 70 hp. All appeared in the village in the early 1970s. The first was introduced by the co-operative. All the rest are privately owned. The first private tractor was bought by a large farmer with over 15 feddans. A farmer with 10 feddans, who guarantees that relatives with 20 or 30 feddans would use it, would buy one. They cost around LE 20,000. Payment is made by instalment over a period of five years with a 25 per cent rate of interest.

Small farmers below three feddans hire tractors locally and pay about LE 24 per feddan. Normally, farmers rent a tractor twice a year for each crop. For machine hiring, the owner decides the price and the farmer the use of the machine. The deal is done orally. Larger farmers might rent a tractor three or four times a year depending on the crop. The owner or his son will drive the tractor. Payment for hire can be made up to a year later. A small farmer growing sugarcane can wait until they are paid by the sugar factory to pay for the hire of machines.

One farmer explained:

> For ploughing, the first pass costs LE 10–12. The second and third passes are cheaper. Altogether around LE 20–25 per feddan. But the traditional plough costs more – around LE 30 (plus a packet of cigarettes). A traditional plough can do one feddan a day, two if the animals are good. But a tractor can do up to five feddans a day. Soil preparation might take a day per feddan, and furrowing a day. Irrigation costs about 500 pounds per year. For one feddan, hire of an irrigation pumps costs LE 25, but if the land is near the canal, it can be cheaper.

In Higaza there are also 25 threshers. The people who own the threshers are the same as own the tractors and they are used together. For the thresher, hiring is by the hour (LE 30). One ardeb of wheat might cost LE 10–12.

This superiority in new technology is also reflected at the governorate and district levels: Qena has a 1.4:1 advantage in tractors (in terms of the 1982–83 stock per 1,000 feddans), a 7:1 advantage in modern ploughs, a 3:1 lead in threshers, and a 6:1 lead with respect to irrigation pump horsepower (see Table 23, Appendix A). In terms of farm use,[1] Table 47 shows that Qena has a 1.6:1 advantage in tractor use, a 2.8:1 advantage in the use of irrigation pumps, and a 2.3:1 lead in the use of threshers. The differences are more striking at the district level. Qus district in Qena has an advantage in farm tractor use of almost 2:1, in threshers of almost 2:1, and a massive lead in irrigation pump use of over 13:1 over Saff district in Giza. In terms of the number of operational units the ratio between Qus and Saff is only 1.3:1.

The ownership of agricultural machinery in Higaza is more heavily concentrated in the larger size classes above five feddans (see Table 48). The 1981 Agricultural Census shows that 72 per cent of tractor owning or sharing farms are located in the above five feddan size classes in Qena as opposed to only 55 per cent in Giza. With regard to irrigation pumps, 52 per cent of owning or sharing farms are above five feddans in Qena, and just 29 per cent in Giza. And 72 per cent of mechanical thresher owning or sharing farms are above five feddans in Qena, as opposed to only 42 per cent in Giza. Clearly, the rich peasant farms in Qena have been able to accumulate and invest in new technology to a much greater extent than in Giza.

The two areas can be contrasted in terms of their level of commercialisation too (see Table 47). Whereas in Saff district, 58 per cent of the tractors and 67 per cent of the irrigation pumps are rented in the private sector (the rest are hired through the co-operative system), the respective figures for Qus district are 98 per cent and 92 per cent. Some 97 per cent of the threshing equipment is hired through the private rental market in Qus as opposed to 80 per cent in Saff. Thus Qus has a significantly more developed private rental market for agricultural equipment than Saff district.

VIII.2 THE EMERGING COMPARATIVE PICTURE AND A
       CONCLUSION WITH REGARD TO THE INVERSE
       RELATIONSHIP

These results provide us with enough evidence to form a picture of what is going on. In an area like Giza, with a relatively low development of the forces of production, and with all farm sizes using more or less the same techniques of production, the higher cropping intensities of poor peasants (less than three feddans) which imply higher labour use intensities and higher value yields, produce the inverse relationship. Rich peasants (above five feddans) have not yet achieved significant scale advantages, although they may be expected to do so in time (as can be seen for the ten feddan farm which is making some progress).

It might be said that the Qena village, Higaza al-Qibli, shows the Giza village an image of its own future. Here, the significantly advanced level of the productive forces has allowed the rich peasants to reap important scale advantages which more than counteract the still higher labour and cropping intensities of the poor peasant farms. Included here in the development of the forces of production is the significantly different cropping pattern as well as use of modern inputs.

Some indication of how such rich peasants were able to do this can be seen in terms of rich peasant domination of the co-operative and village bank system as well as land resources. As we have seen above the leading members of the co-operative are large landowners themselves. The sample data (see Table 46) show that, in Higaza, the top two size classes, representing eight per cent of farm households, own 48 per cent of the land, control 91 per cent of credit disbursements in 1989–90 and 39 per cent of co-operative supplied inputs. In the Shubak sample, they represent five per cent of the farms, own 33 per cent of the land and dominate 56 per cent of credit disbursements and only 14 per cent of co-operative supplied inputs. The mean per capita wealth for large farms over ten feddans is 15 times that of small farms in Shubak, but over 30 times in Higaza.

One large farmer described how large farms have easier access to credit facitiies:

> I have a calf and a cow for milk. The calf gets fed with birseem. A cow or *gamusa* costs LE 800–1,000. Not all farmers can own animals. Only big farmers could keep a calf. To purchase an animal, I borrow from the bank. Big farmers with a lot of land could even borrow to buy a tractor. It's easier to borrow money.

While Giza may perhaps represent something of an anomaly, a semi-rural/semi-urban governorate producing high value fruit and vegetable crops for urban markets such as Cairo, Taylor [*1984*] corroborates the results of the above analysis. She writes that land is highly fragmented in the region. Despite investment in irrigation pumps and livestock, differentiation of farms along capitalist lines has not occurred. Indeed there has been an expansion of the peasant sector which she defines as that composed of family household production, as opposed to wage-labour farming. The nature of the local political economy has meant that accumulation of land has been prevented by rapidly rising land values while tenants have been able to establish security of tenure with low fixed annual rents. Labour migration too has hindered the development of a wage-labour market in the region.

The almost counter-intuitive findings of the above analysis are also corroborated by evidence produced by Esfahani [1988: 157]. He notes that while one would expect mechanisation to advance earlier and faster in areas near urban centres, the evidence shows that the urban and semi-urban governorates are characterised by a lesser degree of mechanisation than all other regions in Egypt and that their mechanisation process has started rather late (see Table 49, Appendix A).[2] Upper Egypt, on the other hand, is characterised by relatively higher degrees of mechanical power, more chemical fertiliser use, and less organic manure use than other regions. He explains that this unexpected pattern of mechanisation is mainly due to the differences in regional cropping patterns and in policies toward different crops:

> the expansion of sugar cane in Upper Egypt was strongly supported by heavy use of fertiliser and machinery from the beginning, while the change in the input composition of other crops came more gradually. In particular, the development of horticulture in the UG [urban governorates] did not require much machinery and could more easily use manure in place of fertiliser.

Waterbury [1979: 132–4; 216–8] too has noted the concentration of investment projects in Upper Egypt, and PBDAC figures [Ministry of Agriculture, 1989: 71, Table 10] show that the distribution of investment loans by governorate on a per feddan and per farm basis have favoured Qena more than Giza: Qena farmers received LE 130 per feddan and LE 270 per holding whereas Giza farmers received only LE 92 per feddan and LE 145 per holding in 1985–86. The latter source [1989: 8] also mentions a study by El Shohna [1970] which shows that Qena and Aswan governorates in Upper Egypt enjoyed a considerable share of subsidised cash loans throughout the 1960s due to the vast plantations of sugarcane. Adams [1986: 60] mentions that sugarcane is regarded as a large farm crop and that credit advances favour the cultivation of sugarcane: a feddan of cotton gets a cash loan of only LE 17, but a feddan of sugarcane gets LE 45. Moreover, if the sugarcane grower plants more than ten feddans, cash loans rise to LE 160 per feddan from the sugar mills.[3]

A noticeable trend in the cropping pattern in Upper Egypt during the post revolution period was the rapid expansion of the sugarcane crop at the expense of other crops [Esfahani, 1988: 137]. Sugarcane is a major industrial crop and its area expanded rapidly from 96,000 feddans in the early 1950s to 220,000 feddans in 1975 [Ikram, 1980: 192]. The area planted under sugarcane increased rapidly under state control by 29 per cent in 1970–73 to 1978–81, due to the increased availability of summer water in Minya, Qena and Aswan [*Radwan and Lee,* 1986: 157].

But sugarcane cultivation in Egypt has a longer history. In areas of Upper Egypt, the creation of perennial irrigation in the nineteenth century led to the cultivation of sugarcane on a large scale. Low population density and the availability of irrigation water for a year-round crop like sugarcane gave rise to a pattern of large estates (at first royal, then later private). This development of agrarian capitalism required more labour for the new cash crops, and labour was recruited from the sedenterizing Bedouin population in estate villages built up by the landowners for this purpose [*Hopkins and Mehanna,* 1981: 9–10].

Most sugarcane was grown under contract to local sugar mills. The joint effort by farmer and mill requires a high level of technical efficiency and support services (sugar production depends not on tons of cane but on sugar content) [*Ikram, 1980: 192*]. In the nineteenth century, local (baladi) varieties were superseded by improved Roumi varieties and in the early years of the twentieth century, the Compagnie des Sucreries introduced a new variety no.105 from Javanese strains [*Foaden and Fletcher,* 1908: 447]. Also the diffusion process for sugar extraction in mills took over from the crushing process in hand mills [*Foaden and Fletcher,* 1908: 453]. Schutz [1987: 8] notes that with sugarcane, the sugar company co-operates with the Credit Bank for the supply of inputs and debt is subtracted from payment (for other crops, credit is via the co-operative or village bank).

The government encouraged the expansion of sugarcane cultivation by setting prices higher than international prices: in 1985, the world price was LE 14 per ton, but the procurement price was 20–24 per ton, and in 1988 prices were raised to LE 38–50 per ton [*Sadowski,* 1991: 179]. Returns per feddan to sugarcane are more than 400 times that on cotton, and because of its annual rotation only rich farmers can grow it [*Adams,* 1986: 71]. In addition, rich farmers who plant non-traditional crops like sugarcane or grapes can get government subsidised inputs that small farmer maize and birseem crops cannot (see Table 50). Thus rich farmers are reaping both subsidised inputs and manage to avoid taxed crops [*Adams,* 1986: 73–4].

We are not suggesting here that the results obtained are crop specific.[4] There is a temptation by some agronomists to classify villages according to their main crop ('sugarcane villages' or 'rice villages' for example). The rational kernel underlying this is that each crop imposes a certain rhythm and discipline on agricultural production, but it is perhaps too easy to exaggerate the influence of a single crop on the total village structure. Certainly though, the major cropping pattern will imply variations in market involvement and in labour intensity [*Hopkins and Mehanna,* 1981: 43–5].

Thus a major impetus to technical and social change in Qena was provided by the close relationship between sugar capital and sugarcane growers. The sugar mill not only locked rich peasants into commercialised agriculture, but furthered the process of peasant differentiation by favouring the large farms with loans and subsidised inputs.

The sugar factories have a great deal of control over production. The sugarcane factory sets up a cutting plan, giving priority to the areas with older plantings and ending with the new plantings. A farmer growing sugarcane will pay an intermediate agent LE 200 to get all the machines and workers, and take the harvested crop to the factory. Then the farmer gets his money from the sugar factory. Here too then we have some indication of why Qena appears to be characterised by a more advanced agriculture than Giza, despite the latter's proximity to the Cairo fruit and vegetable market.

Taylor's thesis above that high land values in Giza have blocked the accumulation of land on the part of rich peasants/capitalist farmers can only be one small part of the story. Indeed, it is perhaps the lack of such proximity to the state centre that has benefited the rich peasants of Qena. Not only were they subject to less supervision in the land reform process, but the state had to depend more heavily on the rich peasant/capitalist farmer strata in Qena to organise and administer the co-operative system in that locality. All these factors may go a long way to explaining the relatively advanced agricultural sector in Qena as compared with Giza.

The paths of development of the two survey villages echo those described and analysed by Hopkins [1987] which we examined in Chapter VII. Two paths of agrarian transition in Egypt are delineated: a capitalist path (using hired wage labour and machinery) and a path dominated by petty commodity production with small farmers producing for the market and agriculture becoming increasingly marginalised. These two paths are manifested in variant forms of village development: (1) land reform villages which have moved in the direction of intensification of petty commodity production; and (2) villages in which capitalist agriculture and the emergence of capitalist relations of production based on the use of wage labour and modern agricultural equipment have appeared.

The village of Shubak al-Sharqi falls into the first category. Land reform in Shubak has created a situation in which less social differentiation and elite land accumulation has occurred. Thus, land reform has actually had the effect of slowing down capital accumulation, inhibiting saving and investment. Shubak has been characterised by small scattered land possessions prohibiting the application of modern technology and leading to the fragile formation of capitalism. Land fragmentation has weakened the ability of large farmers to adopt new agricultural methods, slowing down the intensification of capital utilisation.

The village is dominated by middle and rich peasant farms which have not developed into capitalist farmers. These farms are not fully commercialised and operate with essentially the same techniques of production as the poor farmers with less than three feddans of land. Clearly, the evidence from Shubak shows us that the larger farmers are not qualitatively different from smaller farmers, but only quantitatively differentiated.

In contradistinction, Higaza clearly falls into the capitalist path category. This village has a relatively greater concentration of land, a larger area and population, and higher levels of new technology use, particularly mechanization. The cooperative system was dominated by the rich peasants allowing the large farms to accumulate land and other means of production such as machinery. Thus, Higaza has exhibited a different outcome with increased social differentiation and the potential disappearance of the small farmer rather than his survival.

Higaza has also benefited from development efforts in the form of loans for machinery and other modern inputs because of its integration into an industrialised agriculture dominated by sugar capital. The mode of production has changed because capital has penetrated the village and changed the system of production instead of being merely externally imposed via market relations. The middle and rich peasant family farms have given way to capitalist enterprises organised by the family, but based on wage labour and capitalist accumulation, manifested in the intensive use of machine inputs.

SUMMARY AND CONCLUSIONS

Land reform in Shubak has created a situation in which relatively little social differentiation and elite land accumulation has occurred. Thus, land reform has actually had the effect of slowing down capital accumulation, inhibiting saving and investment. Shubak is characterised by small scattered land possessions prohibiting the application of modern technology and leading to the fragile formation of capitalism. Land fragmentation has weakened the ability of large farmers to adopt new agricultural methods, slowing down the intensification of capital utilisation. Significant elements of semi-feudal agriculture remain to provide the compulsions driving poor farmers to intensify land and labour use, thus generating an inverse relationship.

The village is dominated by middle and rich peasant farms which have not developed into capitalist farmers. These farms are not fully commercialised and operate with essentially the same techniques of production as the poor farmers with less than three feddans of land. Clearly, the evidence from Shubak shows us that the larger farmers are not qualitatively different from smaller farmers, but only quantitatively differentiated.

In contradistinction, Higaza clearly falls into a capitalist path category. This village has a relatively greater concentration of land, a larger area and population, and higher levels of new technology use, particularly mechanisation. The co-operative system was dominated by the rich peasants allowing the large farms to accumulate land and other means of production such as machinery. Thus, Higaza has exhibited a different outcome with increased social differentiation and the potential disappearance of the small farmer rather than his survival.

Higaza has also benefited from development efforts in the form of loans for machinery and other modern inputs because of its integration into an industrialised agriculture dominated by sugar capital. The mode of production has changed because capital has penetrated the village and changed the system of production instead of being merely externally imposed via market relations. The middle and rich peasant family farms have given way to capitalist enterprises organised by the family, but based on wage labour and capitalist accumulation, manifested in the intensive use of machine inputs.

The 'traverse' from Giza to Qena, representing a development of the forces of production both determines and is determined by the development of the relations of production. In particular, rich peasants, either as proto- or fully-developed capitalist farmers monopolise productive resources and dominate access to the new technology through their control of the co-operative and rural credit systems. The utilisation of this new technology accelerates rich peasant accumulation and deepens the process of social differentiation. The productivity advantages thus gained lead to a reversal in the size–productivity relationship characteristic of a relatively backward agriculture.

What implications can we draw from this for the inverse relationship between farm size and farm productivity, and its suggested policy implications such as redistributive land reform? The Egyptian evidence supports the hypothesis that in the static context, the inverse relationship is not the product of superior efficiency on the part of small farms nor is it due to better quality land on the small farms, but arises from the desperate struggle of poor peasants for survival on below-subsistence plots of land in a relatively backward agriculture, and the matrix of exploitative relations within which they operate. Redistribution of land on the basis of the inverse relationship argument therefore, far from alleviating poverty and creating employment opportunities, will only deepen and perpetuate extreme levels of exploitation and poverty.

Furthermore, in the dynamic context of the development of both the relations and forces of production, in the shape of the new technology, the inverse relation is likely to break down and disappear. Rich peasants are able to capture the gains from the new technology, and with increased accumulation develop into capitalist farmers. The evidence from the village of Higaza would tend to support this thesis. Thus, the inverse relationship argument for land redistribution no longer has any rationale in the context of changing production conditions within Egyptian agriculture.

NOTES

1. The latest available (1981) agricultural census does not have figures for current population of agricultural equipment, but does give figures for the number of farms using such equipment on owned, shared and rented bases. The ratio of farms in Qena to that in Giza is 1.6, suggesting the same overall level of use of tractors. This only points out the high level of aggregation inherent in a comparison of governorates.
2. This finding is based on a cross-sectional comparison of the revenue shares of mechanical power and of fertiliser as measures of the degree of mechanisation.
3. Adams [1986: 60, fn. 11] mentions that the privately owned cane presses are all owned by rich peasants.
4. While tomatoes are a very labour intensive crop: 192 man-days per year (compared to 65 for wheat and maize or 99 for birseem and cotton) [*Ikram*, 1980: 193], the general assumption that vegetable cultivation is highly labour-intensive and unmechanised is not borne out by reality: Hopkins [1982: 132] writes: 'vegetable farming did not appear appreciably less mechanized than open field farming'.

APPENDIX A

Statistical Tables

TABLE 1

THE INDIAN FMS SIZE CLASS DATA: GROSS OUTPUT AND FARM BUSINESS
INCOME PER HECTARE BY SIZE CLASS

size	Amritsar and Ferozepur (1954–57) output	FBI	Karnal, Rohtak and Jind Tehsil (1961–62) output	FBI
<5ha	496.69	237.32	751.21	452.21
5-10	459.62	205.10	585.65	316.30
0-15	(		548.58	318.77
15-20	(427.50	200.16	506.27	291.59
20-30	(		462.09	291.59
30-50	(380.55	187.80	373.13	205.10
>50	353.37	185.33	259.46	138.38

size	Uttar Pradesh (Meerut & Muzaffarnagar) 1954–57 output	FBI	Maharashtra (Akola & Amraoti) 1955–57 output	FBI
<5ha	496.69	237.22	259.07	148.86
5-10	459.62	205.10	219.01	119.35
10-15	427.50	200.16	231.00	122.05
15-20	380.55	187.80	201.25	111.69
20-30	(		207.87	116.36
30-40	(		209.25	120.84
40-50	(353.37	185.33	239.40	129.88
>50	(	226.10	116.66	

size	Maharashtra (1955–57) Ahmednagar output	FBI	Maharashtra (1955–57) Nasik output	FBI
<5ha	226.35	78.33	303.20	53.38
5-10	231.79	100.08	295.54	125.04
10-15	145.30	62.02	158.64	52.63
15-20	362.51	137.64	139.62	64.74
20-25	98.35	45.72	129.24	60.29
25-30	128.99	62.77	146.54	82.04
30-50	172.78	69.44	171.49	56.09
>50	81.55	41.27	104.77	37.81

size	West Bengal (Hooghly & 24 Paraganas) 1954–57 output	FBI	Madras (Salem & Coimbatore) 1954–57 output	FBI
.01-1.25	583.18	321.24	(	
1.26-2.50	598.00	316.30	(550.31	86.74
2.51-3.75	573.29	227.34	(	
3.76-5.00	599.16	279.23	(481.12	191.76
5.01-7.50	583.18	294.06	417.12	171.49
7.51-10.0	551.05	321.24	425.52	204.36
10.01-15	400.32	202.63	247.60	88.47
15.01-20	(		175.45	60.05
20.0-25.0	(437.38	239.70	164.82	54.86
>25.00	(		204.11	108.97

TABLE 1 (cont.)

size	Andhra Pradesh (West Godavari) output	FBI	Orissa (Sambalpur district) output	FBI
.01-1.25	1280.02	558.47	(	
1.26-2.50	1126.82	415.14	(328.65	185.33
2.51-5.00	894.53	328.65	316.30	180.39
5.01-7.50	746.27	237.22	(	
7.51-10.0	842.64	192.75	(286.65	140.85
10.01-15	939.01	291.59	254.52	96.37
15.01-20	1008.20	271.82	(	
>20.00	921.72	383.02	(311.36	145.79

size	N. Monghor output	C. Monghor output	S. Monghor output
<2.5	474.45	494.22	439.85
2.5-5.0	370.66	476.92	467.04
5.0-7.5	441.33	442.56	(447.27
7.5-10	486.80	360.78	(
10.0-15	363.25	429.97	632.60
15.0-20	528.81	528.81	454.68
>20.0	407.73	575.76	422.56

size	Bihar (Shahabad) 1960–61 output
<2.5	508.40
2.5-5.0	495.06
5.0-7.5	470.34
7.5-10	478.91
10.0-15	482.39
15.0-20	473.69
20-30	452.01
>30	471.65

size	Rajasthan (Pali) 1962–63 output	FBI	Kerala (Allepey & Quilon) 1962–63 output	FBI
<1.0	(		590.40	96.72
1-2.5	(213.22	142.65	890.62	225.87
2.5-5.0	255.67	188.98	689.78	148.85
5.0-7.5	350.78	162.22	(	
7.5-10	190.98	77.91	(807.30	223.06
10-15	216.76	103.78	768.48	225.28
15-20	260.84	107.96	(	
20-25	166.27	76.65	(741.37	235.95
>25	136.42	37.88	503.19	-90.62

size	Madhya Pradesh (Raipur) 1962–63 output	FBI
<1.0	500.73	321.41
1.0-2.0	409.10	257.40
2.0-4.0	391.82	238.01
4.0-6.0	352.94	212.56
>6.0	377.83	216.32

Source: Appendix III [Department of Agriculture, 1966: 105–14].

TABLE 2

YIELD PER ACRE RELATED TO SIZE: ALL CROP PRODUCTION, INDIAN FMS

Region	Year	Constant term	α	Standard error	R^2	F
Punjab	1954–55	2.08	-0.02	0.005	0.79	11.69[b]
	1955–56	.96	-0.11	0.049	0.83	11.04[b]
	1956–57	2.48	-0.20	0.017	0.96	84.18[a]
West Bengal						
Hooghly	1954–55	2.48	-0.13	0.050	0.55	7.14[b]
24 Paraganas	1954–55	2.40	-0.23	0.145	0.30	2.56
Hooghly	1955–56	2.32	-0.11	0.027	0.72	15.71[a]
24 Paraganas	1955–56	2.31	-0.13	0.057	0.46	5.04[c]
Hooghly	1956–57	2.49	-0.07	0.076	0.12	0.77
24 Paraganas	1956–57	2.35	-0.02	0.066	0.17	0.11
Bombay						
Ahmednagar	1954–55	1.89	-0.30	0.074	0.72	16.28[a]
Nasik	1954–55	2.13	-0.41	0.110	0.71	14.15[a]
Ahmednagar	1955–56	2.02	-0.22	0.166	0.23	1.75
Nasik	1955–56	2.22	-0.31	0.081	0.50	14.69[a]
Ahmednagar	1956–57	2.28	-0.32	0.164	0.41	4.05[c]
Nasik	1956–57	2.28	-0.35	0.089	0.74	16.82[a]
Madras	1954–55	2.27	-0.35	0.191	0.36	3.36
	1955–56	2.42	-0.41	0.091	0.75	20.39[a]
	1956–57	2.68	-0.47	0.104	0.75	20.59[a]
U.P.	1954–55	2.57	-0.13	0.040	0.75	10.43[b]
	1955–56	2.51	-0.12	0.079	0.43	2.26
	1956–57	2.88	-0.21	0.059	0.67	12.17[a]
M.P.						
Akola	1955–56	2.14	-0.11	0.057	0.38	3.71
Amraoti	1956–57	2.18	-0.08	0.065	0.21	1.50
Akola	1955–56	1.83	-0.02	0.059	0.03	0.15
Amraoti	1956–57	1.69	0.14	0.029	0.02	2.10

Note: [a] denotes significance at 1 per cent level
       [b] denotes significance at 5 per cent level
       [c] denotes significance at 10 per cent level

Source: Table B.1 [Bharadwaj, 1974a: 92].

TABLE 3a

YIELD PER ACRE AND SIZE OF HOLDING: INDIVIDUAL CROPS, INDIAN FMS

Region/crop	Year	Constant tearm	α	Standard error	R^2	F
Punjab						
Wheat irrigated	1955–56	0.74	0.20	0.069	0.75	11.04[b]
	1956–57	2.14	0.17	0.028	0.83	14.92[b]
Wheat-gram irrigated	1955–56	2.36	-0.02	0.09	0.74	9.34[c]
American cotton	1954–55	2.06	0.12	0.039	0.76	9.58[c]
	1955–56	2.04	0.12	0.049	0.79	14.42[b]
Desi cotton	1954–55	0.43	0.28	0.068	0.71	16.51[b]
West Bengal						
Aman paddy Hooghly	1955–56	1.20	0.12	0.037	0.61	9.66[b]
Aus paddy Hooghly	1955–56	0.64	0.47	0.053	0.96	77.77[a]
Pulses:						
Hooghly	1955–56	0.38	0.23	0.082	0.55	8.14[b]
Mesta:						
Hooghly	1956–57	0.89	0.18	0.090	0.40	3.97[c]
24 Paraganas	1956–57	0.48	0.69	0.076	0.92	33.73[a]
Bombay						
Irrigated wheat						
Ahmednagar	1956–57	1.00	-0.28	0.120	0.46	5.43[c]
Dry Bajri						
Ahmednagar	1956–57	1.89	-0.30	0.074	0.72	16.28[a]
Nasik	1956–57	2.14	-0.41	0.109	0.69	14.15[a]
Dry gram						
Ahmednagar	1956–57	-0.01	0.33	0.170	0.39	3.82[c]
Irrigated gram						
Ahmednagar	1956–57	0.18	0.42	0.173	0.49	5.95[c]
Madras						
Paddy season I	1956–57	1.59	-0.17	0.04	0.70	15.30[a]
Paddy season II	1955–56	1.42	-0.10	0.05	0.45	4.85[c]
U.P.						
Wheat irrigated	1954–55	1.20	-0.07	0.03	0.36	4.02[c]
Sugarcane ratoon	1954–55	2.73	-0.23	0.06	0.69	13.51[a]
Wheat unirrigated	1954–55	0.98	-0.13	0.03	0.75	21.26[a]

Note: [a] denotes significance at 1 per cent level
[b] denotes significance at 5 per cent level
[c] denotes significance at 10 per cent level

Source: Table B.II [Bharadwaj, 1974a: 93].

TABLE 3b

INTENSITY OF CROPPING AND SIZE OF HOLDING, INDIAN FMS

State/district	Year	Constant term	α	Standard error	R^2	F
Punjab						
Amritsar	1954–55	2.22	-0.04	0.02	0.48	6.75[c]
Ferozepur	1954-55	2.13	-0.05	0.02	0.34	4.25
Amritsar	1955–56					
Ferozepur	1955–56					
Amritsar	1956-57	2.34	-0.07	0.03	0.36	5.34
Ferozepur	1956-57	2.82	-0.19	0.02	0.94	46.65[a]
West Bengal						
Hooghly	1954–55	0.03	-0.03	0.04	0.11	0.76
24 Paraganas	1954–55	0.04	-0.02	0.01	0.30	2.66
Hooghly	1955–56	0.05	-0.09	0.02	0.85	32.09[a]
24 Paraganas	1955–56	0.05	-0.07	0.02	0.64	10.82[b]
Hooghly	1956–57	0.09	-0.51	0.04	0.26	2.11
24 Paraganas	1956–57	0.04	-0.09	0.03	0.55	8.05[b]
Bombay						
Ahmednagar	1954-55	0.08	-0.04	0.01	0.49	6.50[b]
Nasik	1954-55	0.09	-0.03	0.01	0.38	8.35[b]
Ahmednagar	1955–56	0.03	-0.001	0.01	0.02	0.02
Nasik	1955–56	0.19	-0.10	0.02	0.70	14.54[a]
Ahmednagar	1956–57	0.10	-0.04	0.02	0.30	2.62
Nasik	1956–57	0.19	-0.14	0.02	0.83	30.33[a]
Madras	1954–55	2.07	-0.13	0.05	0.37	6.18[b]
	1955–56	0.19	-0.20	0.03	0.90	51.27[a]
	1956–57	0.20	-0.16	0.05	0.66	11.60[a]
U.P	1954–55	0.23	-0.11	0.02	0.86	38.29[a]
	1955–56	0.18	-0.05	0.01	0.71	15.29[a]
	1956–57	0.21	-0.07	0.01	0.86	42.84[a]
M.P.	Double cropping was negligible in M.P					

Note: [a] denotes significance at 1 per cent level
      [b] denotes significance at 5 per cent level
      [c] denotes significance at 10 per cent level

Source: Table B.IV [Bharadwaj, 1974a:95].

TABLE 4a

FRAGMENTS PER ACRE AND SIZE OF HOLDING, INDIAN FMS

State/district	Year	Constant tearm	α	Standard error	R^2	F
Punjab	1954–57	0.50	-0.76	0.045	0.98	282.87[a]
West Bengal						
Hooghly	1954–57	0.64	-0.23	0.040	0.85	33.04[a]
24 Paraganas	1954–57	0.65	-0.50	0.079	0.86	38.72[a]
U.P.	1954–55	0.34	-0.37	0.074	0.79	25.19[a]
	1955–56	0.41	-0.40	0.065	0.85	37.88[a]
	1956–57	0.37	-0.30	0.041	0.90	51.90[a]
Bombay	1954–55	0.30	-0.64	0.102	0.88	39.42[a]
	1955–56	0.17	-0.60	0.065	0.94	92.96[a]
	1956–57	0.29	-0.62	0.088	0.94	49.59[a]
M.P.	1955–56	-0.10	-0.49	-0.31	0.96	244.66[a]
	1956–57	-0.13	-0.48	0.015	0.98	977.92[a]

Note: [a] denotes significance at 1 per cent level

Source: Table B.V [*Bharadwaj*, 1974a: 96].

TABLE 4b

LABOUR DAYS PER ACRE RELATED TO THE SIZE OF HOLDING: ALL CROP
PRODUCTION, INDIAN FMS

State/district	Year	Constant team	α	Standard error	R^2	F
Punjab	1954–55	1.45	-0.10	0.02	0.86	19.40[b]
	1955–56	1.47	-0.10	0.02	0.92	46.16[a]
	1956–57	1.47	-0.15	0.02	0.92	47.32[a]
West Bengal						
Hooghly	1954–55	2.16	-0.11	0.07	0.31	2.75
24 Paraganas	1954–55	1.37	-0.20	0.09	0.44	4.59[c]
Hooghly	1955–56	1.81	-1.13	0.04	0.61	9.62[b]
24 Paraganas	1955–56	1.77	-0.27	0.05	0.81	26.11[a]
Hooghly	1956–57	1.85	-0.04	0.06	0.05	0.29
24 Paraganas	1956–57	1.67	-0.08	0.05	0.31	2.72
Bombay						
Ahmednagar	1955–56	1.79	-0.36	0.09	0.72	16.59[a]
Nasik	1955–56	1.85	-0.36	0.07	0.69	29.92[a]
Ahmednagar	1956-57	1.82	-0.43	0.07	0.83	29.78[a]
Nasik	1956–57	1.89	-0.45	0.04	0.96	101.62[a]
Madras	1954–55	1.95	-0.40	0.125	0.64	10.36[b]
	1955–56	2.07	-0.52	0.10	0.81	27.12[a]
U.P.	1954–55	2.16	-0.49	0.05	0.94	99.62[a]
	1955–56	1.88	-0.18	0.04	0.77	20.93[a]
	1956–57	1.78	-0.01	0.07	0.002	0.02
M.P.						
Akola	1955–56	1.60	-0.22	0.05	0.79	23.74[a]
Amraoti	1955–56	1.51	-0.11	0.09	0.19	1.46
Akola	1956–57	1.15	0.03	0.07	0.02	0.16
Amraoti	1956–57	1.12	0.05	0.13	0.02	0.15

Note: [a] denotes significance at 1 per cent level
[b] denotes significance at 5 per cent level
[c] denotes significance at 10 per cent level

Source: Table C.II [*Bharadwaj*, 1974a: 99].

TABLE 4c

BULLOCK LABOUR DAYS PER ACRE IN RELATION TO THE SIZE
OF HOLDING, INDIAN FMS

State/district	Year	Constant team	α	Standard error	R^2	F
Punjab	1954–55	1.44	-0.16	0.02	0.88	50.51[a]
	1955–56	1.50	-0.12	0.04	0.76	9.86[c]
	1956–57	1.29	-0.20	0.03	0.77	10.09[b]
West Bengal						
Hooghly	1954–55	1.27	-0.03	0.04	0.08	0.50
24 Paraganas	1954–55	1.37	-0.20	0.09	0.44	4.59[c]
Hooghly	1955–56	1.20	-0.03	0.03	0.09	0.75
24 Paraganas	1955–56	1.23	-0.12	0.04	0.56	7.87[b]
Hooghly	1956–57	1.28	-0.01	0.08	0.00	0.03
24 Paraganas	1956–57	1.22	-0.03	0.06	0.04	0.29
Bombay						
Ahmednagar	1955–56	2.10	-0.75	0.33	0.90	22.31[a]
Nasik	1955–56	1.78	-0.35	0.11	0.64	33.77[a]
Ahmednagar	1956–57	1.68	-0.32	0.08	0.79	5.17[c]
Nasik	1956–57	1.89	-0.41	0.07	0.85	10.49[b]
Madras	1954–55	1.89	-0.47	0.09	0.81	25.88[a]
	1955–56	2.14	-0.67	0.09	0.90	51.69[a]
U.P.	1955–56	0.33	-0.13	0.14	0.22	0.88
	1956–57	1.62	-0.12	0.03	0.86	19.24[b]
M.P.						
Akola	1956–57	1.20	-0.04	0.04	0.13	0.89
Amraoti	1956–57	1.06	-0.01	0.08	0.00	0.02

Note: [a] denotes significance at 1 per cent level
[b] denotes significance at 5 per cent level
[c] denotes significance at 10 per cent level

Source: Table F.1 [*Bharadwaj*, 1974a: 109].

TABLE 4d

TOTAL INPUTS PER ACRE RELATED TO THE SIZE OF HOLDING:
ALL CROP PRODUCTION, INDIAN FMS

State/district	Year	Constant term	α	Standard error	R^2	F
Punjab	1954–55	2.53	-0.35	0.24	0.40	2.03
	1955–56	2.43	-0.18	0.03	0.85	31.37[b]
	1956–57	2.57	-0.20	0.04	0.92	36.47[a]
West Bengal						
Hooghly	1954–55	2.49	-0.15	0.05	0.61	9.47[b]
24 Paraganas	1954–55	2.38	-0.32	0.04	0.90	56.99[a]
Hooghly	1955–56	2.26	-0.17	0.05	0.64	10.31[b]
24 Paraganas	1955–56	2.27	-0.18	0.05	0.60	9.54[b]
Hooghly	1956–57	2.49	-0.11	0.05	0.45	4.98[c]
24 Paraganas	1956–57	2.22	-0.01	0.04	0.02	0.11
Bombay						
Ahmednagar	1955–56	2.25	-0.36	0.14	0.52	6.46[b]
Nasik	1955–56	2.25	-0.36	0.09	0.72	15.69[a]
Ahmednagar	1956–57	2.34	-0.48	0.13	0.66	11.66[b]
Nasik	1956–57	2.49	-0.52	0.07	0.90	59.85[a]
Madras	1954–55	2.42	-0.41	0.12	0.66	11.48[b]
	1955–56	2.52	-0.50	0.04	0.96	134.81[a]
	1956–57	2.62	-0.49	0.06	0.90	61.29[a]
U.P.	1954–55	2.74	-0.41	0.04	0.98	102.61[a]
	1955–56	-1.24	1.21	0.25	0.88	23.62[a]
	1956–57	1.04	-0.05	0.02	0.72	7.93[b]
M.P.	1955–56	2.01	-0.07	0.02	0.59	8.66[b]
	1956–57	1.90	-0.08	0.03	0.58	8.08[b]

Note: [a] denotes significance at 1 per cent level
       [b] denotes significance at 5 per cent level
       [c] denotes significance at 10 per cent level

Source: Table F.IV [*Bharadwaj*, 1974a: 112].

TABLE 4e

PERCENTAGE AREA IRRIGATED RELATED TO SIZE OF HOLDING, INDIAN FMS

State/district	Year	Constant term	α	Standard error	R^2	F
Punjab						
Amritsar	1954-55	1.99	-0.05	0.04	0.28	1.21
Ferozepur	1954-55	2.02	-0.11	0.08	0.40	2.06
Amritsar	1955-56	2.01	-0.02	0.02	0.86	20.62[b]
Ferozepur	1955-56	1.85	-0.01	0.08	0.03	0.08
Amritsar	1956-57	1.93	-0.02	0.02	0.10	0.35
Ferozepur	1956-57	1.96	-0.08	0.07	0.13	0.44
West Bengal						
Hooghly	1954–55	-1.01	-0.09	0.93	0.00	0.00
24 Paraganas	1954–55	1.67	-0.67	0.12	0.83	32.45[a]
Hooghly	1955–56	1.08	-0.34	0.20	0.34	2.99
24 Paraganas	1955–56	-0.68	-0.40	1.04	0.02	0.15
Hooghly	1956–57	1.57	-0.85	0.16	0.81	27.83[a]
24 Paraganas	1956–57	0.04	-0.01	0.26	0.00	0.00
Bombay						
Ahmednagar	1955-56	2.03	-0.60	0.14	0.74	17.35[a]
Nasik	1955-56	1.31	-0.43	0.21	0.41	4.26[c]
Ahmednagar	1956-57	1.77	-0.42	0.13	0.62	9.72[b]
Nasik	1956-57	1.75	-0.57	0.10	0.83	27.54[a]
U.P.	1954-55	1.91	-0.08	0.03	0.62	9.52[b]
	1955-56	1.95	-0.09	0.04	0.50	6.26[b]
	1956-57	1.98	-0.06	0.01	0.81	25.77[a]
Madras	1955-56	1.65	-0.32	0.09	0.68	13.55[a]
	1956-57	1.87	-0.54	0.12	0.75	19.51[a]

Note: [a] denotes significance at 1 per cent level
[b] denotes significance at 1 per cent level
[c] denotes significance at 1 per cent level

Source: Table G.I [*Bharadwaj*, 1974a: 114].

TABLE 5a

TOPOGRAPHY AND MAJOR CROPS OF TWO DISTRICTS IN WEST BENGAL

region	land (% total area)			crops (% sown area)		
	high	medium	low	paddy	jute	potato
Hooghly	34.76	26.59	38.65	65.82	15.27	5.58
24 Paraganas	25.16	20.86	53.98	80.47	4.34	0.52

Note: The districts chosen are Hooghly and 24 Paraganas – both essentially wet areas. However, in a comparison between the two, since 24 Paraganas is on the whole in a lower lying area than Hooghly it is generally 'wetter' then Hooghly.

Source: Table 2.5 [*Roy,* 1979: 71].

TABLE 5b

TOPOGRAPHICAL CHARACTERISTICS AND CROPPING PATTERN
FOR SOME SELECTED VILLAGES IN WEST BENGAL

village	high	medium (acres)	low	paddy (acres)	jute pulses	potato
Baliadarga	50.34		14.09	37.91	3.39	
Bolsiddhi	43.46	217.28	173.83	366.44		
Bongaon	834.00	442.00	164.43	1100.00	25.00	350.00^{u}20.00^i
Khau			3092.60	2767.07		
Krishnagar			157.01	80.00	20.00	
Satbaria			1044.02	600.00		
U.Akhrabaua			284.07	224.07		
Srinagar	1301.03	144.60		1140.09	130.04	56.82^{u}28.70^i (41.00)

Note: u = unirrigateed i = irrigated

Source: Table 2.6 [*Roy,* 1979: 73].

TABLE 6
OUTPUT PER NET CROPPED ACRE AND FARM SIZE, PUNJAB

No.	Districts	a (t value)	b (t value)	F-value	n	R^2
1.	Patiala	1648.85 (10.7)	-32.418** (2.3368)	5.46	75	0.07
2.	Ferozepur	956.551 (16.44)	2.7415 (1.0513)	1.105	127	0.009
3.	Sangrur	1361.06 (15.78)	-22.8683*** (2.752)	7.572	72	0.1
4.	Bhatinda	1249.81 (11.98)	-6.9583 (1.1417)	1.303	101	0.013
5.	Jullunder	1695.15 (10.66)	-3.1751 (0.2031)	0.041	42	0.001
6.	Hoshiarpur	1555.67 (34.39)	-11.3808* (1.6828)	2.831	119	0.02
7.	Kapurthala	1605.6 (15.68)	-7.9832 (0.6303)	0.395	20	0.02
8.	Rupnagar	870.16 (14.92)	-13.8832** (2.241)	5.02	58	0.08
9.	Ludhiana	1797.53 (17.25)	-36.717*** (3.482)	12.121	75	0.14
10.	Gurdaspur	1734.53 (20.12)	-15.921 (1.483)	2.199	61	0.04
11.	Amritsar	1555.99 (26.95)	12.098** (2.1488)	4.617	70	0.06

*** = significant at the 1 per cent level
 ** = significant at the 5 per cent level
  * = significant at the 10 per cent level

Source: Table 5.1 [Roy, 1979: 156].

TABLE 7

OUTPUT PER GROSS CROPPED ACRE AND FARM SIZE, PUNJAB

No.	Districts	a (t value)	b (t value)	F-value	n	R^2
1.	Patiala	823.21 (10.80)	-10.3104 (1.5030)	2.259	75	0.03
2.	Ferozepur	552.99 (15.25)	+6.0306*** (3.7102)	13.766	127	0.01
3.	Sangrur	684.05 (15.37)	-3.7555 (0.4897)	0.767	72	0.01
4.	Bhatinda	706.78 (13.45)	+1.4086 (1.2727)	0.211	101	0.02
5.	Jullunder	830.48 (9.74)	+10.6658 (0.5382)	1.620	42	0.04
6.	Hoshiarpur	795.295 (34.80)	-1.8378 (0.5382)	0.289	119	0.002
7.	Kapurthala	736.297 (12.44)	+13.114* (1.793)	3.212	20	0.15
8.	Rupnagar	512.42 (19.35)	-4.2243 (1.5009)	2.253	58	0.04
9.	Ludhiana	908.309 (18.38)	-14.8715*** (2.9723)	8.834	75	0.01
10.	Gurdaspur	957.078 (22.88)	-6.2100 (1.19168)	1.420	61	0.02
11.	Amritsar	872.37 (35.57)	+6.5506*** (2.7831)	7.744	70	0.01

*** = significant at the 1 per cent level
 ** = significant at the 5 per cent level
  * = significant at the 10 per cent level

Source: Table 5.2 [Roy, 1979: 157].

TABLE 8

YIELD PER ACRE OF HYV WHEAT AND FARM SIZE, PUNJAB

No.	Districts	a (t value)	b (t value)	F-value	n	R^2
1.	Patiala	8.3968 (7.868)	-0.07417 (0.7796)	0.608	72	0.009
2.	Ferozepur	7.8759 (7.8511)	+0.04262 (1.021)	1.042	108	0.01
3.	Sangrur	9.8501 (22.21)	-0.071003* (1.6757)	2.808	69	0.04
4.	Bhatinda	10.309 (11.213)	-0.002954 (0.0615)	0.317	77	0.004
5.	Jullunder	11.0091 (23.51)	-0.002954 (0.0615)	0.003	42	0.0001
6.	Hoshiarpur	13.645 (30.387)	-0.18726*** (3.0167)	9.10	54	0.15
7.	Kapurthala	1.356 (0.1833)	+1.8265* (2.0428)	4.173	19	0.2
8.	Rupnagar	10.049 (22.64)	+0.00694 (0.1591)	0.024	49	0.0005
9.	Ludhiana	12.7106 (15.45)	-0.23052** (2.787)	7.769	74	0.1
10.	Gurdaspur	9.339 (17.88)	+0.01443 (0.0643)	0.049	57	0.0009
11.	Amritsar	8.4956 (17.87)	+0.0677 (1.44723)	2.167	70	0.03

*** = significant at the 1 per cent level
 ** = significant at the 5 per cent level
  * = significant at the 10 per cent level

Source: Table 5.2 [*Roy*, 1979: 157].

TABLE 9

YIELD PER ACRE OF HYV RICE AND FARM SIZE, PUNJAB

No.	Districts	a (t value)	b (t value)	F-value	n	R^2
1.	Patiala	12.238 (13.58)	0.01995	0.065	35	0.002
2.	Ferozepur	13.662 (9.377)	0.04648 (0.6156)	0.379	44	0.009
3.	Sangrur					
4.	Bhatinda	15.68 (5.135)	-0.2649 (1.792)	3.212	11	0.26
5.	Jullunder	27.7642 (4.4016)	-0.66396 (1.1523)	1.323	9	0.16
6.	Hoshiarpur					
7.	Kapurthala	12.0658 (6.384)	0.52021* (2.12724)	4.525	18	0.22
8.	Rupnagar					
9.	Ludhiana	19.771 (16.83)	-0.24693** (2.347)	5.508	33	0.15
10.	Gurdaspur	12.8018 (13.47)	0.07446 (0.6435)	0.414	55	0.008
11.	Amritsar	15.282 (30.55)	0.18316*** (3.865)	14.939	67	0.19

*** = significant at the 1 per cent level
 ** = significant at the 5 per cent level
  * = significant at the 10 per cent level

Source: Table 5.6 [*Roy,* 1979: 161].

TABLE 10

PERCENTAGE AREA IRRIGATED AND FARM SIZE, PUNJAB

No.	Districts	a (t value)	b (t value)	F-value	n	R^2
1.	Patiala	0.9818 (31.05)	-0.005235* (1.839)	3.383	75	0.04
2.	Ferozepur	0.89757 (33.21)	-0.00251** (2.0888)	4.362	125	0.03
3.	Sangrur	0.99464 (43.65)	-0.00339 (1.5541)	2.416	70	0.03
4.	Bhatinda	0.8682 (23.19)	-0.00202 (0.9540)	0.910	94	0.01
5.	Jullunder	0.97363 (48.34)	0.00041 (0.02071)	0.037	42	0.001
6.	Hoshiarpur	1.0277 (105.75)	-0.0123** (5.2852)	2.936	19	0.15
7.	Kapurthala	1.022 (17.22)	-0.00201 (1.7137)	0.383	50	0.008
8.	Rupnagar	0.9078 (27.796)	0.00201 (0.6188)	0.383	50	0.008
9.	Ludhiana all farms in the sample have 100 percent irrigation				75	
10.	Gurdaspur	1.0066 (176.21)	-0.00165** (2.3501)	5.606	59	0.09
11.	Amritsar	0.9899 (93.855)	0.000083 (0.08116)	0.014	70	0.0002

*** = significant at the 1 per cent level
 ** = significant at the 5 per cent level
  * = significant at the 10 per cent level

Source: Table 5.4 [Roy, 1979: 159].

TABLE 11

VARIOUS INDICES OF PROGRESS FOR DISTRICTS OF PUNJAB

No.	Districts	a	b	c	d	e
1.	Patiala	40.7	73.4	20.31	87.79	7.64
2.	Ferozepur	66.3	80.2	23.50	91.17	7.54
3.	Sangrur	51.3	71.6	20.42	86.27	6.91
4.	Bhatinda	55.2	53.6	23.07	89.57	7.03
5.	Jullunder	64.1	77.6	17.81	75.76	6.88
6.	Hoshiarpur	15.1	45.7	17.70	53.51	7.46
7.	Kapurthala	62.1	71.5	15.26	73.76	7.15
8.	Rupnagar	17.0	39.0	15.80	49.11	6.11
9.	Ludhiana	59.3	81.6	17.84	80.15	6.80
10.	Gurdaspur	43.5	68.6	19.02	71.07	8.65
11.	Amritsar	87.2	88.9	20.12	86.67	8.11

a = percentage area irrigated 1960–61
b = percentage area under HYVs and American cotton 1974–75
c = agricultural labour as percentage of male work force 1971
d = percentage area of crops with HYV under HYVs 1976–77
e = annual compound rates of growth 1962–65 to 1970–73

Source: Table 5.7 [Roy, 1979: 162].

TABLE 12

RICE BUDGETS AND INTERNAL RATES OF RETURN (LE 1982 PER FEDDAN),
EGYPT

output	unit	quantity		price		income/cost	
		small	large	small	large	small	large
grain	ton	2.56	2.33	130.17	128.45	333.25	299.31
straw	ton	2.63	2.59	9.84	9.22	25.89	23.87
total						359.14	323.18
inputs							
labour	phe[1]	359.14	277.86	0.32	0.32	114.92	88.92
seeds	qirat	2.14	2.2	23.64	21.08	50.59	46.36
fert	kg	79.63	72.19	0.27	0.26	21.5	18.77
machines						48.22	40.48
other[2]						32.63	35.24
total						263.93	231.42
invest							
land opportunity cost[3]						75.71	66.65
IRR					8.16%	11.69%	

(1) phe = person-hour equivalents per feddan: 1 adult male hour = 2 child-hours or 1.5 adult female-hours
(2) saqia and animal-powered irrigation, storage, haulage, interest and depreciation
(3) with government rent fixed at arbitrarily low levels, opportunity cost pricing was used. This is derived from foregone income in maize and cotton for the 5 months that land is planted to rice. The opportunity cost is assumed to be the mean value between government rent levels and parallel market rents, plus foregone production of alternative crops. The opportunity cost for rice land is (152.20+29.66+43.26)/3 = LE 75.71 for small farms; for large farms (23.29+43.26)/3 = LE 66.65.

Source: Shepley [*1985:* 24].

TABLE 13

WHEAT CROP BUDGETS AND INTERNAL RATES OF RETURN
(PER FEDDAN), EGYPT

output	unit	quantity		price		income/cost	
		small	large	small	large	small	large
grain	ardab	9.9	10.25	10.48	10.66	103.75	109.29
straw	ton	4.42	3.82	34.3	45.06	151.62	172.14
total						255.37	281.43
inputs							
labour	phe	165.92	198.09	0.31	0.31	51.44	61.41
seeds	kg	87.2	82.54	0.11	0.12	9.59	10.23
fert	kg	80.41	64.63	0.29	0.285	23.32	18.42
machjnes LE						31.8	35.34
other[1]	LE					10.41	15.80
total						126.56	141.20
investment							
land opportunity cost[2]						103.83	109.62
IRR						6.53%	7.52%

(1) saqia and animal-powered irrigation, storage, haulage, interest and depreciation

(2) with government rent fixed at arbitrariliy low levels, opportunity cost pricing was used. This is derived from foregone income in birseem for thesix months that land is planted to wheat. The opportunity cost is assumed to be the mean value between government rent levels and parallel market rents, plus foregone production of alternative crops. Thus shadow prices for small farms is (207.57+52.05+51.91)/3=LE 103.87. For large farms, the shadow price is (229.43+47.52+51.91)/3=LE 109.62.

Source: Table 7.2 [*Shepley,* 1985: 35].

TABLE 14

COTTON BUDGETS AND INTERNAL RATES OF RETURN
(LE 1982 PER FEDDAN), EGYPT

output	unit	quantity		price		income/cost	
		small	large	small	large	small	large
cotton	qantar	8.39	8.07	59.75	59.48	501.43	480.01
stalks						22.56	15.00
total						523.99	495.01
inputs							
labour	phe	689.76	643.36	0.27	0.27	186.24	173.71
seeds	kg	93.17	125.82	0.04	0.04	3.72	5.03
fert	kg	152.06	198.9	0.35	0.40	53.22	79.56
machines	LE					24.08	23.50
micro nutrients						16.40	17.15
pesticides						21.10	12.01
other[1]	LE					24.53	18.09
total						329.29	329.05
invest							
land opportunity cost[2]						174.	174.
IRR						2.51%	-1.03%

(1) haulage, interest/depreciation, saqia irrigation

(2) LE 7.25 per qirat (weighted mean marginal value product of land in birseem and wheat) x 24 = LE 174 per feddan.

Source: Table 9.4 [*Shepley*, 1985: 76].

TABLE 15

ALL EGYPT REGRESSION MATRIX

dep	a	b	t	n	R^2
y1	1.00	−0.068	−3.041***	425	.0214
y2	0.63	0.036	1.417	425	.0047
y3	0.37	−0.104	−7.377***	425	.1140
y4	1.15	−0.256	−7.062***	415	.1078
y5	0.77	−0.146	−4.097***	415	.0392
y6	0.96	−0.050	−2.233**	425	.0116
y7	0.59	0.054	2.203***	425	.0113

Source: Computed from ILO data.

x = independent variable farm size or operated area, calculated as land owned + land rented in land leased out, and measured in qirats.

y1 = output per net cropped area. Net cropped area is taken as equal to farm size as fallow is negligible in land-scarce Egyptian agriculture. Output is measured in value terms and is the simple unweighted sum of the output values[1] of individual crops.

y2 = output per gross cropped area. Gross cropped area is computed by the simple addition of the areas planted under the crops listed above. Output is as above.

y3 = cropping intensity as the ratio of gross cropped area to net cropped area.

y4 = a second version of output per net cropped area computed by Radwan for his regression. This uses net farm output in the numerator, calculated as the (total value of crop sales + imputed value of own consumption) minus total production costs, including the value of own-produced inputs but excluding the imputed value of family labour.

y5 = a second version of output per gross cropped area based on net farm output as above.

y6 = a third version of output per net cropped area based on Radwan's calculations of total crop value. The latter for the most part agree with my own calculations of total crop value, but there are some discrepancies which may bias the results in favour of the inverse relation hypothesis. In some cases, the total crop values for large farms have been underestimated while for some small farms, total crop values appear to have been adjusted upwards.

y7 = a third version of output per gross cropped area based on Radwan's calculations of total crop value.

(1) Unit farmgate prices were recorded in the original survey. I ran supplementary regressions of producer prices for the major crops against farm size. The results revealed no significant variation in prices across farm size. Indeed the coefficients were weakly negative.

TABLE 16

LABOUR UTILISATION PER HECTARE CULTIVATED, BY CROP PATTERN
AND HOLDING SIZE, EGYPT

crops	<0.8	0.8–2	2–4	>4
CWM[a]	6615	4246	2754	1965
WM[b]	8184	5298	2373	
cotton[c]	7175	4234	2545	1837
rice[d]	7652	3603	2105	1388
veg[d]	9046	4845	2437	
sugar[d]	8029	4410	5608	1960

Notes: a   Cotton-wheat-maize: 15 to 25% cotton
         b   wheat-maize: over 25% wheat, less than 15% cotton
         c   rice and vegetables: over 25%
         d   sugarcane: over 25%

Source: Wilson [1972: 9 tab 5].

TABLE 17

YIELDS BY FARM SIZE, EGYPT, 1983

crop	lt1	1-3	3-5	-10	ge10	all
wheat	1069	1332	1274	1115	898	1215
ssbirs	32	31	32	24	24	29
maize	2303	1568	1213	1209	1350	1439
rice	2320	2670	2623	2855	1914	2541
cotton	796	883	934	765	779	854
lsbirs	91	82	91	72	65	85
potato	0	6035	6009	0	0	6026
onion	5171	5750	7000	2000	5454	4949
tomato	0	6973	2271	2350	4118	4292
fruits	0	860	2927	970	7211	4030

Source: Crouch *et al.* [1983: 20].

TABLE 18

INCOME NET OF CASH COSTS PER FEDDAN, EGYPT

crop	<1	1–3	3–5	5–10	>10	all
wheat	-40.74	53.49	49.33	40.2	39.06	46.19
ssbirs	46.52	37.26	21.53	22.06	21.35	29.88
maize	56.66	60.57	50.04	49.51	30.55	53.73
rice	97.56	110.11	110.76	98.67	.61	99.65
cotton	120.13	121.44	137.57	108.36	122.83	122.34
lsbirs	107.42	123.44	164.12	96.5	.84	120.53
potato	.0	166.82	137.61	.0	.0	157.09
onion	89	114.54	5.82	-49.72	68.36	49.79
tomato	.0	365.27	62.79	72.1	244.81	212.58
fruits	.0	128	45.1	62.08	470.46	205.36

Source: Crouch *et al.* [1983: 21].

TABLE 19

REGRESSION OF YIELDS ON FARM SIZE AND REGIONAL DUMMY, EGYPT

var	constant	dummy	t	size	t
corn1	1294.	349.	3.6	-15.7	-2.45
corn2	94.6	-2.8	-0.51	-0.9	-2.45
cotton1	772.6	249.	4.5	-7.8	-2.42
cotton2	169.2	64.8	5.03	-1.2	-1.57
rice1	2575.	299.9	1.48	-30.6	-2.57
ric2	142.2	32.5	2.84	-2.1	-3.12
wheat1	1394.8	-149.6	-1.71	-13.9	-2.66
wheat2	94.1	0.16	0.03	-0.83	-2.4
all	110.9	29.8	4.33	-0.42	-1.

crop 1 = physical yields primary only
crop 2 = cash yields primary and secondary

Source: Crouch *et al.* [1983: 22].

TABLE 20

REGRESSIONS OF YIELDS ON FARM SIZE AND REGIONAL DUMMIES, EGYPT

corn1	coef	t	corn2	coef	t
int	1675	17.3		82	14.5
z2	-491	-3.4		-5.3	-0.6
z3	102	0.9		19.4	2.8
z4	-462	-3.3		4.8	0.6
z8	-277	-2.1		22	2.8
z9	-380	-1.9		6.5	0.6
size	-12	-2		-0.7	-1.9
r^2	0.28				0.22

cotton1	coef	t	cotton2	coef	t
int	981	15.8		217	13.6
z2	-271	-2.7		-72.8	-2.8
z3	170	2.2		49.4	2.5
z4	149	1.7		14.8	0.6
z8	-292	-3.9		-63.6	-3.3
z9	-374	-4.6		-62.3	-3
size	-3	-0.9		0	0
r^2	0.43	0.34			

rice1	coef	t	rice2	coef	t
int	3555	14.2		246.9	19.3
z2	-1668	-4.5		-134.1	-7
z3	-482	-1.5		-74.8	-4.5
z4	-703	-1.9		-99.3	-5.1
z8	-969	-3.2		-105.2	-6.7
z9	-1636	-4.8		-136.8	-7.9
size	-17	-1.6		-1.3	-2.3
r^2	0.22	0.4			

wheat1	coef	t	wheat2	coef	t
int	1285	14.2		91.4	15.1
z2	-452	-3.1		-27.9	-2.8
z3	52	0.5		19.7	2.4
z4	477	3.4		11.7	1.3
z8	-40	-0.3		-3.8	-0.4
z9	-17	-1.4		-11.5	-1.4
size	-8	-1.7		-0.4	-1.2
r^2	0.29	0.25			

all	coef	t
int	153.6	20.1
z2	-46.8	-3.7
z3	-20.4	-2
z4	-38.4	-3
z8	-45.7	-4.9
z9	-70.5	-6.8
size	-0.1	-0.3
r^2	0.23	

Note: crop 1 = physical yields and crop 2 = value yields
Source: Crouch *et al.* [1983: 25–32].

TABLE 21

REGRESSIONS OF CROP YIELDS ON SELECTED INDICATORS, EGYPT

corn	coef	tvalue	rice	coef	tvalue
int	1212.5	5.5	int	1795.6	3.9
size	8.1	0.9	size	-10.5	-0.6
N	2.3	2.3	N	4.3	1.7
N^2	-1.7	-1.6	N^2	-3.9	-1.3
labour	3.0	0.7	labour	3.0	0.6
SC	-19.3	-0.1	SC	261.1	0.8
cash	-206.3	-1.9	cash	465.6	1.9
NR	-236.3	-2.2	NR	-0.2	0.0
HL/TL	-481.4	-2.2	HL/TL	-184.1	-0.4
r^2	0.23		r^2	0.12	

cotton	coef	tvalue	wheat	coef	tvalue
int	606.4	5.1	int	948.2	4.4
size	-9.4	-2.1	size	-7.9	-1
N	0.7	1.6	N	0.7	0.8
N^2	-0.3	-0.7	N^2	-0.4	-0.5
labour	0.5	1.2	labour	-4.3	-1.1
SC	144.9	1.7	SC	3.2	0
cash	226.4	3.5	cash	186.8	1.9
NR	-136.6	-2.1	NR	192.2	1.9
HL/TL	171.4	1.5	HL/TL	219.6	1.2
r^2	0.22		r^2	0.16	

all	coef	tvalue
int	119.1	7.7
size	-0.2	-0.3
N	0	-0.1
N^2	-0.1	-0.2
labour	1	21
SC	3.2	0.3
cash	2.5	0.3
NR	-2.8	-0.3
HL/TL	-31.8	-1.8
r^2	0.04	

Note: int   = intercept term
       size   = farm size
       N and N^2 = nitrogen fertiliser application
       SC   = sharecropping
       cash   = cash rental system
       NR   = land reform lands
       HL/TL   = proportion of hired labour to total

Source: Crouch et al. [1983: 28–29].

TABLE 22

CROP YIELDS PER FEDDAN, 1984 BY FARM SIZE, EGYPT

size feddan	wheat ardab	cotton qantar	rice ardab	maize ardab
0–1	8.97	7.83	18.86	13.37
1–3	7.97	8.27	21.87	12.83
3–5	7.95	8.90	21.07	12.54
5–10	8.20	8.80	22.67	12.81
>10	6.05	9.50	28.33	13.88
all	8.25	8.21	20.87	12.99

Source: Commander [1987: 174].

TABLE 23

CURRENT POPULATION OF TRACTORS AND AGRICULTURAL EQUIPMENT
PER 1000 FEDDANS OF CROP AREA, BY GOVERNORATE: 1982–83, EGYPT

governorate	tractors	ploughs	sprayers	threshers	trailers (hp)	irrig
Alexandria	6.3	1.3	0.8	0.2	0.4	73.6
Buheira	7.1	5.6	0.2	1.0	1.1	133.3
Gharbiya	9.4	11.2	4.4	2.1	6.4	114.3
Kafr al-Sheikh	5.9	6.4	3.4	1.1	1.1	115.3
Daqhaliya	8.3	10.7	4.5	1.2	4.8	191.2
Dumyat	8.3	5.5	2.9	0.4	1.9	393.1
Sharqiya	6.8	7.0	3.2	1.2	4.8	73.7
Ismailia	9.7	8.9	1.4	0.7	6.5	180.3
Suez	12.7	11.8	1.5	1.5	3.7	379.1
Bur Said						
Menufiya	6.3	5.9	1.7	2.3	1.7	139.8
Qalubia	7.3	8.6	2.7	2.3	6.0	127.4
Cairo	4.4	3.9	0.4		1.4	139.8
Giza	7.7	1.6	0.6	1.5	0.7	129.9
Beni Suef	4.5	1.2	0.4	0.5	0.1	104.6
Fayyum	7.0	5.0	1.1	0.1	2.3	13.5
Minya	6.8	4.2	3.8	1.7	2.1	162.5
Assyut	7.7	10.8	0.2	2.3	9.3	309.5
Sohag	7.7	6.8	0.9	3.1	4.1	266.6
Qena	10.6	7.6	0.4	3.1	4.3	610.0
Aswan	4.3	2.0	0.1	0.1	0.5	30.6
Matruh						
New Valley	6.2	1.0		0.4		139.1
N. Sinai						
average	7.3	6.8	2.4	1.5	3.4	163.9

Source: Table 9A [*Commander*, 1987: 295].

TABLE 24

MEAN VALUE OF MATERIAL INPUTS PER FEDDAN: BY CROP, EGYPT 1984

crop	0-1	1–3	3–5	5–10	>10
wheat	16.60	18.00	14.90	17.60	20.00
sh birs	19.20	17.60	17.10	16.70	25.00
lng birs	18.00	15.80	18.60	15.30	22.30
cotton	24.00	23.40	25.10	22.80	27.00
rice	18.90	21.00	21.00	23.20	21.80
maize	20.20	23.50	20.30	20.30	21.50

Source: Commander [1987: 292].

TABLE 25

DEVELOPMENTS IN LANDOWNERSHIP IN EGYPT, 1952–65

(in thousands)

size class	before 1952 reform				after 1952 reform			
	holdings		area		holdings		area	
(feddans)	no.	%	no.	%	no.	%	no.	%
small								
< 5	2642	94.3	2122	35.4	2841	94.4	2781	46.6
medium								
5–10	79	2.8	526	8.8	79	2.6	526	8.8
10–20	47	1.7	638	10.7	47	1.6	638	10.7
20–50	22	0.8	654	10.9	30	1	818	13.6
large								
50–100	6	0.2	430	7.2	6	0.2	430	7.2
100–200	3	0.1	437	7.3	3	0.1	437	7.2
> 200	2	0.1	1177	19.7	2	0.1	354	5.9
total	2801	100.0	5984	100	3008	100	5984	100

size class	situation in 1961[1]				situation in 1965[2]			
	holdings		area		holdings		area	
(feddans)	no.	%	no.	%	no.	%	no.	%
small								
< 5	2919	94.1	3172	52.1	3033	94.5	3693	57.1
medium								
5–10	80	2.6	526	8.6	78	2.4	614	9.5
10–20	65	2.1	638	10.7	61[3]	1.9	527	8.2
20–50	26	0.8	818	13.4	29	0.9	815	12.6
large								
50–100	6	0.2	430	7	6	0.2	392	6.1
100–200	5	0.5	500	8.2	4	0.1	421	6.5
> 200	–	–	–	–	–	–	–	–
total	3101	100.0	6084	100	100	6462	6462[4]	100

Notes: (1) after the promulgation of Law No.127, June 1961.

(2) excluding government properties.

(3) there is some doubt as to the accuracy of this figure since the average size of ownership in this bracket works out at 8.6 which is clearly inconsistent with the size class of 10 to 20 feddans. The same situation applies to 1961.

(4) the increase in the area of cultivated land between 1961 and 1965 is mainly due to large-scale land reclamation schemes.

Source: Table 1.6 [Abdel-Fadil, 1975: 11].

TABLE 26

SUMMARY OF CHANGES IN EGYPTIAN LANDOWNERSHIP, 1952–65

(in thousands)

size class (feddans)	no. of holdings			area owned				
	1952[1]	1965	change	1952[1]	1965	change	(a)	(b)
small < 5	2642	3033	391	2122	3693 (3353)	1571 (1231)	671[4]	218[5]
medium 5–10	79	78	-1	526	614	88	–	88
10–20	47	41[2]	14	638	527[3]	-111	–	-111
20–50	22	29	7	654	815	161	–	161
large 50–100	6	6	0	430	392	-38	–	-38
100–200	3	4	1	437	421	-16	–	-16
> 200	2	–	-2	1177	–	-1177	-875[6]	-302
total	2801	3191	390	5984 (6326)	6462 (342)	478	-2047[7]	–

(a) = transfers of land as a result of the land reform programme
(b) = private sales and other transactions

Notes: (1) situation before the implementation of the agrarian reform law No.178, 1952.

(2) adjusted figure (see note to Table #).

(3) these are doubtful figures. In the absence of firm evidence, Abdel-Fadil assumes that the decrease in this size class was counter-balanced by sales from public organisations to small farmers.

(4) this represents the cumulative distribution of land reform land up to 1965.

(5) including 110,000 feddans sold by other public organisations to small-holders.

(6) this represents the total area requisitioned from 1952 to the end of 1966.

(7) this represents the surplus of requisitioned area over the actually distributed land.

(8) the number in parentheses under the official figures in the less than five feddan size class are Abdel-Fadil's estimates of the effective increase in the total area of small-holdings derived by referring to the annual agricultural survey published by the Ministry of Agriculture in 1961–64. The official figures for this class reflect scheduled rather than effective transfers.

Source: Table 1.15 [*Abdel-Fadil, 1975: 24*].

TABLE 27

TOTAL POPULATION AND HOUSEHOLDS IN ILO SAMPLE GOVERNORATES

governorate	rural population	share of rural population in sample %	number of households in the sample*
Dumyat	0.32	5.6	56
Gharbiya	1.30	22.6	226
Menufiya	1.22	21.2	213
Giza	1.00	17.4	174
Beni Suef	0.72	12.5	125
Qena	1.19	20.7	206
Total	5.75	100.0	1000

* The number of households with valid answers varies since 132 questionnaires were discarded and another two were not usable for some entries.

Source: Table A2.1 [*Radwan*, 1986: 21].

TABLE 28

NUMBER OF VILLAGES IN THE ILO SAMPLE BY SIZE

governorate	large	small	total
Dumyat	0	1	1
Gharbiya	1	3	4
Menufiya	1	3	4
Giza	1	1	2
Beni Suef	1	3	4
Qena	2	1	3
Total	6	12	18

Source: Table A2.2 [*Radwan*, 1986: 22].

TABLE 29
DISTRIBUTION OF THE ILO HOUSEHOLD SAMPLE BY
GOVERNORATE AND VILLAGE

governorate and village	markaz (district)	population (1976)	total households	households selected
Dumyat				
Meet al-Shiukh	Farskour	2,794	560	56
Gharbiya				
Shubra Blula				
al-Sakhawia	Kutour	5,378	1,045	89
Atf Abu Gindi	"	1,429	321	24
Kamalia	Mahalla	2 460	386	36
Al-Shaheedi	al-Kubra	4,644	178	77
Menufiya				
Tilwana	Al-Bagour	6,121	1,285	111
Manshat Masjid				
al-Khidr	"	1,112	220	18
Kafr Mansur	Ashmoun	3,285	631	46
Manshat Abu Zikri	Quesna	4,047	697	36
Giza				
Shubak al-Sharki	Al-Saff	13,176	2,236	151
Salehia	"	1,793	386	23
Beni Suef				
Al-Maimoun	Al-Wasta	9,321	2,080	62
Telt	Al-Fashn	5 141	1,063	33
Beni Ghoneim	Al-Wasta	1,722	375	11
Kafr Mansur	Beba	3,062	671	19
Qena				
Tafnis	Esna	6,921	1,219	44
Higaza	Qus	17,959	3,327	129
Al-Amiria	Abu Tesht	5,021	1,124	33

Source: Radwan [1986: 18, Table 2.4].

TABLE 30

ALL EGYPT REGRESSION MATRIX

dep	a	b	t	n	R^2
y1	1.00	-0.068	-3.041***	425	.0214
y2	0.63	0.036	1.417	425	.0047
y3	0.37	-0.104	-7.377***	425	.1140
y4	1.15	-0.256	-7.062***	415	.1078
y5	0.77	-0.146	-4.097***	415	.0392
y6	0.96	-0.050	-2.233**	425	.0116
y7	0.59	0.054	2.203***	425	.0113
y8	0.50	-0.062	-2.254**	218	.0290
y9	0.85	-0.118	-3.352***	348	.0315
y10	1.14	-0.153	-2.235**	104	.0467
y11	0.41	-0.041	-1.763*	220	.0141
y12	0.67	0.019	0.727	100	.0054

Source: computed from ILO data.

x=   independent variable farm size or operated area, calculated as land owned + land rented in - land leased out, and measured in qirats.

y1=   output per net cropped area. Net cropped area is taken as equal to farm size as fallow is negligible in land-scarce Egyptian agriculture. Output is measured in value terms and is the simple unweighted sum of the output values[1] of individual crops.

y2=   output per gross cropped area. Gross cropped area is computed by the simple addition of the areas planted under the crops listed above. Output is as above.

y3=   cropping intensity as the ratio of gross cropped area to net cropped area.

y4=   a second version of output per net cropped area computed by Radwan for his regression. This uses net farm output in the numerator, calculated as the (total value of crop sales + imputed value of own consumption) minus total production costs, including the value of own-produced inputs but excluding the imputed value of family labour.

y5=   a second version of output per gross cropped area based on net farm output as above.

y6=   a third version of output per net cropped area based on Radwan's calculations of total crop value. The latter for the most part agree with my own calculations of total crop value, but there are some discrepancies which may bias the results in favour of the inverse relation hypothesis. In some cases, the total crop values for large farms have been underestimated while for some small farms, total crop values appear to have been adjusted upwards.

y7=   a third version of output per gross cropped area based on Radwan's calculations of total crop value.

y8=   winter wheat yields in value terms. The data did include physical measures of output for the different crops, but were measured in different physical units for different households. Some by weight and others by dry measure. Producer prices do not vary significantly over farm size.

y9=   winter birseem yields in value terms.

y10= summer cotton yields in value terms.

y11= summer maize yields in value terms.

y12= summer rice yields in value terms.

(1) Unit farmgate prices were recorded in the original survey. I ran supplementary regressions of producer prices for the major crops against farm size. The results revealed no significant variation in prices across farm size. Indeed the coefficients were weakly negative.

TABLE 31

REGRESSION RESULTS ON ILO DATA DISAGGREGATED BY GOVERNORATE

(i) output per net cropped area (y1) and farm size

governorate	a	b	t	n	R^2
Gharbia	0.88	-0.018	-0.589	125	.0028
Damietta	1.05	-0.047	-1.08	415	.0828
Menufia	1.06	-0.163	-2.865***	71	.1063
Qena	0.82	0.062	1.328	78	.0227
Beni Suef	0.99	-0.128	-1.442	74	.1067
Giza	1.20	-0.099	-2.933***	74	.1067

*** significant at the 1% level   ** 5% level   * 10% level

(ii) output per gross cropped area (y2) and farm size

governorate	a	b	t	n	R^2
Gharbia	0.56	0.037	1.288	125	.0133
Damietta	0.75	-0.047	-1.084	15	.0828
Menufia	0.54	0.014	0.281	71	.0012
Qena	0.58	0.163	3.087***	78	.1114
Beni Suef	0.65	-0.065	-0.682	62	.0077
Giza	0.89	-0.040	-1.082	74	.0160

(iii) cropping intensity (y3) and farm size

governorate	a	b	t	n	R^2
Gharbia	0.32	-0.055	-2.788***	125	.0594
Damietta					
Menufia	0.52	-0.176	-4.661***	71	.2395
Qena	0.23	-0.101	-3.251***	78	.1221
Beni Suef	0.35	-0.063	-1.986**	62	.0617
Giza	0.31	-0.059	-2.271**	74	.0668

(iv) net farm output per net cropped area (y4) and farm size

governorate	a	b	t	n	R^2
Gharbia	1.04	-0.218	-3.706***	122	.1027
Damietta	1.41	-0.291	-3.654***	15	.5067
Menufia	1.34	-0.340	-4.142***	71	.1991
Qena	0.71	-0.042	-0.482	75	.0032
Beni Suef	0.86	-0.170	-1.648	61	.0440
Giza	1.30	-0.204	-2.286**	71	.0704

(v) net farm output per gross cropped area (y5) and farm size

governorate	a	b	t	n	R^2
Gharbia	0.71	-0.163	-3.140***	122	.0759
Damietta	1.11	-0.291	-3.650***	15	.5067
Menufia	0.84	-0.174	-2.050**	70	.0583
Qena	0.46	0.064	0.751	75	.0077
Beni Suef	0.51	-0.109	-1.048	61	.0187
Giza	0.98	-0.136	-1.525	71	.0326

TABLE 31 (cont.)

(vi) output per net cropped area (y6) and farm size

governorate	a	b	t	n	R^2
Gharbia	0.90	-0.034	-1.207	125	.0117
Damietta	1.06	-0.054	-1.203	15	.1002
Menufia	0.90	-0.078	-1.041	71	.0155
Qena	0.81	0.062	1.293	78	.0215
Beni Suef	0.88	-0.068	-1.404	62	.0318
Giza	1.21	-0.106	-2.851***	74	.1014

(vii) output per gross cropped area (y7) and farm size

governorate	a	b	t	n	R^2
Gharbia	0.58	0.021	0.798	125	.0052
Damietta	0.76	-0.054	-1.203	15	.1002
Menufia	0.39	0.098	1.486	71	.0310
Qena	0.58	0.163	3.010***	78	.1065
Beni Suef	0.53	0.005	-0.099	62	.0002
Giza	0.90	-0.046	-1.170	74	.0186

(viii) winter wheat yields (y8) and farm size

governorate	a	b	t	n	R^2
Gharbia	0.37	0.016	0.446	82	.0025
Damietta	0.56	-0.205	-1.566	13	.1824
Menufia	0.59	-0.072	-1.637	58	.0457
Qena	0.21	0.107	1.996*	31	.1208
Beni Suef	0.34	-0.034	-0.696	29	.0176
Giza	0.91	-0.357	-2.506*	5	.6768

(ix) birseem yields (y9) and farm size

governorate	a	b	t	n	R^2
Gharbia	0.38	0.028	0.516	113	.0024
Damietta	0.87	-0.134	-2.179**	15	.2675
Menufia	0.76	-0.105	-2.395**	61	.0886
Qena	0.89	-0.012	-0.193	42	.0009
Beni Suef	0.92	-0.148	-1.547	48	.0494
Giza	1.03	-0.042	-1.794*	69	.0458

(x) cotton yields (y10) and farm size

governorate	a	b	t	n	R^2
Gharbia	0.98	-0.585	-1.266	78	.0206
Damietta					
Menufia	4.86	3.22		2	1.000
Qena					
Beni Suef	1.69	-0.493	-1.868*	24	.1369
Giza					

TABLE 31 (cont.)

(xi) maize yields (y11) and farm size

governorate	a	b	t	n	R^2
Gharbia	0.40	-0.031	-0.775	70	.0088
Damietta					
Menufia	0.36	-0.004	-0.069	40	.0001
Qena	0.24	0.052	0.650	18	.0257
Beni Suef	0.20	-0.002	-0.037	32	.0000
Giza	0.48	-0.030	-0.846	60	.0122

(xii) rice yields (y12) and farm size

governorate	a	b	t	n	R^2
Gharbia	0.66	0.014	0.584	43	.0042
Damietta	0.71	0.060	1.075	10	.0816
Menufia	0.76	0.017	0.407	36	.0048
Qena	0.68	0.074	1.001	10	.1112
Beni Suef					
Giza					

TABLE 32a

AVERAGE LEVELS OF PURCHASED INPUT USE BY GOVERNORATE

governorate	C1	C2	C3	C4
Gharbiya	0.1663	0.0880	0.2056	0.1116
Damietta	0.0778	0.0935	0.0952	0.1178
Menufiya	0.2557	0.2111	0.3081	0.2677
Qena	0.2653	0.6955	0.2896	0.8065
Beni Suwayf	0.1465	0.2608	0.1603	0.2916
Giza	0.1926	0.1411	0.2128	0.1601
ALL	0.1980	0.2548	0.2291	0.3001

C1 = ratio of total outlays on fertilizer, pesticides, seeds and fodder total crop value
C2 = ratio of total outlays on fertilizer, pesticides, seeds and folder to net farm output
C3 = ratio of total cost of purchased inputs to total crop value
C4 = ratio of total cost of purchased inputs to net farm output

Source: computed from ILO data.

TABLE 32b

RATIOS OF PURCHASED INPUTS TO OWN PRODUCED INPUTS
BY GOVERNORATE

governorate	fertilizer	fodder	seeds
Gharbiya	3.7423	0.1480	2.5187
Damietta	0.8161	0.0048	2.7900
Menufiya	1.6423	0.1563	1.1011
Qena	8.0911	0.5318	2.5974
Beni Suwayf	4.6338	0.0366	1.6135
Giza	3.1957	0.1650	7.7747
ALL	3.9049	0.1948	3.3954

Source:computed from ILO data.

TABLE 32c

AVERAGE LEVELS OF MECHANISATION BY GOVERNORATE

governorate	M1	M2	M3	M4
Gharbiya	0.4088	0.1872	0.0071	0.0024
Damietta	0.0000	0.0000	0.0000	0.0000
Menufiya	0.0140	0.0099	0.0055	0.0025
Qena	0.0744	0.0762	0.0044	0.0016
Beni Suwayf	0.0000	0.0000	0.0000	0.0000
Giza	0.1010	0.0127	0.0026	0.0010
ALL	0.1724	0.0442	0.0043	0.0016

M1 = ratio of value of farm machinery and transport equipment to total crop value
M2 = ratio of value of farm machinery and transport equipment to net farm output
M3 = ratio of machinery fuel cost to total cost of purchased inputs
M4 = ratio of machinery running costs to total value of inputs

Source: computed from ILO data

TABLE 32d

POPULATION OF TRACTORS AND OTHER AGRICULTURAL EQUIPMENT
PER 1,000 FEDDANS OF CROPPED AREA BY GOVERNORATE 1981–82

governorate	(1)	(2)	(3)	(4)	(5)	(6)
Gharbiya	9.4	11.2	4.4	2.1	6.4	114.3 hp
Damietta	8.3	5.5	2.9	0.4	1.9	393.1
Menufiya	6.3	5.9	1.7	2.3	1.7	139.8
Qena	10.6	7.6	0.4	3.1	4.3	610.0
Beni Suwayf	4.5	1.2	0.4	0.5	0.1	104.6
Giza	7.7	1.6	0.6	1.5	0.7	129.9

(1) tractors
(2) ploughs
(3) pesticide sprayers
(4) threshers
(5) trailers
(6) mechanical power for irrigation

Source: Commander [1987: 295].

TABLE 33

DISAGGREGATED ILO DATA: BY VILLAGE

	a	b	c	d	e	f
Gharbiya						
Shubra Blula	11	89	57	-1.2	-0.24	-1.67
Atf Abu Gindi	12	22	9	-1.69	0.18	-2.96
Kamliya		13	36	26	2.08	1.18
0.41						
Al-Shahidi	14	77	33	-0.88	0.72	-3.08
Dumyat						
Mit Shuyukh	21	55	15	-1.2	-1.2	0
Menufiya						
Tilwana	31	110	36	-1.09	0.19	-1.76
Manshat	32	18	11	-0.65	0.45	-1.48
Masjid al-Khadr						
Kafr Mansur	33	46	24	-0.12	0.96	-3.2
Manshat Abu Zikri	34	38	1	0	0	0
Qena						
Tafnis	41	44	24	0.5	1.62	-1.92
Higaza	42	129	38	0.09	1.44	-2.16
Al-Amiriya	43	33	16	1.39	0.84	0.73
Beni Suef						
Al-Ma'mun	51	62	33	-0.95	0.27	-1.99
Beni Ghoneim	52	11	1	0	0	0
Telt	53	33	20	-0.48	0.25	-0.4
Kafr Mansur	54	19	9	-0.18	-0.44	0.94
Giza						
Shubak al-Sharqi	61	151	68	-2.58	-1.02	-1.92
Salehia	62	22	6	-0.93	-0.93	0

a = village code
b = sample size
c = sample households with operated area
d = t value (regression with net cropped area)
e = t value (regression with gross cropped area)
f = t value (regression with cropping intensity).

TABLE 34

LAND DISTRIBUTION BY HOLDING SIZE: SHUBAK AL-SHARQI

class	farms	%	owned	%	rented	%
lt 1	263	36.99	216	82	47	18
1–3	395	55.55	287	73	108	27
3–5	44	6.19	36	82	8	18
5–10	8	1.12	4	50	4	50
gt 10	1	0.14	1	100	0	0
total	711	100.00	544	167		

class	land (feddans)	%	owned	%	rented	%
lt 1	172.625	14.56	146.333	85	26.292	15
1–3	744.167	62.79	551.167	74	193.000	26
3–5	188.667	15.92	152.792	81	39.875	19
5-10	64.792	5.47	32.042	49	32.750	51
gt 10	15	1.27	15	100	0	0
total	1185.25	100.00	897.334		291.917	

Source: village co-operative, mushrif zira'i.

TABLE 35

DISTRIBUTION OF FARMS AND LAND BY FARM SIZE IN GIZA
GOVERNORATE, 1981

size	farms	%	area	%
<1	41497	43.46	21041	12.55
1–3	41947	43.93	67416	40.20
3–5	7220	7.56	25390	15.14
5–10	3234	3.39	20829	12.42
>10	1592	1.67	33008	19.68
total	95490	100	167684	100

Source: Table 1a [*Ministry of Agriculture (Giza)*, 1985: 4].

TABLE 36

REGRESSION RESULTS 1990 FIELDWORK

dependent		constant	coeffiicient	r2	n	t	sig.
R1	NY	1745.3	-95.86	0.0605	62	-1.97	0.0539
R2	GY	609.52	13.68	0.0093	62	0.751	0.4558
R3	PY	107.	-5.8	0.01306	40	-0.71	0.4822
R4	PY	8.5	0.3	0.002	58	0.395	0.6944
R5	PY	64.	15.7	0.045	10	0.617	0.5547
R6	PY	8.7	-0.6	0.071	43	-1.78	0.0831
R7	CROPINT	2.89	-0.2199	0.2711	62	-4.724	0.0000
R8	VALACRE	13591.	922.	0.0309	62	1.275	0.2080
R9	LABINT	400.	-65.78	0.2285	62	-4.216	0.0001
R10	NY	1162.74	16.163	0.1069	68	2.812	0.0065
R11	GY	603.15	13.3	0.865	68	20.6	0.0000
R12	PY	7.4	-0.006	0.0000	57	-0.021	0.9834
R13	PY	36.9	0.3	0.076	49	1.967	0.0551

*R refers to the regression equations discussed in the text.

The independent variable is farm size in feddans unless otherwise stated.

NFQ	=	net farm output=total farm output-input costs
GY	=	value of output per gross cropped feddan
NY	=	value of output per net sown feddan
PY	=	physical yield per feddan (see text for unit of measurement)
CROPINT	=	cropping intensity (gross cropped area/net sown area)
VALACRE	=	land value per feddan
LABINT	=	standardised man-days per feddan per year

TABLE 37

SIZE-CLASS AVERAGES FOR SHUBAK AL-SHARQI, GIZA

farm size	nca	nyield	gyield	cropint	labint	valacre
<1	0.61	1522.86	556.66	2.72	369.41	12793
1–3	1.76	1853.16	72.73	2.44	259.27	16454
3–5	3.45	1419.25	607.84	2.36	165.03	14366
5–10	6.13	921.83	561.08	1.59	115.90	20955
>10	10.00	2566.00	938.76	2.73	90.00	0000

	@hyv	fragment	hhnr0	pcq	pcy
<1	0.23	1.47 (2.41)	8.60	131.61	275.15
1–3	0.36	2.45 (1.39)	10.38	351.18	460.76
3–5	0.40	1.80 (0.52)	8.60	751.98	1033.26
5–10	0.13	1.50 (0.24)	12.50	481.40	824.20
>10	0.39	6.00 (0.60)	7.00	3694.29	3848.57

	pcw	@market	@lfam	@lhired	machine
<1	2427	0.44	0.96	0.04	219
1–3	3515	0.44	0.82	0.18	214
3–5	7840	0.45	0.84	0.16	288
5–10	11783	0.56	0.77	0.23	206
>10	37500	0.94	0.17	0.83	550

Source: Giza survey data 1990.

nca = net cropped area
nyield = value of output per net cropped feddan
gyield = value of output per gross cropped feddan
cropint = cropping intensity
labint = labour intensity
valacre = land value per feddan
@hyv = percentage gross cropped area under HYV crops
fragment = number of fragments per farm (in brackets, intensity of fragmentation)
hhnr0 = number of family members in household
pcq = per capita output
pcy = per capita income
pcw = per capita wealth
@market = percentage of output marketed
@lfam = percentage family labour
@lhired = percentage hired labour
machine = machinery inputs (machine rentals+maintenance costs+10% of owned machinery)

TABLE 38

RELATIONSHIP BETWEEN FAMILY LABOUR, LABOUR INPUT INTENSITY AND
CROPPING INTENSITY: SHUBAK AL-SHARQI

1) seasonal yields on seasonal cropping intensity

	constant	b	error	n	t
winter	959	-23.4	252	62	-0.093
summer	592	-124.3	161	62	-0.773
nili	84	338	54	62	6.234

2) seasonal yields on seasonal family labour input per feddan

	constant	b	error	n	t
winter	962	-0.3	0.66	62	-0.456
summer	449	0.2	0.4	62	0.482
nili	173	1.64	0.36	62	4.616
all year	1470	0.457	0.357	62	1.28

3) seasonal yields on seasonal labour input intensity

	constant	b	error	n	t
winter	94	-0.097	0.66	62	-0.148
summer	441	0.25	0.4	62	0.59
nili	165	1.64	0.34	62	4.9

4) seasonal yields on farm size

	constant	b	error	n	t
winter	911	16	27	62	1.396
summer	447	-16	23	62	-0.689
nili	373	-46	22	62	-2.026

5) seasonal land use (cropped area/farm size) on farm size

	constant	b	error	n	t
winter	1.02	-0.05	0.012	62	-4.12
summer	1.06	-0.06	0.017	62	-3.44
nili	0.8	-0.1	0.04	62	-2.736

6) seasonal labour input intensity on farm size

	constant	b	error	n	t
winter	119	-15	4.9	62	-3.22
summer	159	-22.7	6.4	62	-3.56
nili	112	-18.5	7.2	62	-2.56

7) annual net yields on cropping intensity

annual	289	511	99	62	5.158

8) annual net yields on labour input intensity

annual	1442	0.52	0.36	62	1.438

9) net yields on annual family labour input

annual	1561	0.11	0.29	62	0.37

10) net yields on percentage family labour

annual	1605	-10.6	394	62	-0.27

11) net yields on family labour input per feddan

annual	1470	0.45	0.36	62	1.28

TABLE 39

PER CAPITA NET INCOME AND POVERTY LEVELS BY SIZE CLASS,
SHUBAK AL-SHARQI, 1990

CLASS	AVNCA	AVNETINC	AVPCNETY	AVPOVERT
1.00	.61	1786.52	227.15	-137.85
2.00	1.76	3018.11	321.56	-43.44
3.00	3.45	5192.20	599.27	234.27
4.00	6.13	5798.00	472.78	107.78
5.00	10.00	14390.00	2055.71	1690.71

AVNCA = operated area; AVNETINC = net income; AVPCNETY = per capita net income;
AVPOVERT = divergence from poverty line of LE 365

TABLE 40

AVERAGE INCOMES AND THEIR SOURCES, BY SIZE CLASS,
HUBAK AL-SHARQI, 1990

CLASS	AVINC	AVEXINC	AV@EXINC
1.00	2366.32	1234.47	.43
2.00	4828.73	1148.39	.22
3.00	8886.00	2419.00	.24
4.00	10302.50	4285.00	.39
5.00	26940.00	1080.00	.04

AVINC = average income per household; AVEXINC = average outside earnings; AV@EXINC =
average proportion of income earned off-farm

Note that one of the farms in the 5-10 feddan class has a high salaried member who works as a
civil servant.

TABLE 41

AVERAGE LEVELS OF DEBT BY SIZE CLASS, SHUBAK AL-SHARQI, 1990

CLASS	AVLOAN	AVD1	AVD2	AVD3	AVD4
1.00	1177.91	.50	.75	.05	1597.67
2.00	1079.33	.23	.49	.03	643.09
3.00	3450.00	.35	1.06	.05	1076.47
4.00	600.00	.07	.19	.01	120.00
5.00	16000.00	.59	1.11	.06	1600.00

AVLOAN = average loan; AVD1 = debt to income; AVD2 = debt to net income; AVD3 = debt to
assets; AVD4 = debt per feddan

TABLE 42	TABLE 43
AVERAGE LEVELS OF RENT BY SIZE CLASS, SHUBAK AL-SHARQI, 1990	MARKETED OUTPUT PER SIZE CLASS, SHUBAK AL-SHARQI, 1990

CLASS	AV@RENT	AVRENTA	AVRENT	CLASS	AVM1	AVM2
1.00	.80	0.57	258.37	1.00	.55	.50
2.00	.62	1.09	231.59	2.00	47	.45
3.00	.48	1.65	206.90	3.00	.40	.45
4.00	.40	2.00	240.00	4.00	.59	.56
5.00	.40	4.00	45.00	5.00	.95	.94

AV@RENT = average rented area as percentage of total; AVRENTA = average rented area; AVRENT = average rent per feddan

AVM1 = marketed crop (%)
AVM2 = marketed output (%)

TABLE 44

LAND DISTRIBUTION BY FARM SIZE: HIGAZA AL-QIBLI

class	owned		rented		all	
	holdings	area	holdings	area	holdings	area
<1	432	251.75	320	158	752	409.75
1–3	740	1317.34	266	429.5	1006	1746.84
3–5	142	544	39	148	181	692
5–10	120	842	5	31.375	125	873.375
>10	12	158.5	4	42.792	16	201.292
TOTAL	1446	3113.59	634	809.667	2080	3923.257

Source: mushrif zira'i, Higaza co-operative.

TABLE 45

DISTRIBUTION OF FARMS AND LAND BY FARM SIZE IN QENA GOVERNORATE, 1981

size	farms	%	area	%
<1	55243	39.90	24500	7.58
1–3	52051	37.59	87400	27.05
3–5	16506	11.92	59411	18.39
5–10	10292	7.43	67142	20.78
>10	4369	3.16	84619	26.19
total	138461	100	323072	100

Source: Table 1a [Ministry of Agriculture (Qena), 1985: 4].

TABLE 46

SIZE-CLASS AVERAGES FOR HIGAZA AL-QIBLI, QENA

farm size	nca	nyield	gyield	cropint	labint	valacre
<1	0.51	1190	802	1.69	486	11176
1–3	1.85	1225	854	1.51	284	8649
3–5	3.31	1144	839	.41	185	11329
5–10	6.69	1324	999	1.34	170	10339
>10	26.00	1617	1315	1.23	113	12115

	@hyv	fragment	hhnr0	pcq	pcy
<1	0.29	1.86 (3.6)	5.79	126	177
1–3	0.38	3.96 (2.1)	8.33	329	392
3–5	0.38	5.25 (1.6)	7.50	586	716
5–10	0.51	7.67 (1.2)	10.67	914	994
>10	0.64	5.00 (0.2)	6.50	6853	7031

	pcw	@market	@lfam	@lhired	machine
<1	2616	0.44	0.86	0.14	198
1–3	3918	0.54	0.72	0.28	373
3--5	7446	0.58	0.61	0.39	276
5–10	11445	0.64	0.50	0.50	1193
>10	68512	0.89	0.26	0.74	3543

Source: Qena survey data 1990.

nca	=	net cropped area
nyield	=	value of output per net cropped feddan
gyield	=	value of output per gross cropped feddan
cropint	=	cropping intensity
labint	=	labour intensity
valacre	=	land value per feddan
@hyv	=	percentage gross cropped area under HYV crops
fragment	=	number of fragments per farm (in brackets, intensity of fragmentation)
hhnr0	=	number of family members in household
pcq	=	per capita output
pcy	=	per capita income
pcw	=	per capita wealth
@market	=	percentage of output marketed
@lfam	=	percentage family labour
@lhired	=	percentage hired labour
machine	=	machinery inputs (machine rentals+maintenance costs+10% of owned machinery

TABLE 47

FARM UTILISATION OF AGRICULTURAL MACHINERY, 1981

Giza

type	owned/ shared	rented public	rented private	total
small tractors	321	480	5671	6472
large tractors	1657	3398	63344	68399
other tractors	715	739	5384	6838
fixed pumps	3893	247	9379	13519
mobile pumps	4892	248	22514	27654
threshers	695	1357	25277	27329

Qena

type	owned/ shared	rented public	rented private	total
small tractors	149	145	2855	3149
large tractors	2657	2758	98687	104102
other tractors	1468	1283	23606	26357
fixed pumps	4271	2390	33022	39683
mobile pumps	7835	890	64958	73683
threshers	1564	651	59663	61878

Qus district

type	owned/ shared	rented public	rented private	total
small tractors	16	2	444	462
large tractors	196	24	11844	12064
other tractors	34	8	330	372
fixed pumps	476	10	5185	5671
mobile pumps	689	15	7560	8264
thresher	92	11	3506	3609

Saff district

type	owned/ shared	rented public	rented private	total
small tractors	34	80	244	358
large tractors	101	2161	3456	5718
other tractors	40	408	160	608
fixed pumps	204	31	483	718
mobile pumps	77	34	226	337
threshers	28	416	1725	2169

Source: Table 46a [*Ministry of Agriculture, Qena*, 1985: 140] and [*Ministry of Agriculture, Giza*, 1985: 129].

TABLE 48

SIZE DISTRIBUTION OF OWNED FARM EQUIPMENT, QENA AND GIZA

Qena

size	tractors		pumps		threshers	
	n	%	n	%	n	%
<1	222	5	587	5	56	4
1–3	444	10	2777	23	186	12
3–5	531	12	2530	21	194	12
5–10	1167	27	3361	28	410	26
>10	1910	45	2851	24	718	46
total	4274	100	12106	100	1564	100

Giza

size	tractors		pumps		threshers	
	n	%	n	%	n	%
<1	162	6	740	8	59	8
1–3	569	21	3822	44	201	29
3–5	484	18	1693	19	141	20
5–10	664	25	1369	16	140	20
>10	815	30	1161	13	154	22
total	2693	100	8785	100	695	100

Source: Table 46a [*Ministry of Agriculture*, 1985: 129].

TABLE 49
INPUT SHARES IN TOTAL CROP REVENUE IN FOUR REGIONS: 1965–79 (3-YEAR AVERAGE), EGYPT

year	anim	mech	seed	manu	fert	ins	othr	lab	rent	prof	r+p	l+r+p
Delta												
65–67	9.99	0.37	4.66	3.43	5.96	2.62	0.87	19.21	23.59	29.17	52.76	71.97
68–70	7.33	3.94	5.36	3.59	6.82	1.67	0.87	18.34	23.05	29.02	52.07	70.41
71–73	5.02	5.32	4.56	3.25	6.12	1.80	0.84	14.72	19.78	38.60	58.38	73.10
74–76	4.08	5.65	4.13	3.36	4.95	1.32	1.34	15.50	15.82	43.85	59.67	75.17
77–79	3.70	5.33	4.51	3.00	3.89	1.25	1.36	17.36	13.71	45.88	59.59	76.95
65–70	8.73	2.16	5.01	3.51	6.39	2.15	0.87	18.78	23.32	29.10	52.42	71.20
71–79	4.27	5.43	4.40	3.20	4.99	1.46	1.18	15.86	16.44	42.78	59.22	75.08
UG												
65–67	5.97	0.21	3.57	3.86	4.97	1.34	0.88	14.30	19.61	45.28	64.89	79.19
68–70	5.43	2.07	4.10	4.46	6.24	1.27	1.17	16.23	20.74	38.29	59.03	75.26
71–73	3.74	2.12	3.78	4.11	5.32	1.04	0.97	13.10	16.56	49.27	65.83	78.93
74–76	3.27	2.42	4.23	3.58	4.36	0.83	0.95	13.02	13.14	54.20	67.34	80.36
77–79	3.26	3.28	5.97	3.51	3.48	1.01	1.11	15.60	13.72	49.04	62.76	78.36
65–70	5.70	1.14	3.84	4.16	5.61	1.31	1.03	15.27	20.18	41.79	61.97	77.24
71–79	3.42	2.61	4.66	3.73	4.39	0.96	1.01	13.91	14.47	50.84	65.31	79.22

TABLE 49 (cont.)

ME

65–67	4.01	1.20	3.51	3.65	6.51	1.15	1.05	17.16	20.40	41.35	61.75	78.91
68–70	3.97	2.36	3.97	3.79	8.59	1.60	1.26	19.26	23.07	32.13	55.20	74.46
71–73	2.67	2.73	3.77	3.51	7.55	1.32	1.12	15.40	19.43	42.50	61.93	77.33
74–76	2.39	3.25	3.75	3.43	5.62	0.94	1.25	19.54	14.85	44.98	59.83	79.37
77–79	3.07	4.81	4.39	3.12	4.67	0.95	1.41	21.64	13.98	41.95	55.93	77.57
65–70	3.99	1.78	3.74	3.72	7.55	1.38	1.16	18.21	21.74	36.74	58.48	76.69
71–79	2.71	3.60	3.97	3.35	5.95	1.07	1.26	18.86	16.09	43.14	59.23	78.09

UE

65–67	5.59	7.13	4.82	0.81	7.97	0.77	1.27	18.09	22.85	30.70	53.55	71.64
68–70	5.33	9.96	5.92	1.70	9.41	1.44	1.41	19.79	23.53	21.50	45.03	64.82
71–73	4.06	8.53	5.38	1.42	8.28	0.92	1.32	16.45	18.50	35.13	53.63	70.08
74–76	3.56	6.79	6.00	1.48	6.45	0.74	1.45	21.81	13.86	37.86	51.72	73.53
77–79	5.07	6.51	6.19	1.07	5.57	0.59	1.75	28.01	13.45	31.80	45.25	73.26
65–70	5.46	8.55	5.37	1.26	8.69	1.11	1.34	18.94	23.19	26.10	49.29	68.23
71–79	4.23	7.28	5.86	1.32	6.77	0.75	1.51	22.09	15.27	34.93	50.20	72.29

Source: Table 10 [*Esfahani*, 1988: 154].

anim	=	animals	mech	=	machinery
seed	=	seed	manu	=	manufactured inputs
fert	=	fertiliser	ins	=	insecticides
othr	=	other input	lab	=	labour
rent	=	land rent	prof	=	profits
r+p	=	rent plu profits	l+r+p	=	labour+rent+profits

TABLE 50

LENDING CATEGORIES CURRENTLY IMPLEMENTED FOR MAIN
FIELD CROPS DURING 1988, EGYPT

crop	lending sub*1	category non-sub
wheat	12	70
bean	15	50
lentil	15	15
onion	8	
garlic	100	100
potato	300	
tomato		150
cotton	75	50
rice	70	50
maize	40	
sugar	650	50
soya	50	

(1) subsidised interest rate ranges from 3.5% to 6.5%

Source: Ministry of Agriculture, PBDAC [1989: 59].

Bibliography

Abdel-Fadil, M., 1975, *Development, Income Distribution and Social Change in Rural Egypt 1952–1970*, Cambridge: Cambridge University Press.

Adams, R.H., 1986, 'Development and Structural Change in Rural Egypt 1952 to 1982', *World Development*, Vol.13, No.6.

Adams, R.H., 1986, *Development and Social Change in Rural Egypt*, New York: Syracuse University Press.

Agarwala, R., 1964a, 'Size of Holdings and Productivity – A Comment', *Economic Weekly*, Vol.16, No.15, 11 April.

Agarwala, R., 1964b, 'Size of Holdings and Productivity – Further Comments', *Economic Weekly*, Vol.16, No.47, 21 Nov.

Amin, S. (Hassan Riad), 1964, *L'Egypte Nasserienne*, Paris: Minuit.

Ansari, H., 1968, *Egypt: The Stalled Society*, New York: Syracuse University Press.

Antle, J.M. and A.S. Aitah, 1982, *Annual Report. Phase One of the Farm Efficiency Activity*, Cairo: ARE-University of California-AID Economics Sub-Project.

Bachman, K.L. and R.P. Christensen, 1967, 'The Economics of Farm Size', in H. Southworth and B. Johnston, *Agriculture and Economic Growth*, Ithaca, NY: Cornell University Press.

Bagchi, A.K., 1962, 'Productivity and Disguised Unemployment in Indian Agriculture: A Theoretical Analysis', unpublished mimeo.

Baker, R.W., 1978, *Egypt's Uncertain Revolution*, Boston, MA: Harvard University Press.

Barbier, P., 1984, 'Inverse Relation Between Farm Size and Land Productivity: The Product of Science or Imagination?', *Economic and Political Weekly*, Vol.19, Nos.52–3.

Bardhan, P.K., 1973, 'Size, Productivity, and Returns to Scale: An Analysis of Farm-Level Data in Indian Agriculture', *Journal of Political Economy*, Vol.18, Dec.

Bardhan, P.K., 1980, 'Interlocking Factor Markets and Agrarian Development: A Review of the Issues', *Oxford Economic Papers*, Vol.32, No.1, March.

Bardhan, P.K. and A. Rudra, 1978, 'Interlinkages of Land, Labour and Credit Relations: an Analysis of Village Survey Data in East India', *Economic and Political Weekly*, Vol.13, Nos.6 and 7, Annual Number, Feb.

Barraclough, S.L. and A.L. Domike, 1966, 'Agrarian Structure in Seven Latin American Countries', *Land Economics*, Nov.

Barraclough, S.L. and D. Collarte, 1973, *Agrarian Structure in Latin America: A Resume of the CIDA Land Tenure Studies of Argentina, Brazil, Chile, Colombia, Ecuador, Guatemala and Peru*, Lexington MA: Lexington Books.

Basheer, A.M., 1981, *An Analytical Economic Study of Maize Production in Egypt*, EMCIP Publication No.33, Cairo: ARE Ministry of Agriculture.

Berry, R.A. and W.R. Cline, 1979, *Agrarian Structure and Productivity in Developing Countries*, Baltimore, MD: John Hopkins University Press.

Bhaduri, A., 1973, 'A Study in Agricultural Backwardness Under Semi-Feudalism', *Economic Journal*, Vol.83, March.

Bhaduri, A., 1980, 'A Reply to Rao and Ghose', *Cambridge Journal of Economics*, Vol.4, No.2.

Bhaduri, A., 1983, *The Economic Structure of Backward Agriculture*, London: Academic Press.

Bhagwati, J.N. and S.J. Chakravarty, 1969, 'Contributions to Indian Economic Analysis: A Survey', *American Economic Review*, Vol.LIX, No.4, Part 2, Supplement.

Bhalla, S.S., 1975, 'An Analysis of Savings in Rural India', unpublished mimeo.

Bhalla, S.S., 1988, 'Does Land Quality Matter? Theory and Measurement', *Journal of Development Economics*, Vol.29.

Bhalla, S.S. and P.L. Roy, 1988, 'Mis-specification in Farm Productivity Analysis: The Role of Land Quality', *Oxford Economic Papers*, vol.40.

Bharadwaj, K., 1974a, *Production Conditions in Indian Agriculture*, Cambridge: Cambridge University Press.

Bharadwaj, K., 1974b, 'Notes on Farm Size and Productivity', *Economic and Political Weekly*, Review of Agriculture, Vol.9, No.13, 30 March.

Bharadwaj, K., 1979, 'Towards a Macro-economic Framework for a Developing Economy: The Indian Case', *The Manchester School*, Vol.47, No.3, Sept.

Bharadwaj, K., 1985, 'A View of Commercialisation in Indian Agriculture and the Development of Capitalism', *Journal of Peasant Studies*, Vol.12, No.4.

Bhattacharya, N. and G.R. Saini, 1972, 'Farm Size and Productivity – A Fresh Look', *Economic and Political Weekly*, Review of Agriculture, Vol.7, No.26, 24 June.

Binswanger, H.P. and K. Deininger, 1993, 'South African Land Policy: The Legacy of History and Current Options', *World Development*, Vol.21, No.9.

Birks, J.S. and C. Sinclair, 1980, *International Migration and Development in the Arab Region*, Geneva: ILO.

Braverman, A. and T.N. Srinivasan, 1984, 'Agrarian Reforms in Developing Rural Economies Characterized by Interlinked Credit and Tenancy Markets', in H.P. Binswanger and M.R. Rosenzweig (eds.), *Contractual Arrangements, Employment, and Wages in Rural Labor Markets in Asia*, New Haven, CT: Yale University Press.

Byres, T.J., 1972, 'The Dialectic of India's Green Revolution', *South Asian Review*, Vol.5, No.2, Jan.

Byres, T.J., 1974, 'Land Reform, Industrialisation and the Marketed Surplus in India: An Essay on the Power of Rural Bias', in David Lehmann (ed.), *Agrarian Reform and Agrarian Reformism*, London: Faber & Faber.

Byres, T.J., 1977a, 'Output Per Acre and Size of Holding: The Logic of Peasant Agriculture Under Semi-Feudalism', unpublished manuscript.

Byres, T.J., 1977b, 'Agrarian Transition and the Agrarian Question', *Journal of Peasant Studies*, Vol.4, No.3, April.

Byres, T.J., 1979, 'Of Neo-Populist Pipe Dreams: Daedulus in the Third World and the Myth of Urban Bias', *Journal of Peasant Studies*, Vol.6, No.2, Jan.

Byres, T.J., 1981, 'The New Technology, Class Formation and Class Action in the Indian Countryside', *Journal of Peasant Studies*, Vol.8, No.4, July.

Byres, T.J., 1986, 'The Agrarian Question and Differentiation of the Peasantry', Foreword to Atiur Rahman, *Peasants and Classes. A Study in Differentiation in Bangladesh*, London and New Jersey: Zed Books.

Byres, T.J., 1986, 'The Agrarian Question, Forms of Capitalist Agrarian Transition and the State: An Essay with Reference to Asia', *Social Scientist*, Vol.14, Nos.11–12.

Byres, T.J., 1990, 'The Agrarian Question and Differing Forms of Capitalist Agrarian Transition: An Essay with Reference to Asia', in Jan Breman and Sudipto Mundle (eds.), *Rural Transformation in Asia*, New Delhi and Oxford: Oxford University Press.

Byres, T.J., 1991, 'Agrarian Question, The' and 'Peasantry', in Tom Bottomore et al., (eds.), *A Dictionary of Marxist Thought*, (2nd Edition), Oxford: Blackwell Reference.

Carter, M.R., 1984, 'Identification of the Inverse Relationship between Farm Size and Productivity: An Empirical Analysis of Peasant Agricultural Production', *Oxford Economic Papers*, Vol.36.

Central Agricultural Cooperative Union, n.d., *Agricultural Pricing Policies and the Role of Farmers Cooperatives*, Cairo.

Chadha, G.K., 1978, 'Farm Size and Productivity Revisited – Some Notes from Recent Experience of Punjab', *Economic and Political Weekly*, Review of Agriculture, Vol.13, No.9, 30 Sept.

Chandra, N.K., 1974, 'Farm Efficiency Under Semi-Feudalism: A Critique of Marginalist Theories and Some Marxist Formulations', *Economic and Political Weekly*, Vol.9, nos. 32-4, Special Number, August.

Chattopadhyay, M. and A. Rudra, 1976, 'Size-Productivity Revisited', *Economic and Political Weekly*, Review of Agriculture, Vol.11, No.39, 25 Sept.

Chattopadhyay, M. and A. Rudra, 1977, 'Size-Productivity Revisited – Addendum', *Economic and Political Weekly*, Vol.12, No.11, 12 March.

Chayanov, A.V., 1966, *The Theory of Peasant Economy*, edited by D. Thorner, B. Kerblay and R.E.F. Smith, Homewood, Illinois, IL: Irwin.

Cline, W.R., 1970, *Economic Consequences of a Land Reform in Brazil*, Amsterdam: North Holland.

Cline, W.R., 1973, 'Interrelationships between Agricultural Strategy and Rural Income Distribution', *Food Research Institute Studies*, Vol.12, No.2.

Commander, S., 1987, *The State and Agricultural Development in Egypt since 1973*, London: Ithaca Press.

Cornia, G.A., 1985, 'Farm Size, Land Yields and the Agricultural Production Function: An Analysis for Fifteen Developing Countries', *World Development*, Vol.13, No.4.

Crouch, L., Siam, G., and O. Gad, 1983, 'A Descriptive Analysis of Egyptian Agrarian Structure', *ADS/University of California Economics Working Paper*, No.115, Cairo, January.

Dethier, J-J., 1981, 'Food Supply and Agricultural Policy in Egypt', *ADS Project Economics Working Paper*, No.13, Cairo.

Dorner, P., 1972, *Land Reform and Economic Development*, Harmondsworth: Penguin Books.

Dumont, R., 1968, 'Les problemes agraires de la RAU', *Politique étrangère*, Vol.2.

Dyer, G.D., 1989, 'Agrarian Transition in Egypt: Technological Change in Egyptian Agriculture and Its Impact on the Relation between Farm Size and Productivity', unpublished M.Phil. thesis, University of Cambridge.

Dyer, G.D., 1991, 'Farm Size – Farm Productivity Re-examined: Evidence from Rural Egypt', *Journal of Peasant Studies*, Vol.19, No.1, Oct.

Dyer, G.D., 1995, *Farm Size and Productivity in Egyptian Agriculture: An Analysis of Agrarian Structure and Technical Change*, unpublished Ph.D. thesis, London University.

El-Kholy, O. and M. Abbas, 1982, 'A Socio-Economic Survey of Small Farms within the Domain of Selected Village Banks', mimeo, Cairo.

Ellis, F., 1988, *Peasant Economics: Farm Households and Agrarian Development*, Cambridge: Cambridge University Press.

Ellman, M., 1989, *Socialist Planning* (2nd Edition), Cambridge: Cambridge University Press.

El Sahrigi, A.F. and S.C. Shepley, 1984, 'Farm Equipment Manufacture in Egypt', *Egypt Agricultural Mechanization Project*, Cairo: ARE Ministry of Agriculture.

El Sahrigi, A.F. and S.C. Shepley, 1985, 'Socio-Economic Evaluation of Farm Machinery Introduced in Project Villages from 1980 to Dec. 1984', *Egypt Agricultural Mechanization Project, Working Paper No.19*, Cairo: ARE/USAID.

El Shohna, M.R.M., 1970, 'An Economic Analysis of Agricultural Financing in the Arab Republic of Egypt', M.Sc. thesis, Cairo University.

ERA 2000, 1979, *Further Mechanization of Egyptian Agriculture*, Maryland.

Esfahani, H.S., 1988, 'Aggregate Trends in Four Main Agricultural Regions in Egypt, 1964–1979', *International Journal of Middle East Studies*, Vol.20.

Fitch, J.B., 1983, 'Maize Production Practices and Problems in Egypt: Results of Three Farmer Surveys', *CIMMYT Economics Programme Working Paper*, Cairo.

Foaden, G.P. and F. Fletcher, 1908, *Textbook of Egyptian Agriculture*, Vol.1, Cairo: Ministry of Education.

Georgescu-Roegen, N., 1960, 'Economic Theory and Agrarian Reforms', *Oxford Economic Papers*, Vol.XII, Feb.

Ghoneimy, M.R., 1953, 'Resource Use and Income in Egyptian Agriculture', Ph.D. Thesis, North Carolina State University.

Ghose, A.K., 1979, 'Farm Size and Land Productivity in Indian Agriculture: A Reappraisal', *Journal of Development Studies*, Vol.16, No.1.

Goueli, A. *et al.*, 1980, 'Village Institutions, Socio-Economic Characteristics and Economic Indicators from the 1976–77 Egyptian Farm Management Studies', Cairo.

Goverment of India, 1963, *Studies in the Economics of Farm Management in Uttar Pradesh, Combined Report for 1954–55 to 1956–57*, Delhi.

Government of India, 1966, *Farm Management in India: A Study Based on Recent Investigations*, New Delhi: Ministry of Food, Agriculture, Community Development and Cooperation.

Greenberg, B., 1985, *The Changing Constraints to Mechanization in Egyptian Agriculture: From 'Induced' to Reduced Mechanization in a World Price System*, Cairo: USAID.

Griffin, K., 1974, *The Political Economy of Agrarian Change*, London: Macmillan.

Harik, I., 1979, *Distribution of Land, Employment and Income in Rural Egypt*, Development

Committee, Centre for International Studies, New York: Cornell University Press.

Hopkins, N.S., 1987, *Agrarian Transformation in Egypt*, Cairo: AUC Press.

Hopkins, N.S. and S. Mehanna, 1981, 'Egyptian Village Studies', *ADS Project, Economics Working Paper,* No.42, Giza.

Hopkins, N.S., Mehanna, S.R. and B.M. Abdel Maksoud, 1982, 'The State of Agricultural Mechanization in Egypt: Results of a Survey 1982', *Agricultural Mechanization Project,* Cairo: ARE Ministry of Agriculture/USAID.

Hossain, M., 1977, 'Farm Size, Tenancy and Land Productivity: An Analysis of Farm Level Data in Bangladesh Agriculture', *Bangladesh Development Studies,* January.

Ikram, K., 1980, *Egypt: Economic Management in a Period of Transition,* Baltimore, MD: Johns Hopkins University Press.

Imam, S.A., 1983, 'An Economic Evaluation of Farm Mechanization in Egypt', *ADS Working Paper 117,* Cairo.

Kahlon, A.S. and T.R. Kapur, 1968, 'Differences in the Form and Intensity of Input-Mix and Yield Levels on Small and Large Farm Organizations in the IADP District Ludhiana (Punjab) – A Case Study', *Indian Journal of Agricultural Economics,* March.

Kaldas, S., 1984, *Fertiliser Situation in Egypt,* no publication details.

Kamal, M., 1968, 'Feodaux, paysans riches et fellahs', *Democratie Nouvelle,* April.

Kaushik, C.R., 1966, 'farm Adjustments on the Introduction of New Irrigation Facilities in Canal Irrigated Areas of Hissar District', upublished M.Sc. thesis.

Kaushik, CR., 1996 Khalil, M., 1981, 'The Economics of Tractors in Egyptian Agriculture', *ADS Working Paper,* No.39, Giza.

Khan, M.H., 1975, *The Economics of the Green Revolution in Pakistan,* New York: Praeger.

Khan, M.H., 1979, 'Farm Size and Land Productivity Relationships in Pakistan, *Pakistan Development Review,* Vol.XVIII, No.1, Spring.

Khusro, A.M., n.d., 'Some Basic Generalisations in Indian Agriculture', unpublished manuscript.

Khusro, A.M., 1964, 'Returns to Scale in Indian Agriculture', *Indian Journal of Agricultural Economics,* Oct.

Khusro, A.M., 1973, *The Economics of Farm Size and Land Reform in India,* Madras: Macmillan.

Lau, L.J. and P.A. Yotopoulos, 1971, 'A Test for Relative Efficiency and Application to Indian Agriculture', *American Economic Review,* March.

Lehmann, D. (ed.), 1974, *Agrarian Reform and Agrarian Reformism,* London: Faber & Faber.

Leibenstein, H., 1957, 'The Theory of Underemployment in Backward Economies', *Journal of Political Economy,* Vol.LXV, April.

Lenin, V.I., 1967 [1898], 'The Development of Capitalism in Russia', in *Collected Works,* Volume III, Moscow: Progress Publishers.

Lenin, V.I., 1967, 'New Data on the Laws Governing the Development of Capitalism in Agriculture', *Collected Works,* Volume XXII, Moscow: Progress Publishers.

Lipton, M., 1974, 'Towards a Theory of Land Reform', in D. Lehmann (ed.), *Agrarian Reform and Agrarian Reformism,* London: Faber & Faber.

Lipton, M., 1993, 'Land Reform as Commenced Business: The Evidence Against Stopping', *World Development,* Vol.21, No.4.

Lipton, M. and M. Lipton, 1993, 'Creating Rural Livelihoods: Some Lessons for South Africa from Experience Elsewhere', *World Development,* Vol.21, No.9.

Long, E.J., 1961, 'The Economic Basis of Land Reform in Underdeveloped Economics', *Land Economics,* Vol.37, No.2, May.

Mabro, R., 1971, 'Employment and Wages in Dual Agriculture', *Oxford Economic Papers,* Vol.21, No.3.

Mahmood, M. and N. Ul-Haque, 1981, 'Farm Size and Productivity Revisited', *Pakistan Development Review,* Vol.XX, No.2.

Mann, H.S., 1962, 'Co-operative Farming and Family Farming in the Punjab: A Comparative Study', Ph.D. dissertation, Ohio State University.

Mar'ei, S., 1954, 'The Agrarian Reform in Egypt', *International Labour Review,* Vol.69, Feb.

Mayfield, J.B., 1974, *Local Institutions and Egyptian Rural Development,* New York: Cornell University Press.

Mazumdar, D., 1959, 'The Marginal Productivity Theory of Wages and Disguised Unemployment', *Review of Economic Studies*, Vol.XXVI, June.

Mazumdar, D., 1963, 'On the Economics of Relative Efficiency of Small Farmers', *Economic Weekly*, Vol.XV, Nos.28–30, Special Number, July.

Mazumdar, D., 1965, 'Size of Farm and Productivity: A Problem of Peasant Agriculture', *Economica*, May.

Mellor, J.W., 1966, *The Economics of Agricultural Development*, Ithaca, NY: Cornell University Press.

Mellor, J.W., 1967, 'Toward a Theory of Agricultural Development', in H.M. Southworth and B.F. Johnston (eds.), *Agricultural Development and Economic Growth*, New York: Cornell University Press, 1967.

Mellor, J.W. and B.F. Johnston, 1984, 'The World Food Equation: Interrelations among Development, Employment and Food Consumption', *Journal of Economic Literature*, Vol.XXII, No.2.

Ministry of Agriculture, 1989, *Agricultural Financing and the Role of PBDAC in Realizing the Agricultural Development Plan in Egypt*, Central Administration for Foreign Agricultural Relations and the Principal Bank for Development and Agricultural Credit, Cairo.

Ministry of Agriculture, Egypt, 1989, *Nita'ig al-Ta'adad al-Zira'ai 'an al-Sinah al-Zira'aiah 1981–82, Muhafidhah Giza* (Agricultural Census 1981–2, Giza Governorate), Cairo.

Ministry of Agriculture, 1985, *Nita'ig al-Ta'adad al-Zira'ai 'an al-Sinah al-Zira'aiah 1981–82. Muhafidhah Qena* (Agricultural Census 1981–82, Qena Governorate), Cairo.

Ministry of Agriculture, 1989, *Nita'ig al-Ta'adad al-Zira'ai 'an al-Sinah al-Zira'aiah 1981–82, Igmali al-Gumhuriya* (Agricultural Census 1981–82, National Summary), Cairo.

Mohieddin, A., 1977, 'Open Unemployment in the Egyptian Economy', *Institute of National Planning Memo*, No.1184, Jan.

Morsi, M.A.F., 1982, 'An Econometric Study for Factors Affecting Production of Mexican and Giza 155 Varieties of Wheat in the Arab Republic of Egypt', M.Sc. dissertation, University of Menufiya.

Nadim, A., 1979, *The Role of the Village Bank in the Rural Community: A Pilot Study on the Accessibility of Agricultural Inputs to Small Farmers*, Cairo: Al Azhar University.

Narain, D., 1961, *Distribution of the Marketed Surplus of Agricultural Produce by Size Level of Holding in India: 1950-51*, New York: Asia Publishing House.

Nolan, P., 1988, *The Political Economy of Collective Farms*, Cambridge: Basil Blackwell.

Paglin, M., 1965, 'Surplus Agricultural Labour and Development: Facts and Theories', *American Economic Review*, Vol.XV, No.4.

Patnaik, U., 1972, 'Economics of Farm Size and Farm Scale: Some Assumptions Re-Examined', *Economic and Political Weekly*, Vol.7, Nos.31–33, Special Number, Aug.

Patnaik, U., 1979, 'Neo-Populism and Marxism: The Chayanovian View of the Agrarian Question and Its Fundamental Fallacy', *Journal of Peasant Studies*, Vol.6, No.4.

Patnaik, U., 1987, *Peasant Class Differentiation. A Study in Method with Reference to Haryana*, Delhi: Oxford University Press.

Patnaik, U. (ed.), 1990, *Agrarian Relations and Accumulation: The 'Mode of Production' Debate in India*, Bombay: Oxford University Press, for Sameeksha Trust.

Platt, K.B., 1970, 'Land Reform in the United Arab Republic', *USAID Country Report*, Vol.P, June.

Radwan, S., 1977, *Agrarian Reform and Rural Poverty in Egypt, 1952-1975*, Geneva: ILO.

Radwan, S. and E. Lee, 1986, *Agrarian Change in Egypt: An Anatomy of Rural Poverty*, London: Croom Helm.

Rahman, A., 1986, *Peasants and Classes: A Study in Differentiation in Bangladesh*, London and New Jersey: Zed Books.

Rani, U., 1971, 'Size of Farm and Productivity', *Economic and Political Weekly*, Review of Agriculture, June.

Rao, A.P., 1967, 'Size of Holding and Productivity', *Economic and Political Weekly*, 11 Nov.

Rao, C.H.H., 1963, 'Farm Size and the Economics of Scale', *Economic Weekly*, 14 Dec.

Rao, C.H.H., 1966, 'Alternative Explanations of the Inverse Relationship between Farm Size and Output Per Acre in India', *Indian Economic Review*, Vol.1, No.2, Oct.

Rao, C.H.H., n.d., 'Size of Holdings and Productivity: Some Empirical Verifications', unpublished manuscript.

Rao, C.H.H., 1968a, 'Fluctuations in Agricultural Growth: An Analysis of Unstable Increase in Productivity', *Economic and Political Weekly*, Vol.3, Nos.1 and 2, Annual Number, Jan.

Rao, C.H.H., 1968b, 'Agricultural Growth and Stagnation', in A.M. Khusro (ed.), *Readings in Agricultural Development*, Bombay: Allied Publishers.

Rao, C.H.H., 1968c, 'Farm Size and Yield Per Acre – A Comment', *Economic and Political Weekly*, 14 Sept.

Rao, C.H.H., 1972, 'Ceiling on Agricultural Landholding: Its Economic Rationale', *Economic and Political Weekly*, Review of Agriculture, June.

Rao, R.S. and S. Brahme, 1973, 'Capitalism in Indian Agriculture: An Enquiry', (mimeo), paper from Seminar on the Political Economy of Indian Agriculture, Calcutta, March.

Reiss, P., Haddad, Z., Yamani, A. and R. Lutfi, 1983, 'Agricultural Mechanization and Labour: A Look at the Demand and Supply Sides', *ADS Working Paper*, No.9, Cairo.

Richards, A.R., 1981, 'Agricultural Mechanization in Egypt: Hopes and Fears', *International Journal of Middle East Studies*, Vol.13.

Richards, A.R., 1982, *Egypt's Agricultural Development, 1800–1980*, Boulder, Colorado, CO: Westview Press.

Richards, A.R., 1989, *Agricultural Employment, Wages, and Government Policy in Egypt During and After the Oil Boom*, Cairo: ILO.

Richards, A.R. and P.L. Martin, 1981, 'Rural Social Structure and the Agricultural Labour Market: Sharqiyya Evidence and Policy Implications', *ADS Project Working Paper*, May, Giza: ARE Ministry of Agriculture and University of California.

Richards, A.R. and P.L. Martin (eds.), 1983, *Migration, Mechanization and Agricultural Labour Markets in Egypt*, Boulder, Colorado, CO: Westview Press.

Robinson, J., 1964, 'Chinese Agricultural Communes', *Coexistence*, May.

Rochin, R.I. and J.C. Grossman, 1985, *Agricultural Cooperatives and Government Control in Egypt: A Historical and Statistical Assessment*, Department of Agricultural Economics, University of California, April.

Roy, P.L., 1979, 'The Relation between Farm Size and Productivity in the Context of Alternative Modes of Production in Indian Agriculture', Ph.D. thesis, Delhi School of Economics, University of Delhi.

Roy, P.L., 1981, 'Transition in Agriculture: Empirical Indicators and Results (Evidence from Punjab, India)', *Journal of Peasant Studies*, Vol.8, No.2.

Rudra, A., 1968a, 'Farm Size and Yield Per Acre', *Economic and Political Weekly*, Special Number, July.

Rudra, A., 1968b, 'More on Returns to Scale in Indian Agriculture', *Economic and Political Weekly*, Review of Agriculture, Oct.

Rudra, A., 1969, 'Farm Size, Productivity and Returns to Scale', Letter to the Editor, *Economic and Political Weekly*, 30 Aug.

Rudra, A., 1973, 'Allocative Efficiency of Indian Farmers: Some Methodological Problems', *Economic and Political Weekly*, 20 Jan.

Rudra, A. with B. Bandopadhyaya, 1973, 'Marginalist Explanation for More Intense Labour Input in Smaller Farms – Empirical Verification', *Economic and Political Weekly*, 2 June.

Rudra, A. with M.M. Mukhopadhya, 1976, 'Hiring of Labour by Poor Peasants', *Economic and Political Weekly*, Vol.11, 10 Jan.

Rudra, A. and A.K. Sen, 1980, 'Farm Size and Labour Use: Analysis and Policy', *Economic and Political Weekly*, Annual Number, Feb.

Saab, G., 1967, *The Egyptian Agrarian Reform, 1952–62*, London: Oxford University Press.

Sadowski, Y.M., 1991, *Political Vegetables? Businessman and Bureaucrat in the Development of Egyptian Agriculture*, Washington, DC: The Brookings Institution.

Saini, G.R., 1969a, 'Resource-Use Efficiency in Agriculture', *Indian Journal of Agricultural Economics*, Vol.XXIV, April-June.

Saini, G.R., 1969b, 'Farm Size, Productivity and Returns to Scale', *Economic and Political Weekly*, Review of Agriculture, June.

Saini, G.R., 1971, 'Holding Size, Productivity, and Some Related Aspects of Indian Agriculture',

Economic and Political Weekly, Review of Agriculture, June.

Saini, G.R., 1979, *Farm Size, Resource Use Efficiency and Income Distribution*, Bombay: Allied Publishers.

Sau, R., 1975, 'Farm Efficiency under Semi-Feudalism. A Critique of Marginalist Theories and Some Marxist Formulations: A Comment', *Economic and Political Weekly*, Review of Agriculture, March.

Schutz, P., 1987, *The Market of Pesticides in Egypt*, Cairo.

Sen, A., 1981, 'Market Failure and Control of Labour Power: Towards An Explanation of "Structure" and Change in Indian Agriculture', *Cambridge Journal of Economics*, Vol.5.

Sen, A.K., 1962, 'An Aspect of Indian Agriculture', *Economic Weekly*, Annual Number, Feb.

Sen, A.K., 1964a, 'Size of Holdings and Productivity', *Economic Weekly*, Annual Number, Feb.

Sen, A.K., 1964b, 'Size of Holdings and Productivity – A Reply', *Economic Weekly*, 2 May.

Sen, A.K., 1966, 'Peasants and Dualism with or without Surplus Labour', *Journal of Political Economy*, Vol.LXXIV, No.5.

Sen, A.K., 1975, *Employment, Technology and Development*, Oxford: Oxford University Press.

Sen, B., 1967, 'Farm Productivity and Soil Fertility in Indian Agriculture', *Indian Journal of Agricultural Economics*, Vol.22, No.2.

Sen, B., 1974, *The Green Revolution in India*, Delhi: Wiley Eastern.

Shepley, S.C., Shoukry, M. and M. Ismail, 1985, 'Resource Allocation Efficiency in Egyptian Agriculture and General Policy Implications', *Egyptian Agricultural Mechanization Project*, Working Paper No.20, Cairo: USAID/ARE.

Sidhu, S.S., 1974, 'Relative Efficiency in Wheat Production in the Indian Punjab', *American Economic Review*, Vol.64, No.4, Sept.

Singh, R. and R.K. Patel, 1973, 'Returns to Scale, Farm Size and Productivity in Meerut District', *Indian Journal of Agricultural Economics*, Vol.28, No.2.

Sinha, N.K. and R.S. Singh, 1966, 'An Agronomic Enquiry of Cropping Pattern and Input Practices in Ludhiana for the Year 1964-65', *Research Report Series*, July.

Southworth, H. and B. Johnston, 1967, *Agriculture and Economic Growth*, Ithaca, NY: Cornell University Press.

Srinivasan, T.N., 1973, 'Farm Size and Productivity: Implications of Choice under Uncertainty', *Sankhya*, Series B, Vol.34, Part 4.

Srinivasan, T.N., 1979, 'Agricultural Backwardness Under Semi-Feudalism: A Comment', *Economic Journal*, June.

Srivastava, R., 1989, 'Interlinked Modes of Exploitation in Indian Agriculture During Transition: A Case Study', *Journal of Peasant Studies*, Vol.16, No.4.

Taslim, M.A., 1989, 'Supervision Problems and the Size–Productivity Relation in Bangladesh Agriculture', *Oxford Bulletin of Economics and Statistics*, Vol.51, No.1.

Taylor, E., 1984, 'Egyptian Migration and Peasant Wives', *MERIP Report*, No.124.

UAR/INP/ILO, 1965-68, *Research Report on Employment Problems in Rural Areas* (in 10 volumes), Cairo.

United Arab Republic and ILO, 1969, *Rural Employment Problems in the UAR*, Geneva: ILO.

USDA, 1977, 'Major Constraints to Increasing Agricultural Productivity', *USDA Foreign Agricultural Economic Report*, No.120, Washington , DC.

Visaria, P., 1970, 'The Farmers' Preference for Work on Family Farms', in *Report of the Committee of Experts on Unemployment Estimates*, New Delhi: Planning Commission, Government of India.

Waterbury, J., 1979, *The Hydropolitics of the Nile Valley*, New York: Syracuse University Press.

Wilson, R.J.A., 1972, *Rural Employment and Land Tenure: An Egyptian Case Study*, Memo No.304, Cairo: ARE Institute of National Planning.

Author Index

Mar'ei, S. 84
Martin, P.L. 97
Mayfield, J.B. 85, 88, 93–4, 132
Mazumdar, D. 23, 36, 45, 77
Mehanna, S.R. 96, 106, 143
Mellor, J.W. 29, 55
Morsi, M.A.F. 105

Nadim, A. 89, 90, 91, 92, 98
Narain, D. 24
Nolan, P. 29

Paglin, M. 23, 77
Patel, R.T. 56
Patnaik, U. 14, 15–16, 17, 23, 24, 44, 49, 54, 61, 122
Platt, K.B. 72, 82, 83, 85, 86, 91

Radwan, S. 6, 66–7, 74, 76, 83–4, 89, 92, 96, 98, 99, 100ff., 108ff., 112, 143
Rani, U. 55, 62
Rao, A.P. 23, 34
Rao, C.H.H. 19, 23, 25, 27–8, 31, 34, 44, 45, 62
Rao, R.S. 57
Reiss, P. 98
Richards, A.R. 65, 74, 82, 83, 86, 87, 92, 95, 97, 104, 106, 107, 112, 132
Robinson, J. 29
Rochin, R.I. 85–6, 88, 99, 132
Roy, P.L. 17, 18, 23, 24, 32, 33–4, 40, 41, 44, 45, 46, 54, 57– 9, 63

Rudra, A. , 18–19, 20, 23, 24, 25, 36, 38, 43, 45, 48–9, 53, 61

Saab, G. 82, 88
Sadowski, Y.M. 85, 88, 89, 94, 98, 99, 143
Saini, G.R. 20, 23, 24, 25, 56
Schutz, P. 106, 143
Sen, Abijit, 33, 37, 42, 43, 54
Sen, A.K. xvi, 2, 3, 9–10, 12, 14–15, 18, 20, 23, 27, 29, 32, 35–9, 40, 41–2, 44, 45, 46, 47, 49, 50, 53, 62, 69, 125
Sen, B. 35, 44
Shepley, S.C. 65–6, 107–8, 132
Sidhu, S.S. 55, 62
Sinclair, C. 97
Singh, R. 56, 62
Sinha, N.K. 62
Srinivasan, T.N. 39, 45, 62
Srivastava, R. 62

Taslim, M.A. 36, 38–40

Ul–Haque, N. 60

Visaria, P. 45

Waterbury, J. 142
Wilson, R.J.A. 67–8, 74, 75, 76

Yotopoulos, P.A. 23, 62

Subject Index

For Product Safety Concerns and Information please contact our EU
representative GPSR@taylorandfrancis.com
Taylor & Francis Verlag GmbH, Kaufingerstraße 24, 80331 München, Germany

www.ingramcontent.com/pod-product-compliance
Ingram Content Group UK Ltd.
Pitfield, Milton Keynes, MK11 3LW, UK
UKHW042201240425
457818UK00011B/330